Behind the Mask

in Mexico

ehind the Mask in Mexico

Janet Brody Esser, Editor

Museum of International Folk Art

Museum of New Mexico Press   Publishers

This publication was made possible through the generous support of the National Endowment for the Humanities, the State of New Mexico's Office of Cultural Affairs' Publications Revolving Fund, and the International Folk Art Foundation.

The Museum of New Mexico Press and the Museum of International Folk Art are units of the Museum of New Mexico, a division of the State Office of Cultural Affairs.

Published on the occasion of an exhibition sponsored by the Museum of International Folk Art, a unit of the Museum of New Mexico, June 1988–September, 1990.

Book Design: Miho
Studio Photographer: Michel Monteaux
For the Museum of New Mexico Press:
    James Mafchir, Mary Wachs
For the Museum of International
    Folk Art: Charlene Cerny,
    Stephen Becker, Marsha Bol,
    Marilee Schmit, Barbara Mauldin,
Exhibition Design: Christopher Beisel. Video:
Tom McCarthy
Senior Consultant: Janet Brody Esser

Printed in Japan by Dai Nippon.

Library of Congress Cataloging-in-Publication Data

Behind the mask in Mexico / edited by Janet Brody Esser; essays and field photographs by Marsha Bol . . . [et al.].
    p. cm.
  Catalog of an exhibition.
  Bibliography: p.
  Includes index.
  ISBN 0–89013–188–0.
  ISBN 0–89013–189–9 (pbk.)
  1. Indians of Mexico— Masks— Exhibitions.
2. Indians of Mexico— Rites and ceremonies—Exhibitions. 3. Masks—Mexico— Exhibitions. 4. Festivals—Mexico— Exhibi- tions. 5. Museum of International Folk Art (N.M.)—Exhibitions. I. Esser, Janet Brody. II. Bol, Marsha. III. Museum of International Folk Art (N.M.) IV. Museum of New Mexico.
F1219.3M4B44 1988
        730'.8997072'074—dc19   87-34956 CIP

Museum of New Mexico Press
P.O. Box 2087
Santa Fe New Mexico 87503

Front cover: Nuevo San Juan Parangaricutiro, Michoacán. Photo: Miho.
Back cover: San Lorenzo, Michoacán. Photo: Miho

C O N T E N T S

Foreword   vii
Charlene Cerny

Metaphor and Message: On Exhibiting Mexican Masks   ix
María Teresa Pomar

Preface   xiii
Marsha C. Bol

Behind the Mask in Mexico: Meanings and Motivations   1
Janet Brody Esser

Tlaloc Masks as Insignia of Office in the Mexica-Aztec Hierarchy   7
Cecelia F. Klein

Mexican Masks and Ceremonial Dances   29
María Teresa Pomar

Mexican Masked Festivals at the Turn of the Century, as   39
Witnessed by Frederick Starr
Marsha C. Bol

Holy Week in Los Patos, Sinaloa   63
James S. Griffith

Ritual Mediation of the Life-Death Opposition: The Meaning   77
of Mayo *Parisero* Lenten Masks
N. Ross Crumrine

Those Who Are Not From Here: Blackman Dances of Michoacán   107
Janet Brody Esser

Carnival in Tlaxcala   143
Ruth D. Lechuga

Sierra Otomí Carnival Dances   173
James Dow

Dances of the Nahuas and Otomíes of Sierra Norte de Puebla   191
Ted J. J. Leyenaar

Mask Making in Guerrero   215
Ruth D. Lechuga

Mixtec Masking Traditions: Juxtlahuaca, Oaxaca   245
Betty Ann Brown

Catalogue   263

Winter Ceremonial Season at San Lorenzo, Michoacán   275

Carnival at Papalotla, Tlaxcala   287

Lent in the Río Fuerte Region, Sinaloa   295

Festival of the Holy Cross at Zitlala, Guerrero   303

Corpus Christi at Suchiapa, Chiapas   307

Days of the Dead at Acatlán, Puebla   313

Glossary   322

Bibliography   332

Index   344

Contributors   349

F O R E W O R D

Ever since the early Modernist painters took inspiration from African masks, our own society has been fascinated with masks from other, seemingly more exotic cultures. Such masks have been regarded with both distaste and admiration, pronounced "powerful," collected avidly—and often been misunderstood.

When the Museum of International Folk Art undertook to plan an exhibition about the masks of Mexico, it was with the intention of correcting the numerous misconceptions that hindered understanding of them. It is our hope that this and the accompanying publication, both of which are based upon decades of field experience in Mexico, will do just that. We invite you to join us in looking "Behind the Mask in Mexico," from the inside out. What lies there—the essence of masked festival—is rich, complex, and rewarding.

We are very grateful to have had the participation of several distinguished scholars on this project. In addition to the authors themselves, we benefitted from the expertise of those who acted as exhibition consultants: Dr. Barney Burns, Sing Hansen, Dr. Ross Loomis, Dottie Merrill, Dr. Francisco Miranda, Dr. Marshall R. Nason, Dr. Marion Oettinger, Dr. Mari Lyn Salvador, and Sherry Kafka-Wagner. I especially wish to thank Dr. Janet Brody Esser, who served as senior consultant, and project director Marsha Bol, for their remarkable efforts and outstanding dedication to the project.

A particularly gratifying aspect of this project has been the opportunity for increased collaboration with our colleagues in Mexico. Without the direction provided by María Teresa Pomar and Ruth Lechuga, of the Museo Nacional de Artes e Industrias Populares in Mexico City, this effort would not have been possible. Their generosity of spirit has been matched only by that of the villagers in the various towns in Mexico that were selected as case studies for the exhibition. These individuals demonstrated a warm hospitality to our field team. They opened not only their fiestas but their hearts and minds to us. We therefore owe a sincere debt of gratitude to the following communities:

San Lorenzo, Michoacán
Acatlán, Puebla
Zitlala, Guerrero
Papalotla, Tlaxcala
Río Fuerte, Sinaloa
Suchiapa, Chiapas

Also deserving of thanks is Astrid Galindo Sardóz, Mexican Consul to New Mexico, for her kind assistance in many areas during the course of this project. The various lenders to this exhibition are also hereby gratefully acknowledged. Donations from the William and Nancy Anixter Foundation, Ivan and Elliot Schwartz of Studio EIS, and Sauter Lincoln-Mercury-Toyota are also much appreciated.

Deep gratitude must be expressed to the National Endowment for the Humanities, which very generously funded both the planning and implementation phases of this multi-faceted project. Although their support suffused the entire effort, funding in the areas of fieldwork and consultancies by academic colleagues was especially appreciated, as it greatly enhanced not only the overall effort but our own professional growth.

The International Folk Art Foundation continues to play a major role in the development of the Museum of International Folk Art, and for this we are most thankful. The Foundation provided funds for several important collection acquisitions and administered federal grants. They also generously provided funding for this publication, together with the Office of Cultural Affairs Revolving Fund, the Museum of New Mexico Press, and the National Endowment for the Humanities.

Charlene Cerny
Director,
Museum of International Folk Art

Jaguar suit displayed on the wall of mask maker Oliver Velázquez's home. Suchiapa, Chiapas, 1987.

METAPHOR & MESSAGE

On Exhibiting Mexican Masks

Throughout time and space, in many cultures of the world, mask use has exhibited similar configurations. Masks have been used for funerary offerings, propitiatory rites and ceremonies, and entertainment. In our time, as in the past, the use of the mask continues to be profoundly intertwined with the life of man.

Because of its beauty and expressive power, the mastery with which it is elaborated, and its ingenious exploitation of materials (whether these be as common as copper, tin cans, wood, aluminum, cardboard, cloth, stucco, or clay; semi-precious, as the stones found in mosaics; or highly valued, as with gold and silver), the mask is now considered a legitimate art form. Many specialists in the field of art have written, justifiably, that the mask, employing as it does elements of painting, sculpture, repoussé, and many other diverse crafts, has established for itself a secure niche in the world of art. How-

ever, while related to painting, sculpture, and other art forms, the mask is at the same time independent.

The mask is not simply a work from the hands of a solitary creator—it is also the embodiment of the cultural sentiments of the environment in which it is produced. The mask fortifies venerable traditions and ensures their continuity, while at the same time enriching the community's aesthetic and spiritual ambience. The mask by itself, however, in spite of its many aesthetic qualities, is able to reflect only a part of the culture of that society in which it is used. By itself it cannot express the patterns of life, cosmology, needs, or delights of that society. When the mask is extracted from its context it is converted into an object—perhaps beautiful or even exotic, but inert and cold.

We comprehend works of art created by diverse civilizations during various epochs in terms of their relationships

Performers at the Days of the Dead activities. Acatlán, Puebla, 1986.

ix

to those times and places and to the human societies that produced them for use and enjoyment. Today, in fact, we consider such works to constitute the most precious cultural legacies of those societies, whether or not the names of their makers have survived the passage of time.

The traditional mask is not an inanimate object; it acquires life from its user and provokes emotions in those who see it. In Mexico, as in many other places around the world, the mask is used to represent through the medium of dance-drama both real and mythical personages who express the shared beliefs of the community. How different it is to contemplate a mask as a solitary object isolated from its human component than to observe it in its appropriate environment, enlivened by the motivations and intelligence of its wearer, the accompaniment of its special music, and its ability to delight or frighten throngs of small children and to provoke in the adults of the community a contemplation of the content of the dance which it serves and for which it was made.

It is precisely because of this disparity that the exhibition and publication *Behind the Mask in Mexico* was designed to provide us with an understanding of how the mask functions in context. Special care has been taken to present an overview (in spite of the spatial limitations inherent in any museum) of the cultural integration of mask, dancer, and mask maker. The exhibition elucidates, too, the vital roles played by the men and women who create the costumes, those who carefully prepare the food for the dancers or oversee other details of their performance, the little girls who carry flowers to the altar, or the men who ensure the orderly progress of the event. The mask is not produced in isolation from human society but instead is part of a matrix that includes objects of such familiarity that their vitality, in a very special way, is transmitted to the mask itself.

Behind the Mask in Mexico, through the use of photographs and significant accoutrements selected from the many ethnic groups that comprise contemporary Mexico, attempts to recreate or at least give some semblance of cultural environments that include rites and ceremonies, food, homes, choreography, and dress. Portraits of some of the mask makers of Mexico have been included in the exhibition, along with an effort to present the belief systems of the involved communities.

The Museo Nacional de Artes e Industrias Populares has collaborated resolutely and enthusiastically with the Museum of International Folk Art to make this event a reality in the conviction that the efforts of its organizers will result in a new appreciation of Mexican masks—of their authenticity and impact—as fruits of Mexico's rich ethnic diversity. We hope that what is presented here will be of lasting value, rather than simply another exhibition of beautiful or spurious objects, inert and distant from the culture of the universal man.

María Teresa Pomar,
Director,
Museo de Artes e Industrias
Populares del Instituto Nacional
Indigenista,
Mexico City

Dancers performing outside the cemetery on All Souls Day. Acatlán, Puebla, November 2, 1987.

About five years ago, the Museum of International Folk Art became interested in planning an exhibition on Mexican masks, interest due in a large part to the museum's exceedingly large holdings of some six hundred and fifty masks from Mexico. This was a collection, however, with little collection information. In trying to locate further information, we found that reliable published material was sparse and difficult to obtain. Additionally, misinformation was being piled upon the layers of available, and sometimes unverifiable, material.

With numerous individuals and other institutions making inquiries about the same topic and calling upon the Museum of International Folk Art for authentication and verification, the museum accepted the responsibility for addressing the subject of masquerade and acting as a clearing house for information. Knowing in advance the intricacies and complexities of the enormous topic, and well aware of the entangled web of previously published information, the museum elected to go back to the beginning, to determine what we didn't know, and move forward from there.

In 1986 we assembled a group of interdisciplinary humanities scholars from Mexico and the United States to advise and guide our direction and content, led by senior consultant Dr. Janet Brody Esser. This collaboration of consultants and museum staff pointed the project toward the investigation of the full festival complex within the context of its community, rather than focusing simply on the individual object of the face mask.

With literally hundreds of masked festivals to choose from, a second collaboration, growing out of the first, was essential to the successful undertaking of the project. We engaged the Museo Nacional de Artes e Industrias Populares, headquartered in Mexico City and under the direction of María Teresa Pomar. Director Pomar not only has considerable knowledge of her country's folk arts but has accomplished much in the stimulation of those arts. She suggested for our project the framework of the ritual calendar and specific festival occasions in the towns and villages of Mexico, which we might select as representative examples or case studies of Mexican masked dance. Director Pomar offered the resources of her national and regional museums to assist in every conceivable way, including receiving and delivering the considerable field collections that were essential in a project of this nature.

The six communities that were selected offer specific examples of masked festival today in Mexico. They vary in size, geographic location, and language and ethnicity. Many of these festivals are unknown outside their immediate region and have not been presented in exhibition or published form. We have been generously granted permission by each of the communities to present their festival as an example of the tradition in their country. Without the efforts of many individuals from these and neighboring communities this exhibition could not have been possible. In the Tarascan region of the state of Michoacán we especially wish to thank Victoriano Salgado and his son Martín of the barrio de la Magdalena, Uruapan, for permitting us to reproduce their workshop in this exhibition and agreeing to demonstrate their mask-making skills. We are grateful to Antonio Saldaña of Nuevo San Juan Parangaricutiro for advice and information and to Antonio Cruz, Domingo Bautista, and Cecelia Victoriano of San Lorenzo, for their warm hospitality. Joaquín Amaro of Angahuan, who traditionally makes masks for San Lorenzo, agreed to contribute to this exhibition while Maclovia Anguiano of Nuevo San Juan Parangaricutiro drew upon her considerable skills as a needlewoman in making the

Participants perform at festivals in (top to bottom, left to right): Huaspaltepec, Oaxaca; Papalotla, Tlaxcala; Acatlán, Puebla; Zitala, Guerrero; Zitlala, Guerrero; Papalotla, Tlaxcala; Suchiapa, Chiapas; Papalotla, Tlaxcala; Acatlán, Puebla.

Kalalá performer during Corpus Christi activities. Suchiapa, Chiapas.

costumes of San Lorenzo for the exhibit. In Papalotla, Tlaxcala, our efforts to videotape the festival proceedings would not have been possible without the kind help of Dr. Alejandro Lara. We wish to express our appreciation also to Yolanda Ramos, Director, Museo Vivo de la Casa de las Artesanías in Tlaxcala for her valuable assistance in bringing the Papalotla dancers to Santa Fe. Enrique Méndez and other members of the Méndez family from the city of Puebla made the masks used in Papalotla for this exhibition. We are deeply indebted to Victor Seyeli, the indigenous governor of Mochicahue and his assistant, Sisto Bacasegua, for their kind permission to document their community's festival. María Guadalupe Escamilla, Director, and Martín Oscar, Chief of Operations, of the Instituto de Antropología de la Universidad del Occidente in Mochicahue, provided us with valuable information. Dr. Barney Burns and Mahina Drees formed the field collections from the Río Fuerte region for the exhibition and generously shared with us their vast store of knowledge. We wish to thank Juan Godinillo of Zitlala, Guerero, who made the leather mask and costume in the exhibition and provided us with much information. José Colasillo and his son, also from Zitlala, made and collected Tlacololero masks for the exhibition. We appreciate deeply the contribution made by the Archivo Etnográfico del Instituto Nacional Indigenista of Mexico City in lending us their splendid film, *Peleas de tigres*, documenting jaguar dances in Zitlala and Acatlán, Guerrero. We wish to thank Oliver Velásquez, mask maker of Suchiapa, Chiapas, for his guidance and also for making festival costumes for the exhibit. Francisco Cebadua, Director, Instituto de la Artesanía Chiapaneca, graciously placed his car and driver at our disposal in Suchiapa and was hospitable in every way. Our thanks also are to be expressed to

Herón Martínez, the well known potter of Acatlán, Puebla, for sharing with us his information concerning the schedule of festival activities. Of inestimable assistance also were the efforts of Pasqual Domínguez and Efraín Jiménez of Acatlán, and Norberto Simón of nearby Ahuehuetitla, who collected costumes and made masks for this exhibition.

The Mexican Consul to New Mexico, Astrid Galindo Sardóz, offered the assistance of her government in bringing dance groups and artists from the highlighted regions to perform in this country. Such a collaboration among people, museums, and countries working toward commonly shared goals has been an enriching and rewarding byproduct of this project.

In the material contained in this volume, field photos outnumber object photos by nearly three to one. Our emphasis from the beginning has been upon people in their festival occasions, not about objects taken apart from their contexts. The outstanding field photographs that Dr. Ruth Lechuga has taken throughout the years are presented here in further recognition of her outstanding work as a field photographer and ethnographer in Mexico. At all stages in this project, Dr. Lechuga generously contributed information based on her many years of familiarity with Mexico's masked dances, but a special debt of gratitude is owing her for organizing and obtaining the mask and costume collections from Acatlán, Papalotla, Suchiapa, and Zitlala. My thanks also to Drs. Janet Brody Esser, James S. Griffith, and Marion Oettinger for generously sharing their field photos.

Clearly a project of this scope cannot be the work of only one or two individuals. It is the product of many, each lending his or her special talent but, more than that, possessing an excitement, enthusiasm, respect, and commitment for the subject from the beginning and giving a heavy measure of themselves throughout. This was not a project that could be accomplished at a distance. Each participating member was required to become intimately involved with the topic. To this end, a group of Museum of New Mexico specialists, in particular Christopher Beisel, exhibit designer; Tom McCarthy, documentary filmmaker; Marilee Schmit, assistant curator; and myself, under the guidance of three consultants, Dr. Janet Brody Esser, Dr. Ruth Lechuga, and Dr. Barney Burns, visited the majority of the sites in *fiesta*, witnessing and documenting the events through video, photos, sound recording, collections, and notes. The task of developing all of this material in book form fell to Mary Wachs, editor, and Jim Mafchir, publisher, at the Museum of New Mexico Press; and to Jim Miho, book designer. Marilee Schmit contributed immeasurably at every stage, particularly as a Spanish-language specialist, and Barbara Mauldin, assistant curator, was indispensible. Conservation of the field collections was guided by Landis Smith and Bettina Raphael. My heartfelt thanks goes also to Charlene Cerny, director, and Stephen Becker, assistant director, of the Museum of International Folk Art for their continued support and encouragement of this complex project. Most of all, I must express my appreciation to Dr. Janet Brody Esser who guided the conception of this project from the development of the original planning grant all the way through to the actual exhibition and the production of this book. Our considerable progress notwithstanding, we have only begun to open new doors of inquiry into the rich and vigorous tradition of masked festival in Mexico.

Marsha C. Bol,
Project Director,
Curator of Latin American Folk Art,
Museum of International Folk Art

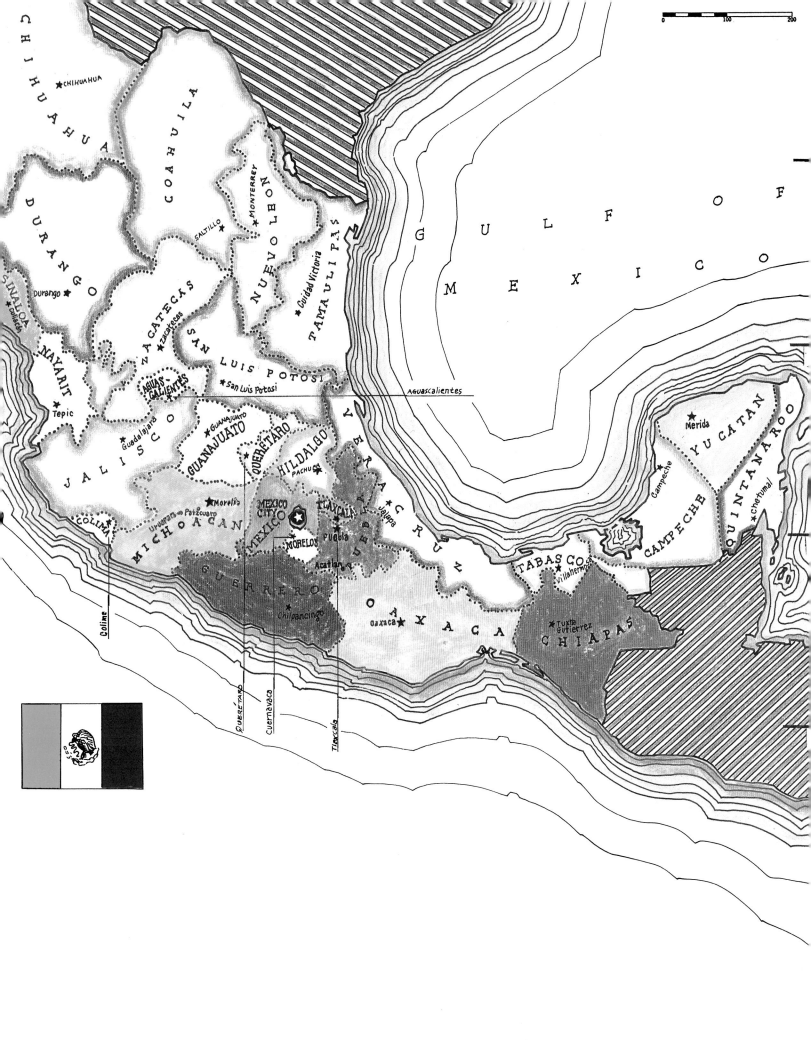

ehind the Mask in Mexico:

Meanings and Motivations

Janet Brody Esser

Mexican masks are regarded with delight and affection by many persons of diverse backgrounds. Americans, perhaps especially, have of late demonstrated their fascination by mounting museum and gallery exhibitions in ever increasing numbers and publishing attractive catalogues and books. Daily, it seems, the list of dedicated collectors swells. Many recent presentations of Mexican masks have focused on the masks themselves as *objets d'art,* emphasizing their formal and expressive qualities. The context in which masks function rarely is alluded to and often totally ignored. To a certain extent this is understandable. Mask use is no longer a central feature of community life in large industrial societies. Mexican masks, with their dramatic insistence, puzzle us and appear somehow exotic and mysteriously "other." We extol, therefore, the supposed rarity, antiquity, and curiously bizarre forms of the masks (because that is how we have come to perceive them) and thereby miss the whole point. Mexican masks are not like paintings and sculptures made by professional artists in our own society. They are made by humble folk, mostly rural, who live at subsistence or near subsistence levels and who make them for their own use and to express their own concerns. Any assumptions with regard to meaning made by uninformed outsiders run the risk of being at best fallacious and patronizing, and at worst unethically exploitive. As a

Note: "Behind the Mask in Mexico" was originally the title of a session on Mexican mask use that I organized for the Latin American Studies Association, Mexico City, in 1983.
1. In 1981 I was fortunate in being able to organize an exhibition, "Faces of Fiesta: Mexican Masks in Context," at the University Gallery, San Diego State University, and the Galería de la Ciudad, Mexicali. While much more modest in execution the aims of that exhibition were similar to those that inform the exhibit "Behind the Mask in Mexico."

result of distorted presentations, the public has been treated to the phenomenon of huge numbers of masks never intended for use but rather wholly invented by artisans in response to manipulation by dealers and collectors. Undeniably, some of these inventions are extraordinary examples of the talent that flourishes in small communities. However, their misrepresentation as genuine cultural artifacts insults Mexican folk artists, denies the value of Mexican folk culture, and ultimately leaves us with only the reflection of our own narcissistic image.

It has been the intention of those involved with this exhibition and publication to set the record straight.[1] Mexican masks are not a thing of the past, nor is their use a fragile archaism in danger of being snuffed out with encroaching modernity. Indeed, it is perhaps the failure of that modernity, even where its tangible signs are evident, to alter life significantly that has fostered the persistence of masked dances and ceremonies in Mexico. Mexican masks are not and cannot be direct survivals of pre-Columbian belief systems. The Conquest set in motion a process that was to change and continue to change the world view of the Mexican people. Today's peasants are not the *caciques,* or ruling elites, of pre-Conquest times. Today's motivations and satisfactions in donning masks are not the same as they were in the postclassic. In the nearly five hundred years since the arrival of people from the Old World, many changes have taken place. Old gods and leaders died off; a new religion and new leaders were imposed from without. Diseases, harsh treatment, and altered use of land all took their catastrophic toll. New ways were introduced, not only by Spaniards, but by immigrants from all corners of the Hapsburg empire and, of course, from Africa, source of at least 250,000 bondsmen brought to Mexico in the Colonial period to do the work of building a "New Spain."

Mexican masks are worn neither to impersonate gods, nor out of fear and trembling in the face of a terrifying and chaotic nature. Rather, they are part of highly structured and carefully organized ceremonials that permit their constituency to celebrate themselves. These masks salute ancestors and honor saints and their living equivalents— those elders of the community who assume responsibility for ritual life. Mask use honors custom but also provides an avenue for new ideas to enter a traditional society without threatening its integrity. Masks can be pleasing or funny; they also can be shocking; they are capable of shaking up the community in order to get it moving again in the right direction. Because mask-using communities are generally small and everyone knows everyone else, masks allow people to express concepts and assume identities beyond the roles generally accessible in the village. And lastly, but hardly least, there is the splendid drama of visual and auditory impact, a splendor generated from means so slender as to suggest the miraculous. But it is only in the context of the community that this impact truly can be appreciated. Resplendent personages in dazzling dress dance in the courtyards of those deserving of respect; lordly jaguars are fought and captured, devils of fantastic mien taunt and preen, oppressors are burlesqued, women are taught (by men) how to conduct themselves, evildoers are put on notice, events in the larger world are acknowledged and assessed. While expressing the varied and profound concerns and values of the community, masks also lift people out of their ordinary, workaday existence and present, for a little while, a very special world where anything is possible.

Masks are used all over Mexico. There are many different kinds of masks, and more are being made all the time. Of all the examples of Mexican folk art made for internal consumption, it is probable that masks are among the most numerous. Rather than irretrievably disappearing, masked dances are frequently resumed by communities that have neglected them for many years. Some encouragement is certainly supplied by various government agencies, mostly in the form of prizes. While the stated motivation of these agencies is preservation of folk culture (an aim certainly not inconsistent with recognition of the importance of the tourist industry), intervention is minimal and its effect still difficult to ascertain. What appears clear, however, is the immense satisfaction afforded by community participation in a world where upward mobility is difficult and comforts, few and far between.

Masks are usually used in conjunction with fiestas on important holidays. These include Christmas, New Year's Day, and Catholic holidays such as Candlemas, Carnival (just before Lent begins), and Holy Week. Corpus Christi, which coincides with the beginning of the rainy (and planting) season in Mexico, and the Days of the Dead at the beginning of November are also occasions for important mask use. Masks sometimes are used at celebrations for a community's patron saint. All these celebrations entail considerable expenditure of wealth and investment of labor and usually involve contracts made with supernaturals. In the essays that follow, the intricate interrelationships between mask use and status, myth, philosophy, religion, historical events, and distribution of surpluses will be examined. These essays, together with their illustrations (the majority of them original field photographs) bring together results of recent intensive investigations of mask use and meaning in a number of different areas of Mexico. It is hoped they will prove valuable to all who are interested in Mexican culture.

The essays have been arranged in chronological and geographical order. They begin with a discussion of the complex symbolism employed by the ruling elites among the Aztecs (Klein). An overview of Mexican mask use and mask manufacture (Pomar) follows. Bol documents the masked dances observed by anthropologist Frederick Starr at the end of the nineteenth century and presents his previously unpublished field notes. A photo essay of Mayo Holy Week celebrations in northern Mexico (Griffith) is next. Crumrine considers Mayo Lenten ceremonies as a paradigm for beliefs concerning death and dying. Representation in the western highland state of Michoacán of the very real contributions made by black Africans in the Colonial period is discussed by Esser, while Lechuga displays the richness of Carnival dances in the central Mexican state of Tlaxcala. Just who is being burlesqued, and why, among the Otomíes of the Sierra Norte de Puebla is made clear by Dow, while Leyenaar presents a survey of dances in the same region performed by both Otomí and Nahua ethnic groups. In discussing mask making in Guerrero, Lechuga documents the making of various fantasy masks while surveying the dances actually performed in that state. The final essay discusses Mixtec mask use in the state of Oaxaca (Brown). By no means have all areas or all instances of mask use been included. Indeed, the process of adequately documenting mask use in the past and present has barely begun. The goal of this volume was to include a number of pioneering studies that by their very nature would generate interest in this vital tradition.[2] The authors of the essays in this volume are all serious students of Mexican history and culture whose preparation and years of systematic study well qualify them to elucidate the intelligence and profundity of meaning that underlie Mexican masks.

And now, because it is truly for all of us, let us seek out and revel in that which lies behind the mask in Mexico!

2. It is not our intention to suggest that our authors comprise an exhaustive list of active researchers in the area of Mexican mask use. We hope that the bibliographies provided by them will suggest further reading.

Blackmen breakfasting at the home of the *cargueros* of the Holy Infant. Corupo, Michoacán, January 1, 1988.

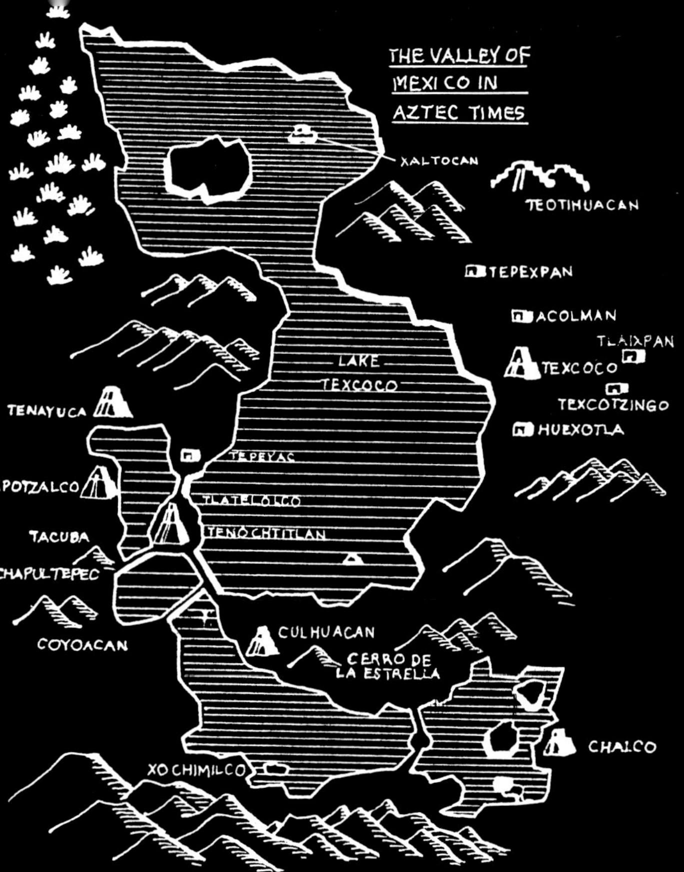
THE VALLEY OF MEXICO IN AZTEC TIMES
XALTOCAN
TEOTIHUACAN
TEPEXPAN
ACOLMAN
TLAIXPAN
TEXCOCO
TEXCOTZINGO
HUEXOTLA
LAKE TEXCOCO
TENAYUCA
TEPEYAC
AZCAPOTZALCO
TLATELOLCO
TACUBA
TENOCHTITLAN
CHAPULTEPEC
COYOACAN
CULHUACAN
CERRO DE LA ESTRELLA
CHALCO
XOCHIMILCO

1. Left side of the Teocalli de la Guerra Sagrada (Pyramid of the Sacred War).

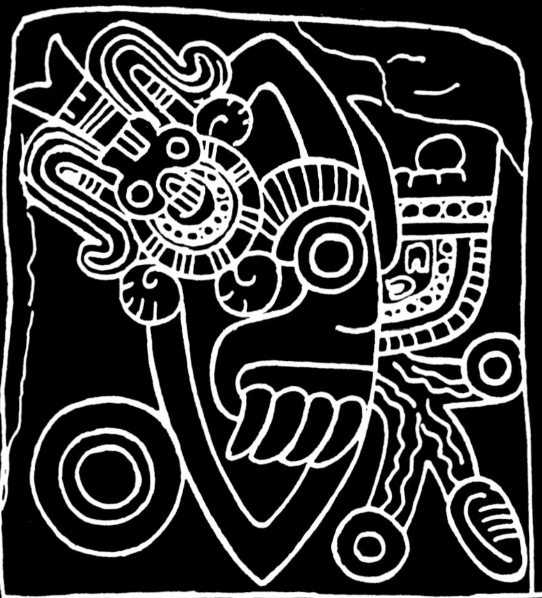
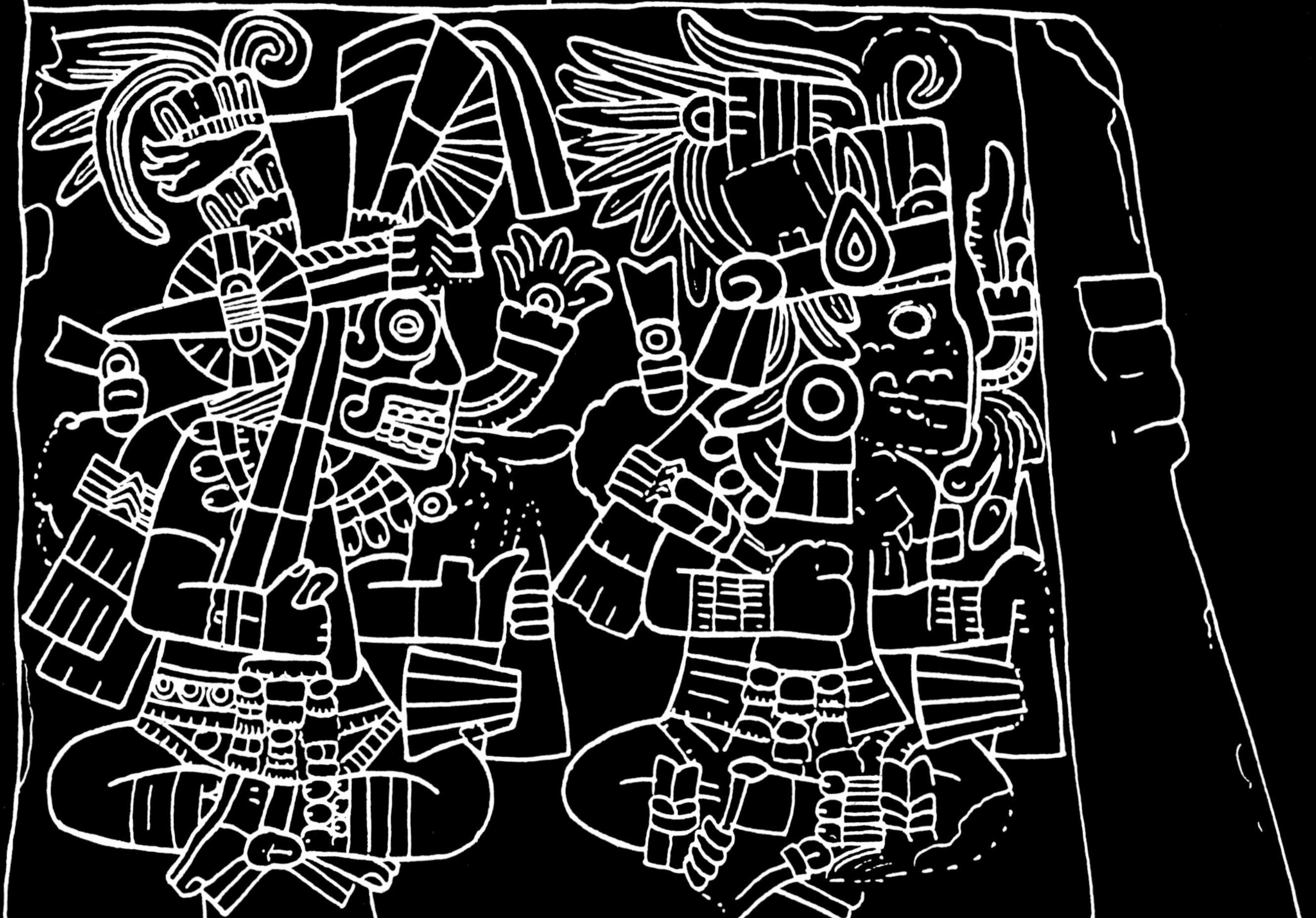

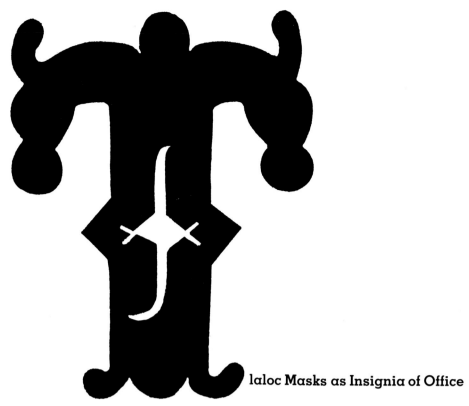

Ialoc Masks as Insignia of Office

in the Mexica-Aztec Hierarchy

Cecelia F. Klein

Note: This essay is a version of an article earlier published in Spanish in *Estudios de cultura náhuatl*; see Klein 1984:

In 1929, Mexican scholar Alfonso Caso (1929: 111) initiated one of the few discussions of Mexica-Aztec masking practices ever published by noting that "masks among primitive peoples have as their principal aim, magic." Masks, wrote Caso, "convert those who use them into new beings and produce by imitation that which is desired." For Caso, as for most scholars who have dealt with the subject, the beings into whom Aztec masks transformed their wearers were always deities, while "that which was desired"—good health and prosperity in most cases—was desired equally for all members of the group. That the Aztecs were a non-egalitarian, expansionist, state-level society some remove from what most scholars mean by primitive was, we know, well understood by Caso and the others. The implication of this for our understanding of the real meaning and function of Aztec masking, however, clearly has not been recognized and remains to be specified and developed.

Arild Hvidtfeldt (1978: 98) challenged the traditional assumption that all Aztec maskers represented deities when he argued in 1958 that magical power, for the Aztecs, resided not in the form of deities per se but in the masks and costumes worn by ritual impersonators and priests. For Hvidtfeldt, the Aztecs engaged in a form of nature worship for which images of all sorts concretized the forces recognized. These images were mistaken by the Spanish conquerors and others as images of gods. Hvidtfeldt's position recently has been revived by Richard Townsend (1979: 23–31), who similarly concludes that the Aztecs had no deities of the Judeo-Christian sort. The mask, the costume, and the impersonator or "idol" were themselves the important, sacred thing. These objects—typically an ensemble of many shapes and materials—thus express their nature by means of the separate elements and their juxtaposition, be these in the form of clothing, jewelry, body painting, or some other accoutrement.

Hvidtfeldt's and Townsend's position has received a fair amount of notice, as scholars have long observed—with considerable frustration—that Aztec masks and costumes, as worn by the

...their ritual impersonators, seldom reappeared with the exact same set of traits. Certain attributes of the god Quetzalcoatl, for example, occasionally appear on the sun god Tonatiuh, while the latter in turn may or may not wear a pair of double eyebands. The central deity of the famous Aztec calendar stone has been shown to wear facial markings and ornaments that refer not just to several different gods but to the discrete phonetic parts of its own distinctive name (Klein 1976). No rules governing the decision to combine certain sets of elements in one case and not the other have ever been discovered, and it would indeed seem that each element of the image's makeup or costume conveyed its own paraliterary message, designed to help create and communicate the distinctive, more complex messages of the whole.

While the Hvidtfeldt thesis "explains" the Aztecs' tendency to shift costume insignia on the most important images, ultimately it has failed to sit well with most scholars. The contention that the Aztecs did not conceive of real deities is implicitly rejected, for example, by both Broda's (1978) and Brown's (1979, 1984) recent arguments that priests and sacrificial victims did indeed ritually dress to impersonate the gods. The concept of deity, in the Judeo-Christian sense of the word, would not be out of place in a class society embarking on a territorial expansion as ambitious as that of the Aztecs. If the curious inconsistencies of Aztec masking practices and depictions of seemingly religious beings must be explained, in other words, the explication should not be sought in denial of the high level of development of the social or religious system. There were probably real gods in the Aztec capital, at least, and these gods most certainly had priests. The real question is not whether there were or were not true deities among the Aztecs, but whether the images that we traditionally have assumed to represent them in fact actually, consistently referred only to the gods.

In a polity based on class divisions and enforced control by an ambitious, exploitative ruling elite, the most expensive state-sanctioned images will almost always reflect the special interests of those who commissioned them. The concern for special rank and status will necessitate changes in the forms and functions of more primitive art objects and themes. When a primitive, essentially egalitarian community evolves into a stratified, expanding state, therefore, the communal, purely magical function of the mask and costume, as projected upon the Aztecs by scholars like Caso, will likely be transformed in such a way that it increasingly reflects the achievements and claims to special status of a small, but power-hungry, group. When this shift to an emphasis on badges or insignia of prestige and office is effected, one can indeed expect more of the important images to refer to individuals and offices rather than only to the gods. The insignia, moreover, in order to effectively reflect the accomplishments of the individual wearer, will begin to take less permanent, more interchangeable and less prescriptive, forms.

Was this, in fact, the case for the Mexica-Aztecs? In an earlier paper I argued that Mexica court carvings of the goddess Cihuacoatl referred directly to, while they did not actually represent, her powerful priest-impersonator, the co-ruling *cihuacoatl* (Klein n.d.). On ritual occasions, this wealthy official actually dressed in the guise of the goddess whom he served. The right to do so, like the title that bore her name, had been taken by the first man to have held that office as a reward for—and symbol of—his conquest of the region where her cult originated. The goddess's costume, in other words, came to mark an important event and major personal achievement, as well as a powerful political position within the Aztec hierarchy. When donned in public by her captor, it must have served to intimidate and deter from rebellion all who may have been chafing under the Aztec rulers' oppressive yoke. Its function here is but an extension of the Aztec practice of awarding trophies or badges after a military victory to the most valiant warriors who participated, these awards in the forms of garments and jewels often referring to, if not actually taken from, the conquered. Aztec deities were themselves reputed to have taken the insignia of other mythic beings whom they had vanquished, thereby designing for themselves a mask and costume ultimately unique in the combination of their assembled parts (Klein, n.d., 1986; Acosta Saignes 1946).

That some Aztec masks, at least, may have had as much socio-political as religious significance, and that the men who administered and performed the Aztec rites through the high-ranking offices they held were the real subjects of the masks and masked images, is supported by several stone images usually identified as the rain god Tlaloc. These images, it can be demonstrated, represent not Tlaloc but a special class of Mexica priest. These priests served not one but many deities, and their images ultimately referred to their own rank and prestige as much as, or more than, to the gods they served. The argument rests both on evidence that certain elements of these figures' costumes were insignia of office, rather than symbols of the deities per se, and on the definitely pre-Hispanic date of their manufacture. While it is certainly conceivable that the numerous post-Conquest images of priest-impersonators are attributable to the artists' lack of first-hand knowledge of pre-Conquest idols, it is inconceivable that Mexica court artists would have shared that handicap.

The first of these images is the best known; it appears to the left on the left side of the famous miniature stone pyramid, the Teocalli de la Guerra Sagrada, or Pyramid of the Sacred War, found in the foundations of Moctezuma II's palace (fig. 1). Here is it paired with another figure as complement to a second pair on the other side. The figure was identified as Tlaloc by Caso (1927: 18), later followed by Palacios (1929: 7–8), on the basis of its goggled eyes and moustache and their mutual conviction that Mexica figural imagery almost always refers to gods. Townsend (1979: 61–63), however, like Nicholson, (1973: 83) has concluded that all four are actually priests. This is patently clear, as Townsend points out, by their incense bags, medicinal back pouches, penitential maguey thorns, and *xicolli* tunics. Townsend argues that the figures represent those priests who conducted the New Fire ceremony, since the monument apparently commemorates the New Fire of 1507; he notes Sahagún's report that priests dressed for that occasion in the guises of gods such as Tlaloc. Townsend even specifically links the figure in question with that half of the dual Mexica priesthood headed by the official called Tlaloc Totec Tlamacazqui, known to have served the rain god's cult among others, and suggests that at least one of the four performed important sacrificial duties.

In support of his contention that Caso's Tlaloc is in reality a priest, Townsend could have cited Caso's (1927: 18) own observation that the moustache we regard as diagnostic of Tlaloc appears here over a mouth quite unlike that of the rain god (figs. 1, 2). Instead of the large, bestial fangs so typical of Tlaloc, this figure sports a fleshless jaw plate with two even rows of exposed human teeth lacking gums. The latter configuration, which appears on the other three personages as well, is a basic feature, as Caso noted, of depicted human skulls. While it is particularly diagnostic of the death deities

1. In those Aztec images that most certainly represent the official *cihuacoatl* in his ritual guise, rather than the goddess herself, the lower part of the face is not covered with a skeletal jaw plate, but instead seems to be flayed or covered with another's skin (e.g., fig. 5). The lips are missing and the gums exposed (see also Townsend 1979; fig. 12). Masks made of flayed skin were, we know, often worn as war trophies and are documented as having been worn by priests of the Toci Tlazolteotl cult during Ochpaniztli (Sullivan 1976: 252; Klein 1986). The connotations of the flayed skin mask were clearly very similar to those of the lower jaw–plate mask, and the two were likely even interchangeable. **2.** This is conjecture, but the bands (*amapeapilli*), as Caso (1967: 130–31) noted, are characteristic of Mictlantecuhtli and, as we shall see, Atlaua and the Chachalmeca, who were sacrificial priests.

Mictlantecuhtli and Micticacihuatl and the closely related war goddess Cihuacoatl, it therefore need not refer to gods at all (figs. 3, 4). Cihuacoatl's own priest apparently wore a bony jaw plate when he performed his official "religious" duties, and his major task was that of human sacrifice (fig. 5).[1] The presence here of skeletal jaws on the Teocalli figures can be explained as a reference to the priestly responsibility of the latter for ritual death.

Caso (1927: 18–19) similarly recognized the Teocalli figure's headdress as inappropriate for the rain god Tlaloc, whose most common headdress took the form of a plumed and crenulated fillet with a pleated neck fan (fig. 2). He related it instead to the death god Mictlantecuhtli, who indeed usually wears the paper rosette and cone element—the *cuexcochtechimalli*—in the Teocalli figure's hat (fig. 3). Caso also realized, however, that the beribboned "staff" of the latter is seen elsewhere in the headdresses of bundled memorial statues soon to be burned on the pyre (fig. 6). The quadruple knot at the front of the Teocalli figure's fillet also appears, he might have added, in a context of both funerary and "new" fire. In Codex Magliabecchiano 60, it secures the bundled grasses that will ignite the statue (fig. 6). In Codex Borbonicus 34, it binds the sticks that distribute new fire to the local temple hearths (fig. 7). The *cuexcochtechimalli* itself need not be regarded as primarily diagnostic of a deity. In Codex Borbonicus 36, it appears, together with the spiral-pleated rosette also often seen on Mictlantecuhtli, as decoration on the so-called year bundle that was ritually burned at the end of the New Fire ceremony (fig. 9).

Numerous attributes therefore support Townsend's assertion that the Teocalli "Tlaloc" figure is in fact a priest. But who *was* the priest? Caso (1927: 21) noted that the Teocalli figure's headdress features a large, inverted eagle's

foot and identified it with that mentioned by Sahagún in his description of the month festival of Tecuilhuitontli. This festival was dedicated to the salt goddess Uixtocihuatl, who was said to be the older sister of the Tlaloque, who is assistant to the Tlaloc.[2] A female impersonator of the goddess, together with a number of male war captives, was sacrificed to the goddess on the platform of the main temple of the rain god. Sahagún wrote that when the feast day arrived, "then were arrayed the priests who would slay the victims. These were called the Uixtoti" (1950–69, 2: 88). It was the Uixtoti who wore the head insignia "made like the claws of eagles." Caso (1927: 22) concluded from Sahagún's ambiguous phrasing that it was the captives rather than the priest who wore the eagle claw headdress, and accordingly identified the small male figure wearing it in Codex Borbonicus 7 as one of those sacrificed to the salt goddess (fig. 8). The figure appears, however, in the context of the seventh *trecena*, a *trecena* always patronized not by Uixtocihuatl but by Chicomecoatl and Tlaloc. Tlaloc appears here, in fact, atop the very mountain from which gushes the water in which the small figure apparently founders. While the figure therefore may represent a child sacrificed to the rain god himself (such children *were* typically dispatched by drowning), its white, rubber-spattered garments are those worn in the ceremonial section of the codex (pls. 25, 31, 32) by priests. The eagle claw element appears on page 29, as Caso himself noted, on two trumpet blowers who are clearly officials and not intended victims (fig. 10).

That the eagle claw device was that of a sacrificer and not the sacrificed is made clear in Sahagún's subsequent description of the month festival of Ueitecuilhuitl. Of the priest who sacrificed the female impersonator of the maize goddess Xilonen, again closely related to Tlaloc, the friar wrote, "he

2. Tlaloc, god of rain.
Codex Magliabecchiano 22.

3. Mictlantecuhtli, god of death. Codex Borbonicus 10.

4. The goddess Cihua-
coatl. Codex Maglia-
becchiano 33.

14

5. The priest-imper-
sonator Cihuacoatl.
Codex Borbonicus 23
(detail).

bore an eagle claw device on his back"
(1950–69, 2: 99). The device does not appear in Sahagún's *Primeros memoriales*
illustrations of either Tecuilhuitontli or
Ueitecuilhuitl, but the sacrificing officer
in the former has both a cone and a
rosette in his headdress (fig. 11). Sahagún expressly stated, moreover, that the
priest who sacrificed Xilonen "carried
a rosette on his back" (1950–69, 2: 99).
The most elaborately dressed male
priest in attendance at the sacrifice of
a goddess impersonator in Codex Borbonicus 30 also wears such a headdress, this one replete with the ribboned staff and quadruple knot of the
Teocalli being (fig. 16). The crossed
paper bands on his chest identify him
with sacrifice.[3] While this individual
lacks the eagle claw device described
by Sahagún for the Xilonen sacrificer,
the ceremony being enacted here is
indeed that of Ueitecuilhuitl (Klein 1980:
191–93).

The exact rank and importance of the
priest carved on the left side of the Teocalli de la Guerra Sagrada is indicated by an image included by Sahagún
in his *Primeros memoriales* illustrations
of the names and dress of the major
Mexica deities (fig. 12). Among those
familiar to us as major Aztec gods and
goddesses (including Tlaloc), Sahagún's informants have included a being
glossed as "Chachalmeca." This being
wears the same *cuexcochtechimalli*
ornament and spiral-pleated rosette
that we saw on the Teocalli figure.
Sahagún's accompanying verbal description of the being refers, moreover,
to the sacrificial band of bast paper as
normally having been wrapped around
the figure's shoulders (Seler 1939, 2, pt.
3: 59). The paper wrap does not appear
on this figure, but it does appear here
on Atlaua, a god of the Chinampa
district of Lake Xochimilco, with whom
our figure shares the cleft reed staff,
or *tlimetl*, and the spiral rosette and
cuexcochtechimalli headdress (fig. 14).
Atlaua wears the ribboned staff of the

3. See page 143,
note 1.
4. E.g., Durán
(1967, 1: 120).

6. Memorial figure of
a deceased ruler
being honored during
Tititl. Codex Maglia-
becchiano 60.

Teocalli figure as well and carries a
bi-zoned shield much like that of Chachalmeca; the red paint said by Sahagún to have been applied around the
lips of the latter appears, like the paper
wrap, only on Atlaua. Seler (1939, 2,
pt. 3: 59) long ago pointed out the obviously close relationship of the two
beings, noting that Atlaua calls himself
inni chalmecatl, "I, the Chalmecatl," in
a song devoted to him. In his *Historia
general,* Sahagún refers to the dress of
the Chachalmeca "deity" as that of
"Atlaua and the gods of Chalman"
(1977, 4: 282). The headdress with the
two rosettes and ribboned staff was, he
says, "the proper dress of that people
of Chalman."

Sahagún implies, therefore, that the
Mexica recognized a god named Chachalmeca. There is, however, little evidence of this. Most other authors fail
to mention such a deity.[4] A goddess
named Chalmecacihuatl *is* mentioned
occasionally and appears among Sahagún's (in Seler 1939, 2, pt. 3: 59) illustrated list of deities; in Codex Ríos (pl. 3)
she appears in concert with seven
"death" deities as the consort of the
death god Tzontemoc. Seler (1939, 2, pt.
3: 82) described her as the wife of all
"the Chachalmeca," who he concluded were actually a group of gods of
death. The pluralistic character ascribed
here was based, however, on the chroniclers' far more frequent mention of a
group of four, sometimes five, priests
called Chachalmeca, whose task was
to hold fast and dispatch sacrificial victims. They apparently belonged to the
most elite grade of Mexica priest, that
of the *cuacuacuiltin,* or *cuauhuehuetque,* who, as the most elderly and
experienced of the priests, enjoyed the
name *tecuacuiltin* (Acosta Saignes
1946: 154; Durán 1967, 2: 159). *Tecuacuiltin* translates as "the god's like-
nesses," and Durán (1971: 91) states
that the leader of the Chachalmeca—
the one who actually wielded the sacrificial knife—changed his name and

7. New Fire priest.
Codex Borbonicus 34
(detail).

8. Uixtoti priest in the
water. Codex Bor-
bonicus 7 (detail).

5. See also Jiménez Moreno (1974: Plate 1, #2). The sacrificing officers in Codex Borbonicus 31 are also probably Chachalmeca, although their headdresses lack the *cuexcochtechimalli.*

6. Durán (1967, 2: 159) actually says that the "supreme priest" was addressed by some as "Papa" and by others as "Topiltzin."
7. The association with the Temple of Tlaloc can be inferred from (1) the combination of Tlaloc and Cihuacoatl insignia on many images of priests; (2) the probability that Cihuacoatl was regarded as the wife of Tlaloc (Klein 1980); and (3) the attendance of the *cihuacoatl* at the Temple of Tlaloc in Codex Magliabecchiano 79. Durán (1967, 2: 311–12), moreover, refers to a specific priest-impersonator dressed as "the lord of the underworld" —surely the *cihuacoatl*—as a fire priest.

8. See also Townsend's (1979) Figure 12, where the figure's crosslegged pose clearly identified it, as Townsend points out, as a (male) impersonator of the goddess.
9. Particularly as Codex Ramírez (1975: 99–100) indicates that the Chachalmeca were specifically active during Panquetzaliztli, the month in which New Fire is being drilled in Codex Borbonicus.

costume for each ritual occasion. Blackened priests who wear the double rosette and/or the *cuexcochtechimalli* headdress clearly assisted at sacrifices during numerous month festivals (fig. 15), and it is thus possible that the Uixtoti sacrificers of Uixtocihuatl and Xilonen were themselves members of the Chachalmeca.[5] Since those officiants wore the eagle claw and rosette headdress that appears on our Teocalli figure, it follows that the figure likewise may represent one of the Chachalmeca.

This identification is supported by the appearance on the *Primeros memoriales* "Chachalmeca" of the heavy eye rings, prominent upper lip or moustache, and long fangs of Tlaloc. The first two, as noted earlier, appear on the Teocalli figure as well. Acosta Saignes (1946: 156) concluded that the Chachalmeca operated under the supervision of the Quetzalcoatl Totec Tlamacazqui, the leader of the second half of the Mexica priesthood, because their leader, the chief sacrificer, was addressed as "Topiltzin." In the myths and histories, Topiltzin is a name usually associated with the historic Quetzalcoatl. After the Conquest, however, the title appears to have had the meaning of "head priest" in general and as such could have been applied to the Tlaloc Totec Tlamacazque just as well. The highest official of the Tlaloc priesthood was, in fact, the *cihuacoatl,* who in Codex Borbonicus is glossed as *papa mayor,* the "supreme priest" (fig. 5).[6] Pomar (1975: 19) similarly identifies the *cihuacoatl* of Texcoco as "the principal priest." Since the *cihuacoatl* is reported by many to have been the sacrificer par excellence, it is even possible that it was he who led the Chachalmeca (Durán 1967, 2: 193). The *cihuacoatl* was associated, like them, with the Chalma *calpulli* (barrio) and with the temple of Tlaloc (Zantwijk 1963: 192, 205–6; 1966: 181–82).[7] The appearance of select features of Tlaloc on his or any

Chachalmeca's visage thus could simply have served to signify affiliation with the Tlaloc branch of the complex priesthood.

The figure bearing attributes of Tlaloc on the left side of the Teocalli de la Guerra Sagrada must therefore directly refer to, and hence represent, one of the Chachalmeca. This means that the carvers of that monument were directed to portray not gods but certain very high-ranking officials. The Teocalli, moreover, is not the only pre-Hispanic monument to do so. A large stone relief carved in the fine style of the Mexica court and now in the Museo Nacional de Antropología e Historia in Mexico City presents a figure with a fleshless jaw plate and fanged mouth much like Tlaloc's and wearing a headdress featuring the spiral-pleated ornament, the paper rosette (here without the cone), and the inverted eagle foot that Caso identified on the Teocalli figure (fig. 13). This being, moreover, bears the monstrous joints, tangled grass hair, cloth earrings, and detached skull normally seen on images of the goddess Cihuacoatl (fig. 17).[8] It wears, however, not the round eye rings of the rain god but distinctive eye plates shaped like a Maltese Cross. These eye plates appear in Codex Borbonicus 34 on the blackened priests who arrive at the hill of Uixachtlan to distribute New Fire (fig. 7). These priests wear the *cuexcochtechimalli* in their headdress, and their mouths are painted red like Atlaua's (fig. 14). Their appearance, in fact, is remarkably like that of the Codex Magliabecchiano 60 memorial statue, which even wears the star-edged black eye mask of Atlaua (fig. 6). Since that mummy also wears the long, drooping, tassled banner that in the *Primeros memoriales* characterizes the "god" Chachalmeca, the New Fire priests may themselves have been Chachalmeca.[9]

In any event they were members of the Tlaloc priesthood. Acosta Saignes

9. Year bundle
wrapped for crema-

10. The Tlaloc Totec Tlamacazqui was, moreover, as Acosta Saignes (1946: 157) notes, also addressed as "Tlalocan Tlenamacac."

11. Sahagún also (1950–69, 4: 45) says of the Tlaloques that they "were like the fire priests."

12. Seler here identified Chalma as a large district encompassing all of Chalco, but both Acosta Saignes (1946: 220) and Zantwijk (1963) assume that it was a barrio, or *calpulli,* within the city.

13. Acosta Saignes (1946: 181) states that the *cihuacoatl* received tribute second in amount only to that received by the king himself.

(1946: 153–58) implied that they were members of the *tlenamacaque,* the rank just below the *cuacuacuiltin* in the priestly hierarchy, whom the chroniclers often referred to as the "fire priests." His opinion is supported by Sahagún's (1950–69, 2: 82) report that the fire priests who officiated at the festivities of Etzalcualiztli (a month dedicated to Tlaloc) "all put on the shoulder rosettes" and had themselves "painted after the manner of Uixtocihuatl"; he explicitly states here, as elsewhere, that they dressed up like the rain god and wore a "Tlaloc mask" as well. Acosta Saignes (1946: 157) concluded that these priests were under the direction of the Quetzalcoatl Totec Tlamacazqui, but they were recruited from the *tlamacazque* priests, who were definitely priests of Tlaloc.[10] The use of Tlaloc insignia among the *tlamacazque* was clearly also common, as Sahagún (1950–69, 1: 75) said that they looked like Tlaloques.[11] All of the Tlaloc priests, however, also wore, as we have seen, a number of insignia referring to other deities and to their office alone. When we look at Mexica images such as the Museo Nacional's stone head of a male with a fanged mouth, large upper lip, Maltese cross eye plates, and rosette headdress, therefore, we must acknowledge them as depictions not of the rain god but of high-ranking priests (fig. 18). Further, the same identification must be applied to those entirely human figures who, like those of the Huitzuco relief identified by Seler (1939, 2, pt. 2: 177) as the souls of dead warriors, wear the same headdress insignia worn by the Chachalmeca (fig. 19).

But just who were these members of the Chachalmeca? Sahagún (in Seler 1939, 2, pt. 2: 177) makes it clear that their name derived from their membership in the Chalma *calpulli* (barrio) which, according to Zantwijk (1963), was the oldest and most prestigious in the city.[12] According to some sources, Chalmecans made up one of the original Aztec tribes to migrate from Aztlán;

Zantwijk links that tribe directly to the seditious Malinalxochitl, upstart sister of the tribal deity Uitzilopochtli, who was banished with her supporters to the Chinampaneca. When that potentially productive region, eventually to provide up to two-thirds of the capital's subsistence requirements, was later forcefully incorporated into the hungry empire, some of its inhabitants apparently settled in the southeast corner of the city (Parsons 1976: 254; Zantwijk 1963). Their patron deity was the goddess Cihuacoatl, almost certainly a version of their founding ancestress, whose head priest was in time the *cihuacoatl,* the very individual who surely headed up the Chachalmeca. Since the *cihuacoatl* appropriated his office and title as reward for his leadership in the conquest of the Chinampa region, those officials immediately under him may well have done the same (Klein 1986, n.d.). Durán (1971: 91) informs us that, unlike the members of the other, lower grades of the priesthood, the high-ranking and "much revered" Chachalmeca passed their titles down "from father to son like our own primogeniture." Such securing of a powerful and obviously economically strategic position within a single descent line matches nicely that effected by the *cihuacoatl* himself. The first *cihuacoatl,* the famous Tlacaelel, is known to have passed his title directly to his son, who transferred it to his own heir in turn (Rounds 1977).[13] Like the king and his powerful assistant, therefore, the Chachalmeca represented wealthy lineages whose relatively recently acquired control of the system was carefully guarded against outside encroachment. If Padden (1970: 90–99), Broda (1978), and Brown (1979, 1984) are correct in asserting that much human sacrifice served by means of intimidation and propaganda to reinforce and justify this control, then Mexica interest in depicting those who performed that sacrifice is at least partially explained.

chachalmeca

12. A Chachalmeca.

13. A Chachalmeca,
stone relief.

15. The Chachalmecas performing a human sacrifice during the month festival Panquetzaliztli.

14. Atlaua, god of the Chinampaneca.

16. Priest-sacrificer for the Ueitecuilhuitl festival. Codex Borbonicus 30 (detail).

17. The goddess
Cihuacoatl, relief on
underside of a stone
sculpture.

18. Head of a Chachal-
meca, stone.

19. Two Chachal-
mecas, relief on a
stone block from
Huitzuco, Guerrero.

exican Masks and

Ceremonial Dances

María Teresa Pomar

*El teatro y la danza son materializa-
ciones de una expresión cultural de
complejos juegos y profundo significado
social.*

—Alfredo Barrera Vázquez (1980)

In present-day Mexico the mask is not an object endowed with a supernatural power transferable to the wearer, nor can its wearer, through contact with the mask, set aside his inhibitions or change himself into another personage. The mask is, rather, an element that completes the costume of the participant in order to more clearly portray a particular character. Participants use masks in a dance, as do good actors everywhere, to identify themselves at any given moment of performance with the personage represented, so as to evoke audience response.

Dance is theater inasmuch as theater is considered a spectacle related to a concrete expression in which actors interpret an author's work. But the traditional ceremonial dance in Mexico is much more than theater because it embodies the mysticism, magic, and tradition of its culture. While professional actors participate in theater, in the ceremonial dance it is the common people who act; it is the baker, the artisan, or the peasant who represents Saint James or the Devil in order to transmit the message, the homage, or the invocation of his society with the obligation and awareness of being the

20. Mask maker Victoriano Salgado roughs out a mask in his workshop. Uruapan, Michoacán.

intermediary between his community and the being or action invoked.

Each man or woman who participates in a traditional dance may be motivated by spiritual concerns but also by the simple desire to participate in front of an audience that understands and enjoys these motivations. It is understood that at the end of the performance the actor will once again become the peasant, artisan, workman, or housewife he or she is in everyday life. Motivations for dancing may include the need to keep religious promises, invoke supernatural aid for the community, give thanks for harvests brought in, or simply express devotion toward a saint. But execution of the dance, whether or not masks are worn, will conform to traditional guidelines.

Masks in Mexico are not isolated objects; they are an integral part not only of costumes but of ceremonial performances. Many of the masked dances in Mexico today are ceremonial theatrical functions that assume choreographed forms in order to express specific themes. As works of popular theater these dances combine acting, costumes, and music to express an entire plot.

In spite of growing interest in Mexican masks, no organization or individual has succeeded in compiling a complete inventory of existing dances in Mexico. Whether one states that two thousand or ten thousand dances exist is irrelevant because some dances disappear and new ones arise that are more appropriate for our time. Even though part of the traditional ceremony may be sacrificed and certain masks may be changed or lost, the new dances continue to be vigorous and use sumptuous costumes. The vitality of dance mask use was demonstrated most effectively in 1980 in the city of Guadalajara, where more than 150 dance groups gathered to honor the Virgin of Zapopan. The majority of them performed dances of the type called

conquista (Conquest). In these the *bartolos* or *batos* (masked characters that dedicate themselves to keeping order among the spectators) still live, now transformed by plastic masks into monsters of the Frankenstein type. The motivation, however, is still the same: to render homage, fulfill vows made in return for miracles, and petition the Virgin of Zapopan.

The Mexican mask, like many other phenomena of our popular art, is not the product of influences either wholly indigenous or occidental. Alfonso Caso has characterized the national culture—mestizo—as a mixture of three basic plant foods: Indian maize, European wheat, and Asian rice. To this list I would add the African yam, which black ethnic groups, torn from their home by slavers, brought with them, along with their singular sense of music. Numerous dances, masks, and musical instruments used in many regions of Mexico attest to the vigorous influence of these settlers of Mexico. Without question, it is these four great cultural currents that have helped to form the characteristics of our present-day masks and dances.

Masks are fashioned of diverse materials: of wood of various kinds, from the soft *parota* to cedar and the soft coral tree (*colorín* or *tzompantle*); of leather, wax, cotton, felt, and even delicate tulle; of cardboard, wire mesh, clay, alloys of iron and aluminum, gourd, tin, natural fibers, and turtle or armadillo shell. They are decorated with vegetable and industrial paints, lacquer, or shellac, and adorned with *ixtle* (agave fiber), human hair, horsehair, wild boar bristles, lamb or goat pelts, beads and sequins, natural horns of deer, goats, cows, and sheep, or iron, wood, and even rags.

In the southern state of Morelos and towns bordering the Pico de Orizaba in Veracruz, masks of wire mesh adorned with beards fashioned of human hair are used for the dances of *chinelos*

21. Antonio Saldaña at work on a mask in the courtyard of his home. Nuevo San Juan Parangaricutiro, Michoacán.

(long-robed dancers with large head-dresses) and *moros y cristianos* (Moors and Christians). Wax masks, sometimes painted, sometimes decorated with beards, are used for the *cuadrillas* (quadrilles or court dances) performed at Carnival in various towns of the state of Mexico—Chimalhuacan, Los Reyes, and La Paz, among others. In Zapotec towns in the Valley of Oaxaca—Zaachila, San Martín Telcajete, and San Bartolo Coyotepec, among others—they are used for the dances of the *jardineros* (gardeners), where they are decorated only with paint.

Masks are of various shapes: *caretas* (face masks) serve to cover the face; helmet masks rest on top of the dancer's head; *media caretas* (half-face masks) cover only the upper or lower half of the face; and the *casquetes* (skullcaps) are placed on the upper part of the skull. There also exist back masks that, by means of suspenders and belts, are hung waist-high on the wearer's back.

Long fringes attached to the hat sometimes serve as masks, as in the case of the *negritos* of Papantla, Veracruz, and Sierra Norte de Puebla. Sometimes strings of beads in the form of curtains are joined to crowns and almost completely hide the face, as among the *matachines* of Jalisco, San Luis Potosí, and Zacatecas. Thick black veils are worn by the Holy Week centurions among the Mayos and Yaquis of Sonora and Sinaloa and by the *diablos* (devils) of religious theme plays of Colima. In the state of Colima monstrous faces are embroidered with colored sequins that trace eyes, noses, and mouths on pieces of black tulle.

Among the Otomí Indians of San Pablito, Puebla, and the Tzotzil and Tzeltal peoples of Chiapas, large dark glasses are used that cover part of the face. In some places in Mexico face and body paint substitute for masks. When the Coras paint their bodies they speak of "erasing" them; that is, losing their sense of individuality. The Tarahumara

Pascoleros utilize face and body paint which, along with a crest of feathers, a loincloth, a sash, and *tenivares* (cocoon leggings) on their ankles, make up the costume of those who participate in the dance.

Although face masks are those used most frequently in almost all the dances of Mexico, helmet masks abound. In the Museo Nacional de Artes e Industrias Populares there is a wood helmet mask of a Moor from the state of Mexico that has been dated between the seventeenth and eighteenth centuries. Today, for this same character, a helmet made of cardboard and fabric is used in the dance of the *segadores* (harvesters) and *negros sordos* (deaf blacks). In the town of Acapetlahuaya, Guerrero, wooden helmet masks representing *tigre* (jaguar) and *perra* (bitch) are made for the dance of *tecuanes* (jaguars; literally, "man-eaters").

Today, helmet masks made from hollowed logs with fabulous carvings of four faces and hunting scenes or zoomorphic figures carved on the back have proliferated, but to date no trace of use of these masks from the state of Guerrero or elsewhere has been found. Some of them, as objects in themselves, are of extraordinary beauty.

Masks such as those of the *tastoanes* of Tonalá and the *diablos de pastorela* of Cajetitlan (both in the state of Jalisco) and also some from the state of Guerrero that are adorned with abundant *ixtle* hair are firmly attached to the headdress, forming a type of helmet that rests on top of the head. Helmet masks of goat or lamb skin which the *chapayecas* (Pharisees) use during Holy Week among the Yaqui and Mayo groups of Sonora and Sinaloa also exist. For these masks the whole skin is used. The face is shaved and eyes, nose, and mouth are painted. Sometimes the face is made of wood and attached to the helmet. Masks may then be decorated with two or three horns, ears, hats, paper flowers, or ribbon topknots. At the end of Holy Week masks are burned in fires kindled in front of the churches.

In the zone of Pahuatlan, Puebla, and Tenango de Doria, Hidalgo, *voladores* (flyers) until recently were dressed in bird outfits made of feathers. In the zone of Tenango a wooden mask of the helmet type is still made representing the head of an eagle. At the museum we are familiar with two examples of these masks which resemble pre-Columbian carvings.

In some states of the republic, helmets of tin plate with visors cover head and face. In the state of Mexico, in the town of San Martín de Pirámides, a helmet mask made of an iron and aluminum alloy representing the head of the apostle Saint James is used for the dance of the *archareos*. The men who compete for the honor of wearing this mask (which weighs just under five kilograms) are called *sabarios*. A rigorous reckoning of the religious and social contributions they have made to the community is used in making the decision. Señor Santiago in this dance of the *archareos* is accompanied by other dancers who use felt masks that resemble African masks. These masks are joined to lambskin, converting them into helmets. In the town of Zitlala, Guerrero, there is a dance of *tecuanes* which employs jaguar helmet masks made of numerous layers of green and yellow leather, possibly with the objective of protecting the wearers from the blows that they give each other with a rope during the dance. Often a painted leather helmet is added to a wooden face mask to complete the head of a jaguar or other animal. Such masks are still used in the state of Guerrero.

In the Mixteca zone of the coast of Oaxaca, small wooden masks measuring no more than fifteen centimeters tall by a little less in width are used for the dance of the *tejorones*. In the Zoque region of Ocozocuantla, Chiapas, a large helmet mask—eighty centimeters in diameter—that represents a jaguar is made by stretching painted fabric over a reed frame, umbrella fashion. Half-face masks are also common in some dances, especially in the Atzompa region of the Veracruz sierra and in Zapopan, Jalisco. Skullcap masks are worn among the Tzotzil of Zinacantan, Chiapas, who use the dried muzzle of a jaguar as though it were a hat. Among the Zoques of Suchiapa, Chiapas, a wooden jaguar helmet worn on top of the head is used for the dance of the *kalalá*. The feline's mouth is left open to serve as a visor.

Back masks generally take the form of a serpent among the Chontal people of San Miguel and San Pedro Huamelula, Oaxaca. In the latter town a very beautiful example of this type of mask, which the townsfolk assert dates from Colonial times, is zealously guarded in the church. This type of mask is also used among the Huaves of San Mateo del Mar, Oaxaca, as well as among the Zoques of the region of Ocozocuantla, Chiapas, where in addition to the figure of a serpent the head of a pig carrying an ear of corn in its mouth is used.

The gourd (*lagenaria vulgaris*), that natural product so useful as a container in rural settings, is used by the *hortelanos* (gardeners) of Uruapan for comical masks that are adorned with beards, moustaches, and hairdos of *ixtle* or lambswool. The Pames of Santa María Acapulco, San Luis Potosí, also use masks of this material for their ceremonial dances. Masks made of papier-mâché are used by the Cora Indians of Nayarít (Jesús María, Nayar, and Santa Teresa) during Holy Week. These are shaped over clay molds and adorned with vegetable fibers and deer horns, then painted white, black and white, and finally many colors on the successive days of the festival. At the conclusion of the ceremonies masks are thrown into the river in an act symbolizing termination of evil. There are also the simple carnival masks of Celaya, Guanajuato, which together with Prussian helmets and swords of the same material are the delight of children during the September fiestas or at local fairs. With wastepaper, paste, and paint a marvelous world of clowns, devils, goats, witches, old people, sultans, monkeys, frogs, skeletons, and beautiful ladies arises from the hands of humble craftsmen. The Otomí people of El Doctor, Querétaro, make masks of old rags to which *ixtle* headdresses or paper flowers are added to convert them into the devils and animals that, commanded by the scoundrel *Barrabás,* swarm about the town on holy days.

In recent times masks of painted, embossed copper or silver have become popular. The Museo Nacional de Artes e Industrias Populares has conducted an extensive investigation into these masks and concluded that they are spurious. Although very beautiful, they are made to order and do not correspond to traditional use. The investigation yielded similar results with regard to some very elaborate masks that were painted in imitation of an antique painting technique of the state of Guerrero. These extraordinary wooden masks incorporate serpents, lizards, devils, and other figures in the same carving. As works of popular art they are outstanding, but they are not masks intended for use.

With the possible exception of Baja California and Quintana Roo, masks are used throughout the entire republic with varying frequency. Masks in conjunction with dances of *moros y cristianos* are the most often used. Some of these masks exhibit cruel expressions, while others have the beautiful, gently smiling faces of saints.

In numerous traditional performances, many with biblical themes, the Devil is portrayed by masks and outfits of diverse styles, the only common feature being horns. In Huasteca, San Luis Potosí, the masks are made of fabric and filled with hay; in Uruapan, Michoacán, bull horns are used; generally, throughout the country, horns of goats and cows are used. The multiple-horned devil of the dance of the *diablos* of Telolopan, Guerrero, and the more westernized Devil of Juxtlahuaca in the Mixteca region of Oaxaca demonstrate the diversity with which this evil character is conceptualized.

Death is also a common character in the dances of Mexico. He appears in numerous plays with religious content, such as *siete vicios* (Seven Vices), especially in the states of Guerrero, Zacatecas, Hidalgo, Mexico, and Michoacán. On the Day of the Dead in Pinotepa de Don Luis, Oaxaca, however, only youngsters wear masks of death as they go merrily from house to house in search of handouts.

Masks of blacks are also used widely and there are many dances in which they figure importantly. In the Juárez sierra of Oaxaca there are the *negritos comilludos* (tusked blacks), and among the Mixteca of the coast a mask with exaggeratedly flattened nose and everted lips is used in the dance of *tejorones.* In Michoacán blacks are portrayed with delicate features (aquiline nose and dimpled cheeks), and in Guerrero characters representing blacks participate in many of the traditional dances. In Jalisco old clay masks of Tonalá and Tlaquepaque have survived that represent blacks with curly hair. In the dance of the *negritos* of Puebla and Veracruz all the dancers are costumed as blacks but without masks; only two or three dancers wearing black-painted face masks participate.

Another character that appears in many different dances is the *viejo, viejito,* or *huehue* (old man). In the dance of *viejitos* in Michoacán, all the characters wear masks of old people, despite the full energy and strong rhythm of the dance. In Guerrero, in the dance of *huehues,* wrinkles are carved in the wood.

Of enormous importance is the character of the *tigre.* The immense variety of masks depicting these felines in many dances is notable. The jaguar masks of Guerrero, Zacatecas, Oaxaca, Chiapas, Tabasco, Puebla, and Hidalgo are particularly well known. Dances of *tecuanes* are very popular in the state of Guerrero. In Olinala, Guerrero, jaguar masks are painted with lacquer and adorned with boar bristles. In the state of Chiapas they are made of cloth over a reed framework. Jaguar masks of the coastal Mixteca characteristically include large eyes made of mirrors that, by reflecting the sun, bewilder the "dogs" and "hunters" who kill the jaguar. Today these masks imitate the style of a noted mask maker from Huazolotitlán, Oaxaca, who carved magnificent and realistic jaguar heads of *parota* wood.

Costumes worn by dancers are as varied as the dances themselves. Some costumes are made of very modest elements, intended merely as symbolic representations, while others are extraordinarily luxurious. Dance outfits such as those worn by the *matachines* of Chihuahua may be improvised with simple bandanas and brightly colored fabrics or, as with those used in the *cuadrillas* of the state of Mexico, embroidered with gold and silver thread and cost more than 100,000 pesos.

Dancers carry or wear objects whose significance may have become lost or with which the spectator is unfamiliar, such as the little wooden horses used by Santiago Apostol or San Martín Caballero. These little horses are part of a wooden frame that encircles the body and from which the head, feet, and tail of the horse project. In the dance of the *pescado* (fish), the dancer wears a large mermaid tail fashioned of cardboard. In other dances such as the *concheros* (also known as "Aztec" dancers) of Guanajuato and Mexico City, the *pluma* (feather) of the Valley of Oaxaca, and the *paragüeros* (umbrella bearers) or *charros* (horsemen) of Tlaxcala, immense headdresses of feathers of peacocks, ostriches, or even chickens are worn.

In some dances, participants carry dolls or dried animals, generally squirrels or badgers—while in others jaguar, deer, or boar skins are worn on their backs. In warrior dances such as *las varitas* (the little rods) of Huasteca, San Luis Potosí, dancers use small, highly decorated canes to fence with during the course of the dance. Small bows are carried in dances of *conquista.* Tambourines, bells, seeds, or *tenivares* lend rhythmic emphasis to many of the dances.

But what of those who make the masks? The mask maker himself is a man who works for his own community and who lives within its cultural sphere. He is a man who exhibits a profound creativity that permits him to shape his work to meet the exigencies of his time, but who has the wisdom not to alter the roots of national consciousness. He is a man who makes abundantly clear his love for his craft, expressed in the form of his masks, which are created and recreated almost daily.

The tendency to believe that crafts produced in the past are superior to those of the present is a mistake, because each object is related to its own time. Changes in form may very well reflect accelerated changes in society itself. But such evaluations certainly influence the manufacture of Mexican masks. The buyer avidly seeks to acquire masks that have been labeled *bailadas* (danced), scorning new ones even though they may correspond to more genuine traditions. Generally, it is the artisan, not the dancer, who makes the mask and is the guardian of tradition. It is he who organizes the paraphernalia of the dance and possesses knowledge of the characters. Commercial demand and the desire to

22. Masks in various
stages of completion
hang above mask
maker Antonio

Saldaña's work bench.
Nuevo San Juan Paran-
garicutiro, Michoacán.

sell his product have resulted in some artisans, inspired in some instances by the consumer himself, disguising modern masks as old ones by applying patinas. In this way extraordinary woodcarvings have been created that do not correspond to any dance, but rather are the fruit of a carver's inventiveness. This has led some collectors to attribute masks to nonexistent dances, characters, and even towns. Nonetheless, these carvings sometimes turn out to be fine examples of popular art. Whether a collector desires a beautiful, decorative mask or one that corresponds to a traditional dance, the best way to obtain it is simply to commission a mask maker to produce it.

Some mask makers, because they are leaders of the dances, feel obligated to make masks for the other dancers in order to give them the correct characterizations. Depending upon his skill, he may become the village mask maker without compromising his time-consuming role as dance leader. Sometimes a dancer makes his own mask. In some instances it is the town *santero* (carver of religious images) who, as he is a very skillful carver, is charged with fashioning the masks.

Although a mask adheres to a predetermined form, each mask maker will endow it with a different expression and character irrespective of material. For this reason, the Mexican mask persists as one of the most exciting manifestations of contemporary popular art. The mask is not an object solely created and utilized in the past, to survive only in collections, behind display windows, or in photographic archives. Surely hundreds of masks are produced daily throughout the length and breadth of our territory in order to satisfy local needs first and those of collectors second. While the mask may lend itself to aesthetic contemplation, it plays a central role in traditional dances. We admire Mexican masks, therefore, not only for their intrinsic

plastic value but because they are so closely linked to the fervor, the ethic, and the vigor with which a town dresses itself in order to define itself—to show in the thousand faces of its masks its expressive capacities and its deep cultural roots.

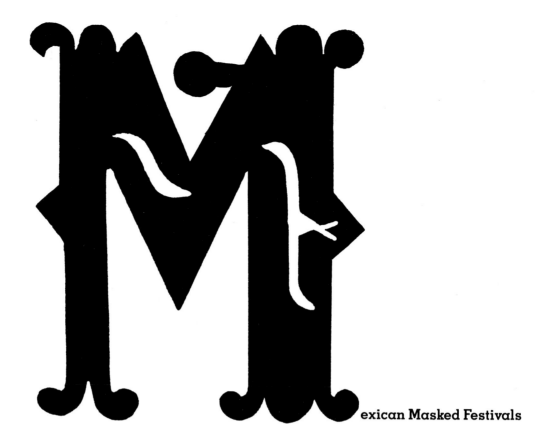

Mexican Masked Festivals

at the Turn of the Century,

as Witnessed by Frederick Starr

Marsha C. Bol

The Columbian quincentenary, the five hundredth anniversary of the arrival of Columbus in the Americas, will be observed in 1992. One hundred years ago the world was preparing for a similar celebration, the 1893 World's Columbian Exposition in Chicago.

A massive effort went into the preparation of exhibits for the 1893 exposition, particularly in the still-fledgling field of anthropology. Certainly the names associated with that fair, among them Franz Boas and Frederick W. Putnam, are those today associated with the foundations of American anthropology.

In Chicago, simultaneous with the preparation of the exposition, the University of Chicago created a new depart-

ment of anthropology and appointed Dr. Frederick Starr (1858–1933) its first and sole anthropologist, a position he held from 1892 to 1923. Born in Auburn, New York, the fourth son of a Presbyterian minister, Starr had received his Ph.D. in geology from Lafayette College in 1885 and was one of the self-trained anthropologists of the period.

In 1894, immediately after the fair closed, Starr set off for Mexico to begin his research into the living cultures of the region, an area of investigation largely ignored by scientists up to that time. What little was known of nineteenth-century Mexico outside the country was provided by popular travel accounts published in a variety of forms and in surprising numbers. For

23. The Moors. Mesquitán, Jalisco, Saint James Day, July 25, 1895.

Notes

1. Some of the scientific work going on in Mexico was presented in Chicago at the 1893 exposition. Carl Lumholtz, a Norwegian who was one of the earliest natural scientists to work in Mexico, presented some of his findings at the Chicago Exposition. He said, "I am enabled to continue my researches alone until August, 1893, when I took my Tarahumare and Tepehuane collections to Chicago and exhibited them at the World's Fair" (Lumholtz 1902: xii).

2. Starr (1899: 7) said, "The chief object in the author's journeys into Southern Mexico has been to study the physical types of the native tribes. In January and February, 1896, he made a horseback journey from the city of Oaxaca to the city of Guatemala. Most of

the most part, however, nineteenth-century travel accounts of Mexico exhibited little or no interest in the diverse ethnic cultures of Mexico and their folk festivals and arts. The visitors were far more interested in the urban delights of Mexico City. When brief mention was made, the comments often were derogatory. Madame Calderón de la Barca, in describing a mask worn for a Holy Week drama, said, "One who represented the spy, with a horrible mask like a pig's face, was seen looking through the trees where the Savior was concealed" (1843: 360).

It remained until the late nineteenth century, when a few scientists began to investigate the various cultures of Mexico, for the living traditions to begin to be systematically recorded.[1] From 1894 to 1904, Starr traveled to Mexico on a series of field trips, the results of which were recorded in numerous field notebooks and published articles, books, and lectures.

The reading public may well ask, Why another travel book on Mexico? Few countries have been so frequently written up by the traveler. Many books, good, bad, and indifferent, but chiefly bad, have been perpetrated. Most of these books, however, cover the same ground, and ground which has been traversed by many people. Indian Mexico is practically unknown. The only travel-book, regarding it, in English, is Lumholtz's "Unknown Mexico." The Indians among whom Lumholtz worked lived in northwestern Mexico; those among whom I have studied are in southern Mexico. The only district where his work and mine overlap is the Tarascan area. In fact, then, I write upon an almost unknown and untouched subject (Starr 1908: v).

Starr's stated plan of work included the following: "The work I planned to do among these Indian towns was threefold: 1. The measurement of one hundred men and twenty-five women in each population, fourteen measurements being taken upon each subject; 2. The making of pictures—portraits,

dress, occupations, customs, buildings, and landscapes; 3. The making of plaster busts of five individuals in each tribe" (1908: vi).

This interest in measuring individuals and making plaster casts of heads was an emphasis of late nineteenth-century anthropology clearly in evidence at the Chicago exposition. It was this work of measuring, photographing, and making plaster busts of various ethnic groups which propelled Starr, traveling by mule, horse, canoe, coach, ox cart, train, and on foot, into some of the remote areas of indigenous Mexico, where he found his subjects to be quite "unreasonably" reluctant to undergo the procedure.[2]

Starr eventually completed some one hundred busts, which he brought back to the University of Chicago. The results of his primary work in physical anthropology, however, proved to be of little interest to the scientific community, and there is no record indicating that the busts were ever put to scientific use. Eventually they disappeared altogether.[3]

If his plaster busts were lacking in enduring scientific value, Starr's secondary accomplishments, while not central to his work, have proven to be a valuable resource duplicated by no one else.[4] His collections of late nineteenth-century Mexican folk arts, although relatively unknown and unseen outside his publications, taken in combination with his field descriptions and photographs of indigenous costume, architecture, and arts, are unique.[5]

On occasion, neither by plan nor design, Starr and his party stumbled upon villages that were in fiesta. His descriptions, photos, and collections, although unsystematic, constitute the best documentation that remains from that period. His fascination with the festivals of Mexico was clear: "The student of folk-lore can nowhere find a more interesting field for the study of popular celebration than our sister republic. We find there a most curious mingling

25. Group of *Tas-toanes*. Mesquitán, Jalisco, Saint James Day, July 25, 1895.

44

26. The Throne. Mes-
quitán, Jalisco, Saint
James Day, July 25,
1895.

the Journey was through purely Indian country. Although aware of the diversity of languages in this area, the author was not prepared for the accompanying diversity of physical types, which he found. This appeared so important that another journey was planned for its investigation." The plaster bust-making procedure involved the following: "He was put flat on the floor, face down, on a little piece of matting. At this stage some objected. . . . The Mexican plaster worker, who has followed the caravan from its start, goes to work. He makes a cast of the back of the head and shoulders, and the Indian is turned over, face up. Another cast of the breast and neck and chin is made, and yet another of the front half of the head and the face, with little tubes for breathing, sticking through it" (Starr 1908: 408–9). Starr described several of the bust-making sessions: "Some weeks later we were again at Huixquilucan, this time to secure some busts. . . . Everything went well until the moulds were removed; it is true that in the removal a good deal of hair was pulled out, but no serious damage was done" (Starr 1908: 65).

3. The Field Museum purchased the series of one hundred plaster busts in 1905. They

of native American ideas and practices with those of medieval Europe" (Starr 1896a: 161).

The masked combat drama between the personages of Santiago and the *tastoanes* held at Mesquitán, a suburb of Guadalajara, prompted Starr to document the event in 1895. He took photographs, collected masks and figurines, and made field notes.

In 1894 we accidentally learned that a popular drama was celebrated at Mesquitan, a suburb of Guadalajara, on Saint James Day, July 25. The fact that some of the players masked, that words of Aztec were frequently in the dialogue and that the name was itself Aztec aroused our interest and in 1895 we were on hand to see the *Tastoanes*. Unfortunately there had been some disturbances the preceding year and we found the drama prohibited. After a world of trouble the government permitted the play for our benefit. It was impossible to note the details as fully as desirable but we saw a hastily prepared rendition and received a general idea of it (Starr Field Notes, Box 19, Folder 17, p. 1).

Starr described the event:[6]

as rapidly as we could get sets ready we photographed them. The *personal* was— Santiago, Three Kings, Two Moors, Two Capitans, One Queen. Tastoanes including one as *Perro*. Each of these different grades was specially costumed. Santiago was rather prettily dressed in pink and purple satins and with a great broad brimmed brightly-plumed hat. His horse was also quite gayly caparisoned. The three kings were individually different in dress. Each wore a mask of terra cotta painted, supposed to represent (but certainly very indifferently) three racial types, black, white and Mexican. The white king was very early dressed and was very decidedly unsteady in his movements and actions. The queen was the tallest man of the lot and looked very ridiculous in her expressionless mask and her dingy dark blue dress. The moors with red jackets, turbans with high bright plumes and queer red trousers with laces around the legs were not masked but had heavy black veils before

their faces [fig. 23]. The capitans had pretty red satin caps and rather elaborate jackets built up on a leather base [fig. 24]. The Tastoanes were masked in queer masks of leather painted brightly to which were attached great headdresses of cowtails and raveled rope. These enormous wigs hung down their backs. Old black coats some with gift, lace epaulets, etc. and red trousers cut up along the sides completed their costume. One of their number was differently clad with a queer little jacket and an ugly pig's mask. He was the *perro*— or dog [figs. 25, 35–38] (Starr Field Notes, Box 20, Notebook 6, pp. 39–41).

An enormous wooden structure was erected which served as a throne.

All were, by this time, facing toward the throne; with much fol-de-vol and wavering they went up onto it. At first only two or three of the Tastoanes went up and they appeared to test the strength of the structure [fig. 26]. All this in a clownish way. They then all piled pell mell up— kings, queens and Tastoanes. The drunken white king and the queen meddled considerably with one another. The moors acted as pages for the royal personages—preceding them with elaborate gestures of invitation, striking of sticks against shields, and then trailing the sticks along on the ground before the personages. When all were settled the kings and queen each on the higher and farthest back seat with one tastoan at each end; the rest were seated down below on the cross beams, and were a sad looking crowd [fig. 27] (Starr Field Notes, Box 20, Notebook 6, pp. 42–43).

At the end of the same year, 1895, Starr witnessed *Los pastores* at Chapala, Jalisco, on December 25.

The Pastors celebrates the birth of Christ, and is rendered at the Christmas holidays. We saw its last rendition at Chapala. It was danced at evening, by moonlight, in the little plaza. The whole town had gathered to witness it, and the people sat or squatted on the ground in circles about the players; all the spectators steadily munched sugar-cane as they watched. The pastores (shepherds) were about a dozen in number; the parts were

27. Group on the
Throne. Mesquitán,
Jalisco, Saint James
Day, July 25, 1895.

were later transferred to the University of Chicago and then to the Indiana University Museum. Somewhere along the line the set was partially dispersed and separated from its documentation.

4. "While doing this work in physical anthropology many photographs and data of ethnographic interest were secured. . . . They make no claim to completeness, but it has seemed worth while to publish them; other travellers may pass them by and many customs and practices will soon be gone" (Starr 1900: 3).

5. Starr's collection of 575 ethnographic objects from southern Mexico was sold to the Field Museum in 1905. His "folklore" collection of 630 objects from northern and central Mexico was given to the Folk-Lore Society in London in 1899 and housed at the University Museum of Archaeology and Ethnology at Cambridge. A few pieces that Starr retained were later sold from his estate, some of which are now in the collections of the Taylor Museum of the Colorado Springs Fine Arts Center. Each of these collections contains some dance masks that Starr collected in the field.

6. See Starr 1896a and Starr 1902 for published versions of his account.

7. Field notes for this performance are located in Box 20, Notebook 9, pp. 13–15, 57–108.

taken by boys from twelve to seventeen years of age. In clean white shirts and trousers, they wore blue girdles about their waists and broad-brimmed hats, gay with flowers and ribbons, upon their heads; each bore a wand or staff adorned at top with tinsel and artificial flower wreaths. Three men took the part of devils and bore the names of Pecado, Astucia, and Luzbel. They were dressed in black velvet spangled with gilt and silver, and had horns upon their heads. Two men played the clown under the names of Bartolo and Hermitaño. The former wore a brown face-mask, a black coat, and yellow trousers; he carried a great pin-cushion, a make-believe armadillo, and rode a hobby-horse. The hermit wore an aged-man mask, a great calico gown that nearly swept the ground, and a long rosary with a cross, made of large spools strung on a cotton cord. Two men were "Indians." Three little girls dressed in white with lace decorations, and wearing wreaths of flowers, took part,—one representing an angel. The play was mostly sung, and many of the tunes were bright and pretty. At the beginning the devils plan the destruction of mankind. Luzbel learns that the Saviour is to come and defeat his plans. At first he is in terror, but soon recovers and renews his scheming. Through the greater part of the play the pastores stand in two lines, facing, with a space between them. Those who speak stand at one end between these lines [figs. 28, 29, 30]. A blind harper supplies the music and sits at the other end. The old hermit, who is supposed to be a missionary of good, is really a coarse old fellow, between whom and Bartolo there is an almost constant interchange of rude jokes and coarse by-play. The pastores several times go through with a pretty processional, with a peculiar halting dance-step. The wands are used in these evolutions for beating time and forming quite artistic figures. The birth of the Christ-child is announced and hailed with joy. One and another advance to the little girl who represents an angel and do obeisance. The devils and the clowns come last. At the close is a quaint cradle-song to the baby Christ, while a pretty figure is made with

the crossed wands. This little play is rendered throughout the week, in the streets before houses, and the performers are invited inside to simple refreshment, —cakes, *cigarros*, liquor. The play is fairly recent at Chapala. Only a few years ago a young fellow from the village saw it at some other town; he learned it by heart and trained his band of actors. This illustrates the way in which such dramas travel—even in Mexico—from town to town (Starr 1896a: 167–68).[7]

In the town of Juquila, Oaxaca, Starr witnessed two dances taking place simultaneously in observance of San Marcos day on January 29 and 30, 1896. One of the dances included the use of masked costumes. The other he termed the *danza de la conquista* (dance of the Conquest).

While this drama [*danza de la conquista*] was being enacted under the shade-tree, another amusement, in connection with the *fiesta* of San Marcos was in progress in front of the church. The musicians with the long horns made doleful music; a dozen gayly-costumed dancers took part. They wore dark trousers slitted up the sides; bright kerchiefs, with the point hanging down in front, were tied about the waists; crowns of plumes were on the heads; red vests and kerchiefs, crossed at the neck, completed the costume. One player, who seemed to be a leader, carried a tricolored flag; another represented a man on horseback, by creeping into a frame of sticks, covered with cloth, in the shape of a horse. They danced in the full sunlight for hours; their movements were varied and pretty, quite different, too, from the figures in the danza de la Conquista. Two outside characters played the clown. One of these was a little lad dressed in a garment representing a tiger-skin, while over his face he wore a heavy, old wooden mask, imitating an animal's head. The other was older, dressed in a leather suit with a wooden mask like a vacant-looking human face [fig. 31]. These two were very popular, and indulged in many acts that bordered on the obscene. We got no satisfactory explanation of this whole performance. The *cura* said that

28–30. *Pastores*. Chapala, Jalisco, December 25, 1895.

8. For Starr's field notes of this event, see Box 20, Notebook 10, p. 26, and Box 19, Letter 3, January 29–30, 1896, n.p.

it represented the conflict between Christ and the Jews; this we greatly doubted (Starr 1908: 31).[8]

Starr visited Santa Fé de la Laguna, Michoacán, located on the shores of Lake Pátzcuaro, planning to make some physical measurements. Here is his account of events on December 25, 1897:

No cases came in and we lost time constantly until mid-afternoon. Then on my sallying out in some desperation to see if I could find some cases, I found a first lot of the *viejos*. These we photographed. The rest of daylight was devoted to watching the *viejos* and taking refreshment with the crowd. . .

The viejos: These bands of masked figures were some six in number. The first one I saw consisted of five or six persons. One only represented a woman. She probably was really so and was dressed quite in the usual fashion though of somewhat unusual height: she was barefoot and had her rebozo so gathered about her face as to completely cover it. Above it a hat. The rest were dressed in long dresses or robes of bright colors, red, purple, green. These were buttoned down the front. The head was covered with a white cloth over which was fitted a little clay mask. These little masks were peaked and retreating and made the heads look remarkably like microcephalic idiots. About the neck passed a woman's faja so brought together in front as to suggest a rosary. The legs were stockinged with long white stockings and on the feet were shoes with high and solid heels. One or two of the party had common guitars of local and native construction. They strolled through the street playing and dancing. The dancing was true clog dancing with considerable gusto and was either by the single dancers in turn—or else by one of the males and the female at once, in the manner of the jarabe.—We soon saw that the interest centered in the yard and house connected with the little *templo* behind the church. Going in there we found the town gathering. Men came in and sat down on benches or against walls: women came in one or two at once, all carrying something. The crowd continued to gather until the place was full. Then women with little children all squatted down in the open and laid their burdens down by them. These proved to be great

pots full of atolli [*atole*], bundles of large sweet, tortillas, masses of *tomallis* [tamales] or great sacks full of little earthen vessels. When the place was well filled, the bands of viejos began to appear. They would dance and sing as they came up the central path to the Templo, would then look into the sacred building and then move out into the crowd. Presently the officials came in all their grandeur: those who should with canes. They seated themselves in two reserved benches at the upper end of the common. The dancing parties coming in paid their respects to these and then went about through the crowd causing fun. Everywhere they made jokes, begged food and carried on generally. No food however was being eaten but a lot of waiters were busying carrying it first to the officials, who had a table improvised before them, on which it was placed— then to the rest. When nearly all were supplied—including the strangers, we fell to and while the mass were eating the parties kept up their lively and funny time. Two of these were such as we have already described. The others were far more quaintly and antiquely got up. They wore in general extremely large and old wooden masks of most comic form. Some of them are so old as to show long continued signs of use and abuse: one represented a long, warty, bearded face and was painted purple: some others were painted brown: most however were plain and uncolored. With them were wigs of cornhusk or matting: the clothing was ragged and tattered. In most cases an attempt was made at the ancient slit trousers and in some the material was well worn skin of *tigre* or other animal. In each party there was one who was *maestro* or leader: often he had some tattered paper in his hand as if it were a book of directions or a part book. He had it open much of the time but also used it to slap his hand with and to make a great noise and flourishing. He calls out the individual dancers, who are to perform and seems to lead in the jocularity. The movements of two of these bands—those with the most grotesque masks and representing the oldest men— were particularly vigorous and lively. At times two would leap at or strike at each other and then leap apart in a very funny way. Again the whole party would get into a little ring and would dance sidewise with very vigorous leaps. The

31. Fiesta of San
Marcos. Juquila,
Oaxaca, January
29–30, 1896.

32. *Viejos*. Santa Fé
de la Laguna,
Michoacán, December
27, 1897.

jokes appeared to be impromptu and we could not well make them out. Among the sets one was composed of little fellows in rough matting and distressful combinations of dress, who had however most of their wooden masks, small and badly made and probably the cast off ones of some former time when they were used by the less conspicuous dancers in some much larger party than any of these. The party of hosts, guests, and dancers dispersed with darkness though the dancers went around from house to house during the night (Starr Field Notes, Box 20, Notebook 15, pp. 51, 53–56).[9]

Two days later, on December 27, Starr described this scene: "The different bands of *viejos* came to display themselves. They were seven more given to lively antics than before. Padre Tomás, who was formerly cura here gave orders to appear tomorrow for photographing. . . . [The next day] the *viejos* appeared and were photographed [fig. 32]" (Starr Field Notes, Box 20, Notebook 15, pp. 65–66).[10]

The Starr party traveled on to Cherán, Michoacán, on January 1, 1898:

As we were about to leave the *negritos* began a celebration before the townhouse. There were sixteen boys dressed in black suits, with negro masks and elaborate headdresses of colored tissue paper with streamers of the same. There was at least one girl—I think two—gaudily gotten up and a wee boy besides the negritos. I was sorry we had no time to see this *Pastores* celebration (Starr Field Notes, Box 20, Notebook 15, pp. 85–86).

In the spring of 1901, while traveling in southern Mexico, Starr arrived at Mérida, Yucatán, during Carnival season. He was particularly taken with a band of dancers called the *xtoles*.

The last day of our stay in Merida we saw the *xtoles*. These are bands of Indian dancers who go from house to house during the carnival season; they are dressed in costumes which reproduce some features of the ancient Indian dress. In the little company which we saw were fifteen dancers, including the standard-bearer; all were males, but half of them were dressed like females and took the part of such [fig. 33]. The male dancers wore the usual white *camisa* and drawers, but these had a red stripe down the side of the leg; jingling hawk-bells of tin or brass were attached to various parts of their dress; a red belt encircled the waist; all wore sandals. The "female" dancers wore white dresses of the usual sort, with decorated borders at the arm and neck; also necklaces of gold beads and gold chains with pendants. Two of the dancers were little children, but the rest appeared to be young men up to about thirty-five years of age. All wore crowns upon the head; these consisted of a circlet of tin, from which rose two curved strips which intersected over the middle of the head; from the circlet rose four feathers—either natural or made of tin. Two of the crowns of special size, with real feathers, marked the king and queen. Under the crowns, covering the top of the head and hanging down from the shoulders, were gay handkerchiefs of red or blue. All the dancers were masked. The men wore bandoliers of cotton, worked with bright designs representing animals, birds and geometrical forms; the square ends of these were hung with marine shells. In their hands, the dancers carried curious rattles and fans, which they used in making graceful movements as they danced. The handle of the fan consisted of the leg and foot of a turkey, while the body was composed of the brilliant and beautifully spotted feathers of the ocellated turkey, a bird peculiar to Yucatán and the adjacent country. There were two musicians, one with a long *pito*, or fife, and the other with a *huehuetl* or drum, which he struck with his hands. Hanging to the side of the drum near the top was a turtle-shell, upon which the drummer beat, from time to time, with a deer's horn. A standard was carried by the company, which bore representation of the sun, with dancers and a serpent; the pole by which it was carried was surmounted with a tin disk representing the sun's face. The music was apparently of Indian origin and the words of the song were Maya. The dancing itself was graceful and accompanied by many

9. For the published description, see Starr 1908: 71–72.
10. See also Starr 1908: 83.

curious movements (Starr 1908: 317–18).

Traveling on to Progreso, Yucatán, Starr witnessed Carnival there as well.

Certainly the Carnival at Progreso was more interesting, more lively, and more enthusiastic than in Mérida. As "Manuel" would say there were plenty of *abusos*. Men and boys went around the streets with ribbons and flowers in their hats and with their faces painted or daubed: many had their hands full of flour or of blue paint with which they dashed the faces and clothing of friends they met on the streets. Strolling bands of masked persons danced and [text missing in original] the street. Parties of boys nearly naked—and daubed to a browner tint than natural played toro with one who was inside a frame of wood and cloth [fig. 34]. A completely naked man, painted over his body, pranced through the streets on all fours as a "*caballo*". Young fellows dressed in women's clothing and with faces covered or masked or painted wandered about singly and addressed people on the street in high falsetto with all sorts of tales of woe or absurd questions. One band of trained dancers was really pretty. They had a standard, leader, music— pretty dances. Each carried two *palitos* which they used in a variety of pretty forms and there was a song with Spanish words. Manuel called my attention to the fact that in movement etc. it was almost identical with the xtoles" (Starr Field Notes, Box 21 Notebook 34, pp. 27–29).[11]

Starr witnessed a number of festivals, both masked and unmasked, recording his impressions, taking some photographs, and collecting a few masks. The number and variety of festivals and celebrations which he witnessed are disappointingly few, however, when compared to the countless festivals taking place in the diverse regions and among the varied ethnic groups of Mexico. He himself recognized that "there are no doubt hundreds of them in the aggregate, many of which are local and interesting. At present they may be studied perfectly" (Starr 1896a: 169).

As were so many students of Mexico before him and since, Frederick Starr was convinced that "especially the plays in which masks, ancient musical instruments, and native dance-steps occur, must, in many places, soon disappear" (Starr 1896a: 169). In his field journal he noted: "Chiapas is rather a place for fiesta: look into the baile de Calalá with its calalá, its tigre, and venado: is it at Carnival? What signification attributed to it?" (Starr Field Notes, Box 21, Notebook 35, p. 23).[12] Ninety years after he wrote this, in 1987, a group from the Museum of International Folk Art in Santa Fe, New Mexico, witnessed a masked dance in Suchiapa, Chiapas, that had the same masked elements as Starr had investigated in 1901 and 1902. Contrary to Starr's prediction, Mexican masked festival has neither disappeared nor diminished and shows no signs of doing so. On the contrary, masked festival appears to be exhibiting signs of increased vitality as it continues to be a dynamic essential in the life of the Mexican people.

11. For the published account, see Starr 1908: 324–25.
12. Starr (1902: 67) answered his questions with a brief description: "In the dance called *calalá*, there is dialogue in the old Chiapanec language. This dance takes place during carnival season, and among the dancers are the *calalá*, the *tigre* (tiger), and the *venado* (deer)."

33. *Xtoles*. Carnival, 1901. Mérida, Yucatán.

34. Carnival, 1901.
Progreso, Yucatán.

35–38. *Tastoan* Masks. Guadalajara, Jalisco. Painted plaster on leather. Collected by Dr. Frederick Starr, 1895. Loaned from the Taylor Museum, Colorado Springs Fine Arts Center.

* (Editor's note: The first of the evangelizing missionaries arrived in what is now Mexico just a few years after the Conquest. These early Augustinians, Franciscans, and Dominicans were followed by members of other orders. As men of their time, their teachings frequently expressed a deeply ingrained anti-semitism. Friars and colonists (who, after all, shared the same prejudices) introduced the various *judios, fariseos, caifases,* etc. into indigenous masked dances. These characters were represented as killers of Christ, enemies of humanity, and synonomous with the Devil. That which the friars sowed rooted itself very deeply; the association of Jews with evil persists into our own time. It should be understood, however, that the practitioners of folk drama make no identification between masked impersonators of evil and members of an actual group of people such as the Jews. Ironically, few of the participants have ever met or are aware of having met anyone who is Jewish. The characters in the dances who bear titles and assume roles inspired by European medieval hatred have been pre-empted by indigenous communities to express concerns that antedate the arrival of Europeans by many centuries. JBE)

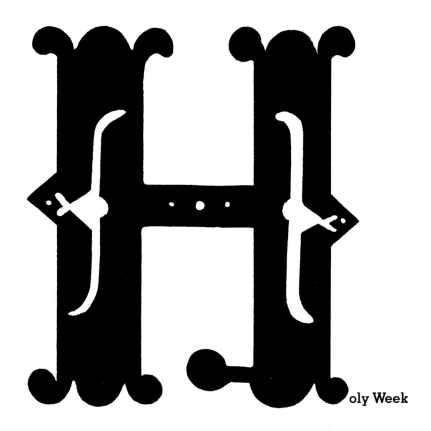

Holy Week

in Los Patos, Sinaloa

James S. Griffith

The Mayo Indian Lenten and Easter ceremonies of southern Sonora and northern Sinaloa are related to similar events created by the Yaqui and other native groups in northwest Mexico. Basically a Passion Play introduced by Jesuit missionaries in the seventeenth and eighteenth centuries, the ceremony varies from community to community throughout the region. A constant feature, however, is the presence of masked participants who serve as clowns, as persecutors of the godly, and as crucifiers of Christ.* These beings frequently appear early in Lent, accompanying religious processions and preparing for their role in the culminating drama of Holy Week. They are menacing clowns who often deliberately violate accepted codes of behavior, especially in such areas as aggression and sexuality. During Holy Week they find, capture, and crucify Christ and are then defeated on Holy Saturday, the very moment when they seem to be winning. Their final defeat usually takes place in or near the village church in a dramatic confrontation with the forces of good. It is frequently accompanied by the ritual burning of their masks.

In most Mayo communities, these masked beings (often called *fariseos,* or Pharisees) also visit villages and towns throughout Lent, gathering alms with which to pay for the culminating Easter fiesta (which involves the hiring of specialists and the feasting of all participants). They are in charge of the Lenten and Holy Week events and con-

Notes

1. For a listing of works relating to the Yaquis in general, the Yaquis in a single Arizona community, the Mayos of Sonora, and the Pascolas, see Bibliography.
2. Both trips were self-supported and were part of a project, since discontinued, of documenting the traditional arts and ceremonies of northern Sinaloa. On the second visit to Los Patos I was accompanied and aided by my wife, Loma. I am grateful to her beyond that fact for the encouragement and assistance she has invariably given me. I also wish to state my gratitude to and love for the late Edward H. Spicer, who introduced so many of his students and others to so much. My debt to the villagers of Los Patos I have already expressed.

tinue to be in control on Easter Sunday. They are the most noticeable of the different sets of participants in the traditional drama.[1]

The photographs in this essay were taken during Holy Week, 1968 and 1970, in the Mayo Indian village of Los Patos (a pseudonym) in northern Sinaloa, Mexico. They were taken with the permission and the active cooperation of the villagers involved in the ceremonies. I was able to attend on Holy Thursday, Good Friday, and Holy Saturday of 1968 but had to leave the village before Easter Sunday itself. The Sunday activities, therefore, have been . filled in with photographs taken in 1970. The 1968 pictures were later used as a starting point for interviews with various participants concerning aspects of the ceremony.

It must be emphasized that the pictures were taken, selected, and printed by an outsider and necessarily reflect an outsider's view of the ritual. Documentation by a participant in the local cultural and ceremonial system would doubtless be very different both in scope and emphasis.[2]

Judíos outside the house of one of their number on Holy Thursday, April 11, 1968 (fig. 39). _Judíos_ (Jews) play a major role in the Lenten and Holy Week drama. They portray, as the Pharisees, the slayers of Christ and appear each Friday of Lent, accompanying religious processions and harassing the people as they walk, sing, and pray. At these times they are said to be searching for Christ. Their duties culminate in the Holy Week activities shown in this series. The role of _judíos_ involves clowning and inverted behavior. Another duty of the _judíos_ is to visit nearby towns and settlements during Lent, collecting alms for the Easter fiesta.

Men serve as _judíos_ for three or more years, having vowed to do so. _Judíos_ are organized in military fashion and are considered to be soldiers. At the head of the organization in this village is the _joyero mayor_, assisted by two officers, a _capitán_ and a _guarda de espaldas_. Other _cargos_, as they are called, include the _chicoteros_, who preserve discipline with rawhide whips; _tamboleros_, who drum for the dancing; _venados_, who carry rattles and mimic the deer dance; and _soldados razos_, or the "rank and file." All these _cargos_ except the _soldado razo_ are ranked internally, as, for example, _primer_ (first) _venado_ and _segundo_ (second) _venado_.

In figure 39, the two _judíos_ on the right are _tamboleros_. To their left is one of the three leaders of the _judíos_. The two characters on the far left are _soldados razos_. The _judíos_ have just finished a meal and are beginning to resume their weapons and roles. Directly behind the left-hand figure is a cross of the sort that participating Mayo families place outside their houses during Lent. During the meal, _judío_ equipment had been . stacked around it. Several lances remain.

These _judíos_ are posing for the camera. The _soldado razo_ in the rear is standing at attention in a posture typical for this rank and role. The masks are all of goat hide and are typical of the style of this village, with their tendency toward long hair and facial features indicated by scraping and cutting, rather than by applying extra pieces. The masks and other equipment are made in a group session at the beginning of Lent.

Uprooting a house cross, Good Friday, April 12, 1968 (fig. 40). On Good Friday morning the _judíos_ divide into two companies and proceed to uproot all the house crosses in the village and its surrounding countryside. A band of _judíos_ approaches a house cross on the run (their usual traveling pace). With their lances they remove the foliage surrounding the cross and loosen the soil around its base. Meanwhile the _chicotero_ loops his whip around the neck of

the cross and tugs it out of the ground. It is then laid gently on a bench or board provided by a householder. The *judíos* then dance around the fallen cross while one of their number collects food and other necessary fiesta supplies from the householder. At some houses they are offered a meal or coffee.

In figure 40 the *tambolero* (far left) is drumming and a *venado* (with rattles) is dancing. Several *judíos* are digging at the cross base while the *chicotero* is trying to pull it up with his whip. A gunnysack for contributions of food, skyrockets, and other necessary supplies is visible at far right.

Carrying the Santa Cruz down the hill, Good Friday, April 12, 1969 (fig. 41). After all the house crosses have been uprooted, the *judíos* run to the top of *Kao O'ola* (old hill), where a cross is planted. This cross is one of several near the village. The others are on the old trails leading from the village, at places where, according to local belief, God's footprints are visible in the rock. These latter crosses do not figure in the Holy Week ceremonies, but they are visited on May 3, the day of the finding of the Holy Cross, by a procession bearing the cross from *Kao O'ola*.

After "shooting" the cross with rockets tied to their machetes, the *judíos* remove it and carry it into the village on a litter made of their lances. It is dressed in one of the houses, placed on a bier, and carried around the Way of the Cross. On Easter Sunday it is placed by an altar in the fiesta *ramada* (bower), wearing a white habit and straw hat. Later on Good Friday afternoon, the *judíos* uproot and "shoot" the cross in front of the fiesta *ramada* and uproot the crosses on the Way of the Cross around the plaza. They also "kill" Christ by shooting Him, then stabbing Him with their lances.

In figure 41, one of the leaders walks in front of the groups carrying the San-

ta Cruz on their lances. *Tamboleros* and *venados* are playing and dancing out of the picture. The unmasked man to the rear of the group is the *mandón*, or official sponsor of the fiesta, and he wears in his hat the Mexican government permit necessary to hold a public religious procession.

Praying at one of the Stations of the Cross, Good Friday, April 12, 1968 (fig. 42). Late in the afternoon of Good Friday, a procession leaves the *ramada*, which serves as a church, there being no permanent church structure in the village. It consists of the *maestro*, or lay prayer leader, women carrying small boxes with the local saints' images (the boxes with their doors closed), and four men carrying the bier with the Santa Cruz. There are also four boys ("Josés") and four girls ("Marías"), dressed in white with red sashes, and a large number of women. The procession goes around the Way of the Cross, stopping at each fallen cross while the *maestro* recites prayers. The procession is accompanied by the *judíos* in two long files, herding the people along with whips cracking. At each stop, drummers play while the *venados* dance. One of the three leaders of the *judíos* kneels with the *maestro*, attempting to distract him at his prayers by thrusting a book (in this case, a text on engineering) into his face.

In figure 42, the *maestro* is praying out of a small book in front of the fallen cross. (The cross is obscured behind the women and the girls kneeling in the right foreground.) A *judío* attempts to distract him by showing him another book. In front of him, to the far right, women, "Josés," and "Marías" hold the saints and other ritual objects. The *mandón*, machete bared as usual and his permit in his hat, watches on the right, while two *tamboleros* play for a *venado*. Other *judíos* watch and clack sticks on their lances in time with the drumming.

Loading Judas on his burro, Holy Saturday morning, April 13, 1968 (fig. 43).
Early on Holy Saturday morning, the *judíos* are busy cleaning the area in front of the *ramada* in preparation of the *gloria*. Others are hauling water and fetching supplies to the rear of the fiesta *ramada,* where they are to live until Easter Sunday afternoon. At about nine in the morning, one group of *judíos* fetches an effigy of Judas from the house where he had been made ready; others get a burro. They play with Judas for a while, pretending to give him beer, tweaking him in the crotch, threatening to strike him, or fanning him with his hat. They then place him on the back of the burro, along with one *judío* to hold him in place, and lead him at a gallop around the Way of the Cross, goosing the burro with their lances in an attempt to get the riders bucked off. Judas is then carried over to a stump at the far end of the cleared runway in front of the fiesta *ramada* and propped up to watch the proceedings.

At about half-past ten the *pascolas* and their music arrive. The *pascola* is the ritual host of every Mayo and Yaqui fiesta. He prays to open and close the fiesta, makes comic and serious speeches, and dances and clowns during the course of the celebration. Each *pascola* dances a short dance to the violin and harp. By shortly after eleven, the *judíos* have stacked their lances around Judas and taken all their other equipment, including leg rattles, rattle belts, whips, and wooden machetes, to their quarters in the rear of the *ramada*. By half-past eleven they are in two lines in front of the *ramada* by the resurrected church cross.

Figure 43 shows Judas being placed on his burro. He is dressed as a Mexican or an Anglo, in work boots, khaki pants, denim shirt, and blue blazer. Various *judíos* steady him and adjust his costume, while one man in the background waves a clenched fist at him.

The *gloria*—charging the church on Holy Saturday morning, April 13, 1968 (fig. 44). After the *judíos* have been waiting in front of the fiesta *ramada* for awhile, the church bell starts ringing. At that, the *judíos* charge the *ramada,* waving the wooden switches that each carries, only to be pelted with green leaves by the *pascolas.* They run back to the cross and charge again, this time through the front of the *ramada* and out the side doors. After the third charge they rip off their masks and toss them toward the end of the pathway, by Judas. They then run once more to the *ramada,* where they kneel in two long, huddled lines while the *pascolas* whip them lightly with switches and the *maestro* sprinkles them with a corncob dipped in holy water. Then each *judío* is joined by his godparents and the long process of re-entering them into the Christian community begins. Meanwhile, the *pascolas* start dancing in the *ramada,* and Judas, who is stuffed with straw and fire crackers, is set on fire by two of the *judíos.*

In figure 44, *judíos* are seen charging the fiesta *ramada.* The standing cross is out of the picture to the left, as is a rack with one bell. To the lower right is part of the line of green twigs which marks off the pathway in front of the *ramada.* The leaves thrown by the *pascolas* can be seen in the air.

Pascola dancing, Easter Sunday, March 29, 1970 (fig. 45). With the unmasking of the *judíos* on Holy Saturday, the Easter fiesta begins. *Pascolas* dance all afternoon and night, and there is an evening social dance behind the *ramada* as well. On Easter Sunday, the altar is decorated with artificial flowers and color is evident in all the decorations and the clothes of the villagers. On Easter Sunday morning, while the *pascolas* dance, most villagers very formally crack *cascarones* (confetti-filled eggs) over each other's heads.

Figure 45 shows a *pascola* dancing to the music of a harp and two violins.

Pascolas' costumes may be more or less elaborate. The *pascola* in this picture wears a minimal costume. Around his legs are *ténovaris* (strings of dried moth cocoons filled with small pebbles). His wooden mask, decorated with goat hair, is on the back of his head. He is performing a stepdance to the violin and harp music while spectators look on.

Taking the saints home, Easter Sunday, March 29, 1970 (fig. 46). All through the course of the fiesta, the *judíos* have been in charge, keeping some order and providing supplies as needed. On Easter, they wear their best clothes, with scarves over their heads and faces, and carry their wooden machetes as badges of office. They have been living in quarters in the rear of the *ramada*. After a meal of *wakavaki,* or special fiesta stew, they form up inside the *ramada,* each holding a wax candle stuck on the end of his wooden machete. After speeches and a closing ceremony they accompany one last procession around the village. As the village does not have a permanent church, the local saints' images are kept at private houses where they are cared for by family members. On Holy Thursday they had been brought to the church in a series of processions, accompanied by the then-threatening *judíos.* Now they are taken back. First go two women carrying banners (an important part of most Yaqui and Mayo processions), followed by the women carrying the privately owned images and the Santa Cruz from *Kao O'ola.* Following them are more women with processional arches, the *pascolas* and musicians, and the rest of the people. As before, the *judíos* flank the procession, this time holding their machetes with candles stuck to the ends. Men walk in front, setting off homemade skyrockets—a constant feature of the celebration ever since Saturday noon. Finally, each image has been returned

to its house, and the Santa Cruz is once more atop its hill. The fiesta is over, and the tired participants have fulfilled their obligations.

In figure 46 the banner carriers are at the far right. In the middle are two women with wooden boxes containing small holy images. The boxes are also filled with cut paper and paper flowers and are being carried closed because of a high wind. The woman on the right carries the Santa Cruz, dressed in a white habit and decked with ribbons. The *judíos* are visible in the background, heads and faces covered with scarves, carrying their machetes and candles. At far left are two processional arches consisting of bundles of supple sticks wrapped with cloth and decorated with paper flowers.

A Final Word

It is not possible to convey more than a vague impression of a ceremony such as this with a handful of photographs. Much has been left out: all the *judíos'* activities before Holy Week, several processions, a good deal of dramatic activity on Good Friday and Holy Saturday, and much of the Easter fiesta that follows the charge on the church. The importance of the saints and of the Holy Cross during the rest of the ceremonial year has only been hinted at. The work of a large number of specialists who contribute in one way or another to the ceremony—potters, cooks, fireworks makers, the *maestro* or lay prayer leader, musicians sacred and secular, ritual dancers—has likewise been glossed over. I have tried to concentrate on the role of the masked *judíos,* but even here I have been able to offer little more than a hasty sketch.

There is a sense in which this is appropriate. The masks are central to the identity assumed by the men and boys who take on the role of *judío,* and the *judíos* are certainly central to the drama that is re-enacted during the forty days of Lent. Yet the masks are sel-

44

45

dom at rest—they are on the heads of people who are in almost constant motion. Among the neighboring Yaqui, in fact, they should not even be looked at closely by spectators. They are certainly never isolated and displayed as objects of aesthetic contemplation. And at the end of their usefulness they are burned.

Incomplete though this visual and verbal statement may be, I hope it conveys some of the drama and intensity of this particular ritual use of masks in this part of Mexico. That the ceremonies are important to their communities is evident in the mere fact of their survival. The ceremonies I witnessed and photographed in this and other villages in the 1960s and early 1970s had changed in the centuries since their introduction and have doubtless changed more in the years since my visits. But they persist, and through their persistence are a living part of the intricate mosaic that is Mexican—and human—creativity. My respect and gratitude go to those villagers who not only preserved these and other traditional ways of creating beauty but have so freely shared them with outsiders.

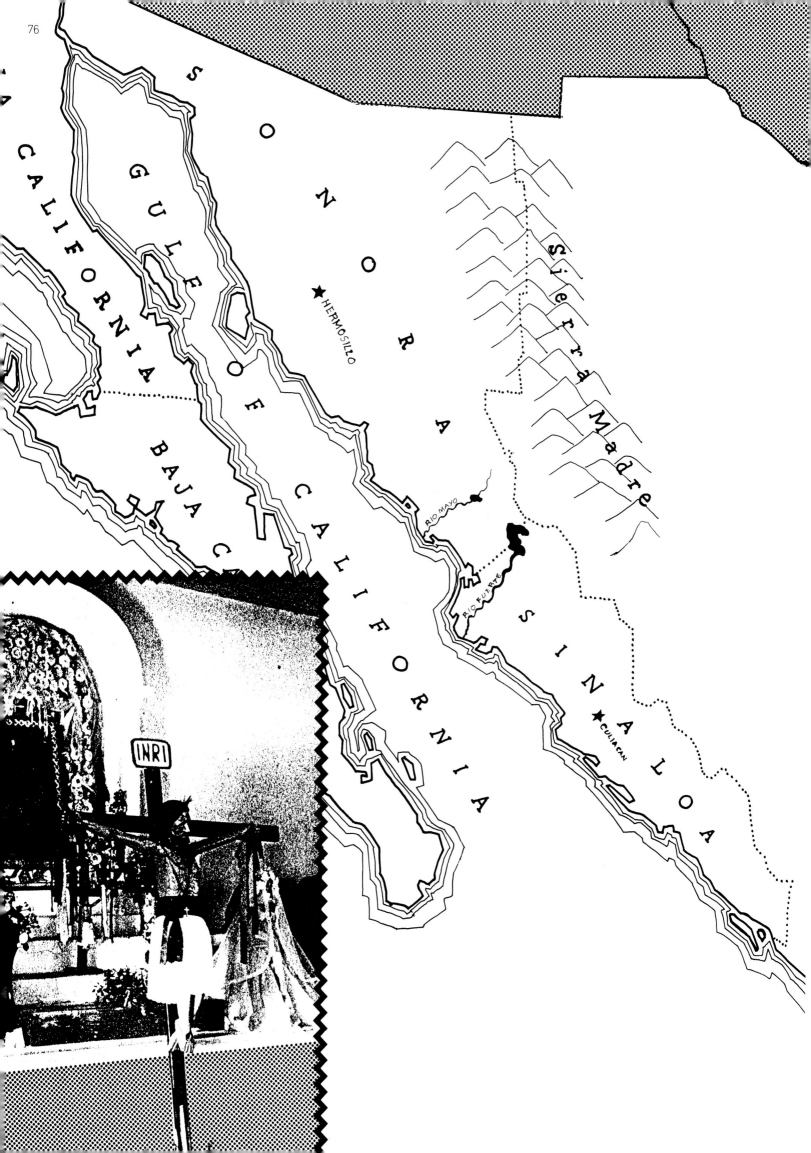

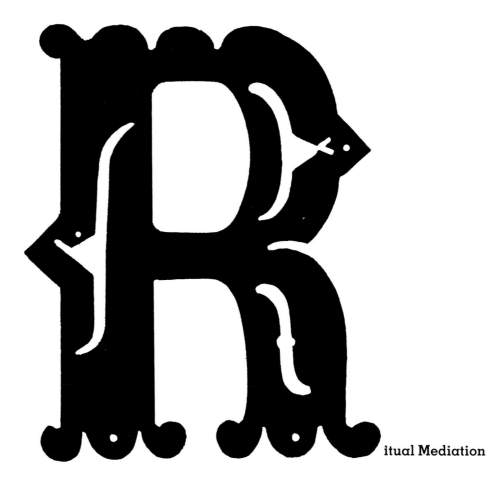

Ritual Mediation

of the Life-Death Opposition:

The Meaning of Mayo *Parisero* Lenten Masks

N. Ross Crumrine

1. See page 102.

At first sight the masks used by the Mayo Indians of southern Sonora and northern Sinaloa[1] in Lenten and Holy Week ceremonies may appear strikingly alien, certainly non-Christian, and strangely out of place during the Christian Lenten season. Yet as one sees and learns more about the Mayo Easter rituals, the masks and behavior of those who wear them become less exotic and seem to fit naturally into the developing Easter drama. The rituals must be understood as serious folk drama that present and expand upon a single theme while performing and re-enacting sacred history.[2] For the Mayos, rituals surrounding death and burial, whether for family members or Jesus, are extremely sad, serious, and emotionally exhausting and are perceived by them as "real." In some sense *Itom Achai Usi* (Our Father Child, or Jesus Christ) actually dies and is resurrected each Lenten season in the Mayo area.[3] The Mayo Easter masks must be understood within the contexts of life, death, and salvation. In this sense the masks transcend our desire to distract ourselves with what is strange and exotic and come to represent instead an aspect of our shared humanity, of what it means to be human and to work out by mean of creative performance the basic human problem of transition. Among the Mayos, as elsewhere, the reality of death and loss to society of deceased members provide some of the most difficult emotional and intellectual problems. The impact of these problems is ameliorated, in part, through

47. Guarding the
altar before the last
Friday procession. The
small Crucifix is
covered with a white
cloth. An image of
Christ's head protrudes
through the cloth. All
photos taken in the

performance of folk drama. It is the task of this essay to relate myth, or sacred history, dealing with death as transition to the use of masks.

A typical solution to the Lenten subject of death first generates the concept that life stands in opposition to death, replacing the concept of unitary death with that of life and death as parts of a duality.[4] This solution requires a mediating function to provide a transition or link between the oppositions. The mediating function might emerge either in the form of dramatic roles in an oral narrative or in performance of a ceremony. Once realized, this type of structural solution will generate specific roles to expedite the mediating function, an achievement which, when philosophically and aesthetically successful, reinforces the acceptance of the original solution. Within this general framework, the mediating function will produce a group of specific structural variants[5] and a range of specific functions.[6]

In analyzing Pueblo mythology Claude Levi-Strauss (1963:226) noted a "series of mediating devices" generated in response to the life-death opposition:

"messiah > dioscuri > bisexual being > sibling pair > married couple > grandmother-grandchild > four-term group > triad."

Although Mayo masked Lenten participants often appear as tricksters, it is believed that the characters they represent were created as a result of the acts of a kind of dioscuri comprised of God and *Caifás*[7]—the Devil (see editor's note for Griffith). Participants assume at random male or female roles and exhibit bisexual behavior.[8] The fact that they fulfill a mediating function would place them in the early section of Levi-Strauss' series. The specific forms of the mediating function also prove readily applicable in other social roles, such as social unification, reduc-

tion of tension through inversion and rituals of rebellions, rites of passage—especially initiation and funeral rituals, and reinforcement of ethnic and political identity. The Mayo Lenten ritual as directed by the *pariseros*[9] (literally, Pharisees), who serve as ritual hosts in the Lenten ceremonies, can be shown to involve all these social functions.[10] In discussing the complex Mayo solution to the dilemma posed by death, we shall focus upon the anomalous character of the *pariseros* and their role in the death and resurrection of Jesus.

Since modern Mayo Lenten ritual represents a complex fusion of seventeenth-century Catholicism and pre-Hispanic indigenous traditions, several key events in the history of Mayo contact with non-Mayos and of Mayo development must be presented.[11] From the Mayo point of view, their ceremonialism reaches back to their own cultural roots and is a uniquely Mayo system that provides direct communication with God and the saints. Although Spanish contact was initiated in the mid 1500s, Jesuit missionaries did not successfully convert and missionize the Mayos until the seventeenth and eighteenth centuries. The missionaries learned and taught in the Mayo language, lived in Mayo communities without elaborate military support, worked through Mayo leadership, and established a string of mission villages. Except for the period in 1740 when there was a widespread Indian revolt, the Jesuits remained in the area until 1767 when they were expelled from the New World. From the time of their expulsion until the late nineteenth century political authority in the Mayo area was not firmly established and Mayos experienced a period of relative autonomy. Gradually, as the numbers of mestizo colonists and their power grew, Mayo resistance waned and they were pacified in the late 1880s. Having gradually lost their lands and autonomy, Mayos joined the Mexican Revolution in 1910 hoping to regain freedom. During and after the disruption caused by the revolution, Mayo churches were burned and the cycle of major village ceremonies was curtailed or discontinued. However, by the 1930s some expropriated land had been returned to Mayos in the form of *ejidos*,[12] many local churches had been rebuilt, and the ceremonial cycle had been reestablished. The Mayo Easter ceremonialism under consideration in this essay, therefore, represents a cultural system that has survived for nearly four hundred years by means of dynamic modification and adaptation to broader historical and ecological changes taking place in the Mayo River Valley.

Today, Mayo Easter ceremonialism is maintained in spite of considerable general ecological constraints.[13] Characterized by nearly complete technical and economic assimilation, modern Mayos live in a high-yield irrigation agricultural zone. Many Mayos hold and farm small areas of land, approximately four to six hectares, either as members of *ejidos* or as owners of privately held plots. The time, amounts, and crops to be planted are essentially dictated by the banks, which lend monies for water, seed, etc., and by the hydraulic commission that supplies irrigation water. The everyday Mayo way of life now includes modern technology such as use of insecticides, spray planes, fertilizers, cloud-salting to produce rain, and introduction of the latest hybrid crops. This technical and economic assimilation stands in contrast to the persistence of Mayo language, ritual, and ceremonialism. The Mayo religious and ceremonial system also constitutes a crucial aspect of identity insofar as Mayos conceive of themselves as separate from mestizo Mexico. One of the major and most complex examples of this system is manifested in Lenten ceremonialism.

The following myth, still told today by modern Mayos, represents a pre-Contact mediating function that has survived as a variant to the masked *parisero*, or *chapakoba*.[14] It exemplifies, then, both the structural and historical processes as discussed earlier. Possibly linked to the ancient indigenous practice of burial in pots,[15] the myth not only reveals one type of mediating device that may be applied to the life/death opposition, but also emphasizes the deep respect which the modern Mayos feel toward God and the saints. Retold over the years, its modern form furnishes additional insight into the present meaning of Mayo Easter ceremonialism. The following is a free summary of the Mayo text, which is included in the endnotes.[16]

> Myth 1, The Loss of the Resurrection Pot. An old *sabio* (man of knowledge) wanted to remake himself into a child. He had himself chopped up and placed in a huge pot. The pot was tightly closed. Since he was a good *sabio* many people came looking for him. They looked and looked but nobody found him because he was sealed in the pot being renewed into a child. Still more people came looking for him but found nothing. A Mayo man was guarding the pot so it would not be opened. Nobody had permission to open the pot as it would kill the little child. However the guard went off to cut firewood. While he was doing so, the pot was opened and the little child forming in there died. He needed nine months to be fully formed just as children need nine months to form inside their mothers. The people killed him because they opened the pot and the wind blew in on him; the wind killed him.

The Ceremony and the *Parisero* Costume

Mayo Lenten ceremonialism focuses upon a local ceremonial center, relies upon individuals living within the general area of the center, and unifies local people, in contrast to saints' day celebrations that draw participants and observers from broad areas of northwest Mexico. Numerous Easter ceremonials take place simultaneously throughout the Mayo region. However the information presented in this article relates to the pueblo of Banari,[17] or Jupare, which is a Mayo ceremonial center and also a mixed mestizo and Mayo village of some 250 permanent residents. Each year during Lent local Mayos converge upon their small church in order to produce the following major events as organized by the *parisero* sodality:

(I) The Friday *Konti,* or Way of the Cross Procession, performed on each of the first six Friday afternoons of Lent (figs. 47–53).

(II) Holy Week:

(1) Palm Sunday, the capture of the *O'ola* (an old man who represents Jesus) by the *pariserom;*[18]

(2) Wednesday evening, the *Tinieblas* ceremony in which twelve candles in the church are extinguished and relighted while the *pariserom* cry in the darkness like wild animals, terrifying the women and children (fig. 54).;

(3) Thursday afternoon, the chasing of the old man around the second Way of the Cross by the *pariserom* and a procession later that evening (figs. 55–58);

(4) Late Friday afternoon as the sun is setting, the symbolic crucifixion of Jesus by the *pariserom,* followed later Friday evening by two processions around the Way of the Cross. The first accompanies the image of Jesus in an elaborately flowered coffin, while the second is split into two groups which, when joined, enact the meeting of Jesus and Mary (figs. 59–65);

(5) Saturday morning, the symbolic burning of the *pariserom* and their return to humanity again via baptism (figs. 66, 67);

(6) Sunday morning, the meeting of the resurrected Jesus with Mary and the return of the image of Jesus to the church, thus ending *Warehma* (Lent) and the Easter ceremonial (fig. 68);

The Mayo myth of Jesus' life of curing and travel in the Mayo River Valley, His capture by the *pariserom* in the forest, His crucifixion along the Mayo River, the burning of the *pariserom,* and Jesus' return from the dead articulate these events into a sacred ritual drama. The *pariserom* sodality, which serves as the Army of Pilate, assumes the major responsibility for the production of the ceremonial, although it is assisted by the *paskome* (low-ranking ritual hosts who guard Christ's tomb during Holy Week) and other church sodalities. In the weeks of Lent the *pariserom* play the pursuers of Christ. Finally, during Easter week, they symbolically crucify Jesus and in turn are destroyed themselves. During Lent the *pariserom* take over many of the political and ceremonial functions and duties that are controlled by other sodalities during the rest of the year. After the destruction and baptism of the *pariserom,* the secular and church organizations regain the power that they had relinquished to them.

The following myths explain this Lenten ceremonialism from the Mayo point of view, placing it within a sacred temporal cycle:

Myth 2. Joseph and Mary fled, out of shame it is said, because Mary was pregnant, and Joseph knew that he had nothing to do with it. But the angel appeared to Mary and told her not to be ashamed because she was going to give birth to Jesus; he told her and Joseph not to be ashamed for it was the work of the Holy Spirit. He talked to Joseph alone, then, and told him not to leave Mary because of this. So Mary and Joseph came back to Bethlehem, but there was no room for them anywhere so they had to go to a stable. And there the Child was born and the *Bahi Reyesim* (Three Kings) came to see the Jesus Child. The animals made special noises signalling his birth. The cock crowed, the donkey brayed, and the dog barked. Then Pontius Pilate started pursuing the Christ Child, it is said because he was afraid. Since the Three Kings had visited Jesus, Pilate thought the child must be pretty important. So the army of Pontius Pilate pursues the Christ Child every year, and kills him, but in the end He arises and He and the Three Kings triumph on the Saturday of Glory.

Myth 3. Jesus taught, cured, was pursued, crucified, and arose in the Mayo River Valley as He did in all parts of the Earth. Jesus travelled around the river valley (the Mayo Area) curing the sick and teaching. The *pariserom* finally chased Him into the desert, the mesquite forest. They captured Him there in the mesquite forest, and took Him to the river to the *abaso* (cottonwood) forest where they crucified Jesus.

Myth 4. The *pariserom* followed and killed Jesus because they wanted to command. They did not want Him, Jesus, to command them. *They* wanted to command. But even through they won when they killed Him, they did not win. Because due to their killing Jesus, they themselves had to die. He arose and ascended to heaven. The army of Pontius Pilate is destroyed. Jesus' will is supreme and the *pariserom* must die because they have disobeyed His will. The *pariserom* took power but forgot that only Jesus commands.

In these myths, Mary stands for *Itom Aye* (Our Mother), the Mother of Jesus and the Mother of all Mayos. Pontius Pilate stands for the *parisero* group and is head of the *pariserom*. Several *pilatom* (soldiers of Pilate) command the *pariserom*. The *pariserom* are symbolic of the pursuers and crucifiers of Jesus and at the same time are repositories of a somewhat self-focused and individualistic religious and political power. Mayos often comment, "When a man wants to do something he alone wants for himself, and he cares for no one else, he is like that then." The *chapakoba* masks and *pilato* headdresses add to their physical height, and the black *pilato* capes, swords, and weapons of the officers suggest power, natural and supernatural. Their unsuccessful attempt to dominate Jesus ultimately proves that only God rules and that He has much greater power than they.

Since Mayo Easter ceremonial costume and material apparatus is rather complex, I will focus upon a description of the masked members of the *parisero* society, the *pariserom*. In general, all members of the *parisero* society wear cotton shirts and wash pants as well as rosaries and sandals, except on Easter Sunday when the sandals are replaced by shoes. The rosary is concealed under the shirt or mask and the cross on the end is held in the mouth when the mask is pulled down over the face. The *parisero* "eats" the rosary and repeats the *Credo* or another prayer while the mask is over his face. Good Friday, when the *pariserom* knock down the house and church crosses, they also paint their forearms and lower legs with red stripes, symbolic of the blood of Jesus. The well-attired *parisero* also wears *tenebarim* (cocoon rattles) around his lower legs just above the ankle. The *tenebarim*, like those worn by the *paskola* and *maso (deer)* dancers,[19] are moth cocoons strung in strings that are long enough to make several wraps around each leg of the *parisero*. Over their shirts they wear a blanket that extends down below the waist, over the hips, to the mid section of the upper leg, and is like a shawl over the back with the two ends pulled up underneath the arms. Above the blanket, a huge white cloth is wrapped around the head and hangs out beneath the mask, draping over the shoulders. Finally, the mask worn over the cloth-wrapped head tops off the *parisero* attire.

Four types of head coverings are utilized in the Easter ceremonial in

Jupare: hats, scarves, face coverings, and masks. An extremely common item of male clothing in the Mayo River Valley is an ordinary flat-topped, broad-brimmed straw hat. Out of respect to God and the saints, men remove their hats when they enter a church or stand within a sacred Way of the Cross or in a procession. The *pariserom* refuse to show this respect and wear their hats within the church and during processions. They respect only themselves.

The *parisero ya'uchim* (officers) wear large colored scarves, often purple or pink, around their necks, which they pull up over their noses and mouths in ritual contexts. On Easter Sunday, the day after the burning of their masks, the former *chapakobam* also wear scarves in this manner. This scarf, when placed over the face, contributes to the sense of mystery and power surrounding the role of *parisero*. Much more powerful are the full face covers of the *pilatom*. These are tied with a colored ribbon at the top of the hat and fall completely across the face and down to the neck, both in the front and the back. The cloth is light enough in weight to permit the pilato to see out, but it greatly conceals his features and facial expressions and gives him the appearance of a faceless, expressionless being.[20] On Thursday they wear pink or red face coverings. From Friday afternoon until the end of the ceremonial they appear with black face coverings and white ribbons.

The most striking head covering used by members of the *parisero* sodality is the *máscara* (mask of the *chapakoba*). Perhaps the most outstanding characteristic of the Jupare masks is their long black, brown, or white hair. They sport long, narrow, pointed ears and shorter, yet narrow, pointed noses made of pieces of scraped hide sewn to the masks, which flap as the *chapakoba* turns his head. The face is produced by scraping an oval area clean of hair and painting eyes and a mouth. Other masks may have an especially delicately carved wooden face attached. *Chapakoba* masks also exhibit individual as well as group differences. Mayos easily recognize a local mask from one of another ceremonial center. This may relate to a strong desire on the part of certain ceremonial centers to maintain a separate community identity. Thus differences in masks reflect sociological and political divisions between neighboring communities. While individual masks may employ different kinds of decorations, construction of masks is basically consistant. For example, one mask was observed with a pair of glasses and another had a deer head decorated like that worn by the *maso* dancer. Masks are made either by the individual *chapakoba* or purchased from persons who are practised in this folk art.

In describing the hand-carried accouterments I will focus upon those utilized by the *pariserom*. The *Pilato* carries a banner of red or black cloth and occasionally a sword, the *capitán* (Captain, second ranking officer, second in command beneath Pilate) a metal sword and sheath, and the *cabo* (corporal or third in command, lowest ranking officer) a machete and a whip. All the *chapakobam* carry wooden swords and knives and about half of them also bear drums. The three-foot- to four-foot-long wooden *lansam* (swords) and the eight-inch- to twelve-inch-long wooden knives are decorated with red and green designs with the cutting edges painted red to symbolize the blood of Jesus. To attract attention or "talk," the *chapakoba* will clack his knife against the sword, as he never actually speaks. When a number of *chapakobam* begin to make this clacking noise at the same time the volume is arresting, especially when it and the sound of their drums drift through the silence of the night. The double sheepskin-headed drums are often painted with red and green motifs such as trees,

48. Prayers at a
Station stop during the
last Friday procession.

49. Prayers at *Kalbario* with the large Crucifix resting on the low table just in front of the three crosses.

50. *Paskome* protecting *Kalbario*, the last Station, from the *pariserom*.

51. Pulling up the crosses of this first *Kalbario* after the prayers.

five-pointed stars, and even a nude pinup girl wearing high heels. The drums are held in the left hand and played with short wooden sticks held in the right hand. Like the clacking of swords and knives, the beating of *chapakoba* drums creates a sound that commands attention.

Chapakobam also make ingenious use of items accidentally found or made for the occasion. The finding of a ball results in a *pelote*-type game played with two lines of *chapakobam* kicking the ball back and forth. On other occasions, a dead bird or a dead snake may become an object of play. A piece of bread and a comic book discarded beside the church are used as props for a *chapakoba* pantomime of eating and reading. A small metal bucket and small discarded wine bottles become receptacles for the collection of human "feces" in other *chapakoba* pantomimes. Other items are carried, especially for performances, such as money with which they try to bribe the little boys dressed as the Three Kings and the girls dressed as angels. Toy guns, a rubber doll's leg and foot which is placed on the end of a sword, a baby bottle with a rubber nipple, a violin, and carefully carved wooden phallic representations are carried by individual *chapakobam.* Anything that might serve as a prop in a pantomime of traditional activities may be utilized by *chapakobam.*

The most important images carried in many of the Jupare Easter ceremonial processions are the large and small crucifixes which are named respectively Our Father, or Santo Cristo, and Our Mother, or Mary, and the image of San Juan (Saint John). The image of Christ crucified is the patron saint or supernatural guardian of the *parisero* sodality. This image must include a cross which is dark gray or black in color. Many *pariserom* have a dark colored crucifix resting on their home altars. They also pay special homage to the *urna* (coffin of Jesus),

which generally rests in a smaller room just off the altar area in the Jupare church. The old man, who is finally captured, "runs" around the Way of the Cross because he is thought to be like Jesus. He too may be conceived as a sacred image. The old man wears a crown of greenery around his head, similar to those placed on Mayo house crosses; to those placed on the crosses of *Kalbario* (the place symbolizing Calvary, the last station on the Way of the Cross) for the sixth Friday procession; and to that placed around the head of the large crucifix. Mayo house crosses, with their crowns of greenery and flowers, also play an important part in the Easter ceremonial, representing as they do the old man and Jesus.[21] Candles, too, are important and after the crucifixion are carried by almost everyone walking in the evening procession. The flame originates in the church and is passed from one person to the next. After the ceremony is over Friday evening, Mayos take their candles home where they place them beside the pulled-up house crosses to burn for the remainder of the night. Both during the time of the crucifixion and during the last Friday procession when the Way of the Cross has been removed, the church altar is decorated with four large white candles and six tall vases of *sunni* (cane). At this same time the *tumba* (a mound of earth that symbolizes the tomb of Christ) is constructed around the glass coffin for the image of Jesus. All these sacred objects— cane, candles, bowers, coffin, and mound of earth—are symbolically part of the tomb and death of Jesus.

During Lent, three sacred areas are prepared and protected: *Kalbario,* which is used for the Friday processions; the Way of the Cross around the church, used during the week; and *Loria Ultima* (the last *Gloria*) or *Sewateri,* used on Easter Sunday for the meeting of Jesus and Mary. These three sacred ways provide the material contexts and the boundaries, the stages on

52. *Pariserom* accompanying the procession.

53. *Pariserom* in procession.

54. The *tinieblas* ceremony with the *O'ola* and his *madrinas* sitting before the altar. The *madrinas* hold switches with which they strike the church floor after the candles are extinguished, thus fending off the *pariserom* who yell and run around in the dark.

55. Running the *O'ola*,
who is just behind the
pariserom flutists and
flanked by two
masked *pilatom*.

56. *Pariserom* investi-
gating one of the
Stations where the
O'ola will kneel and
rest during the
running.

57. Carrying the large
Crucifix in the evening
procession after the
running of the *O'ola*.

58. *Pilatom* on horse-
back gallop between
the two branches of
the procession carrying
the large Crucifix and
the image of Mary.

which a great deal of the ritual of the Jupare Easter ceremonial takes place.

The *Parisero* Organization and Ritual

Although a number of sodalities are involved in the production of the Easter ceremonial, the *pariserom* are directly accountable and responsible only for the Lenten ceremonial, in contrast to other Mayo sacred sodalities for whom the Easter ceremonial is only a part of their ritual duties. The cooperating groups include the *maestro* (lay minister), *sacristan* (sexton), *cantora* (female church cantors), altar women, *bahi mariam* (little girl angels and their godmothers), the *Santisima Tiniran* and *Santa Kurus paskome* (ritual hosts) and a *Mo'oro* (advisor) of each, the *matachini* dancers (a church dance society), *bahi reyesim* (the Kings, comprised of little boys, the civil-church governors, and the men of the pueblo), and the *paskola* and *maso* dance groups.[22] With the exception of the *paskola* and *maso* dance groups, and the positions of *maestro, cantora, sacristan,* civil and church governors, recruitment for most sodalities is based on the making of a *manda* (a vow to serve God or a saint or the Virgin). A Mayo makes a *manda* to a saint when he calls on the saint to cure or aid him. If the petitioner is cured, then he or she must fulfill the promise and perform ritual labor in honor of God or the particular saint to whom the *manda* was made. In most sodalities, such as the *pariserom* and the *paskome,* the *manda* is made for three years, although these do not have to be consecutive. The *chapakobam* usually serve for three years, although the officers of the *pariserom* sodality are obligated for longer periods of service which may last a lifetime.

In Jupare in 1961 the *pariserom* was an all male sodality with over one hundred members organized into groups with more than twenty-five *ya'uchim,* men in their thirties through fifties, and seventy-five *chapakobam,* youths between the ages of fifteen and nineteen.[23]

All were members of the local community of some 2,500 to 3,500 Mayos. The fact that the younger men served for three years resulted in perhaps one in every two or three young men serving in this sodality.

The major structural principle within the sodality is that of hierarchical authority or dominance/subordinance. The hierarchy of statuses consists of *Pilato, capitán, cabo* (corporal), *flautero* (flutist), and *tampalero* (drummer). These are the leaders of the *ya'uchim.* Lowest in rank are the *chapakobam,* who are also called *Pilatotom o'owim* (men of Pilate) or *soldados* (soldiers).

The activities of the *pariserom* during Lent build to the Crucifixion, Defeat, and Resurrection. Their portrayal is that of a power struggle in which an egoistic type of power is defeated by the power of *Itom Achai O'ola* (Our Father Old Man God) and Jesus. On the other hand, *pariserom* are called *costumbre ya'uchim* (protectors of custom), and are responsible for producing the ceremonial. Their activities and roles are dual in nature: they are protectors of custom, as opposed to destroyers of established order. The *Pilato* role is one of extreme authority. Ultimately it is *Pilato* who is responsible for the death of Jesus, and his dramatic role evolves with the development of the ceremonial.[24] During the Friday processions and up to the time of the Crucifixion, the *pilatom* remain highly visible yet aloof and inactive. During the crucifixion and bid for ultimate power that follows they

59. Good Friday morning. The *pariserom* have pulled up the crosses near the church.

become the main actors. Afterwards they appear as the passive recipients of action. As second in command, the *capitán* protects the *Pilato* and walks on the outside of the *Pilato* in the procession. He either carries out the orders of the *Pilato* or sees to it that these are executed by passing them on to a *cabo*. Like the *Pilato* and *capitán*, the *cabo* is also expected to retain and serve as a repository of ritual knowledge. In practice, however, his role focuses upon the practical problems involved in the production of the ceremonial, carrying out commands, and policing the ceremonial area. A *Pilato* or *capitán* usually does not carry out an order, while the *cabom* and *chapakobam* are constantly running about performing the physical labor required by the ceremonial. Each *cabo* has a group of *chapakobam* as his specific charge. At the bottom of the hierarchy, the *chapakobam* are expected to do most of the physical labor and burlesque, as well as enforce, the customs. In moving down through the sets of roles, the expectation of ceremonial knowledge decreases; all, however, are expected to obey and enforce the customs and behave in traditionally sanctioned ways. The *chapakoba* role is extremely ambiguous.[25] First, the *chapakoba* protect the customs by enforcing proper kneeling form with respect to ritual, making sure that nobody in or around the church sleeps on Good Friday, and by guarding the sacred way used on Easter Sunday. Second, they work extremely hard on the ceremonial, and are expected to sweat under their masks and to suffer as Jesus did during the last days of his life. Before each of the six Friday processions they must run around the Way of the Cross three times. This exertion is termed "the *parisero* confession for the whole community." Lastly, the *chapakobam* ritually impersonate Mayo sacred symbols and acts. Links between the *chapakobam* and the dead exist. Dead animals fascinate them and

are used as objects of burlesque. The often backward performance of their actions may be symbolic of the world of the dead and definitely is symbolic of witchcraft behavior. Besides using their left hands to cross themselves and to shake hands, they also pantomime defecation on sacred objects. In small cans they pretend "collection" from the other *chapakobam* of "feces," and the "eating" of "feces" is a common pantomime. Lastly, *chapakobam* are fascinated with sex. They "kiss," "hug," "dance" with each other, and carry wooden male phalli. All this behavior is quite deviant for Mayos. When the *pariserom* have their masks on "they are without shame." For this reason they must be baptized to become men again.

After a formal planning session on Sunday before Ash Wednesday, the first of six Friday Lenten processions takes place on the first of the sacred roads. During the six weeks of Lent the smaller of the two crucifixes is carried by the *pariserom* to homes in the community. Household members take the image into the house and make a small contribution to the cost of the Easter week ceremonies. The "resting of Jesus" that occurs during this period repeats the pattern of visiting households. This ceremony, however, is more complex and Jesus remains in the home overnight. These rituals involve cooperation between the *pariserom* and the *paskome*, since the former burlesque

61. The *pariserom* pull apart the bower to reveal the body of Christ.

0. The *maestro* and *cantora* pray and sing beside the cottonwood bower housing the Crucifix.

62. The body of Christ, removed from the cross, is carried to the coffin.

and protect the group and the latter care for the image. Often Deer and *paskola* dances are included in this ceremony. The "resting of Jesus" refers to Jesus' travels, teaching, curing, and stopping at individual homes.[26]

After the sixth Friday procession the *paskome* pull up all of the crosses on the sacred road as they return to the church. Relief and relaxation are experienced by participants. With the completion of the six Friday processions many of the most difficult rituals of the Jupare Easter ceremonialism have been realized. The structure of each Friday procession is replicated on a broader scale in the Easter Week ritual. Thus each Friday procession exists both as an independent ritual and as part of the developing Lenten ceremonialism. The differences in each procession become apparent as the weeks of Lent advance. All of the processions, however, exhibit similar patterns in the kinds of preparations made around and within the church; in the paths taken out to *Kalbario* and back to the church; and in the closing rituals. Structural replications of the Lenten cycle are embedded in the Friday processions that serve as precursors of the activities of Holy Week. The capture and running of the old man and the Crucifixion of Jesus focus the community's attention outward toward the specialness of these events. The Resurrection, burning of the masks, and the meeting of Mary and Jesus represent the return to the church, while the final procession and the "feeding" of the *pariserom* are rituals of closure.

Parisero Symbolism and Meanings of the Ritual

Coupling explanations offered most frequently by Mayos concerning Lenten rituals with a myth about the origin of the *pariserom* may suggest a method for analyzing this ceremonial. Mayos have been most willing to discuss the rituals; the subject came up repeatedly in informal conversations, and concern was expressed for their understanding. Four clusters of partial explanations emerged from these conversations. The first and most general Mayo response concerning Easter ritual and especially *chapakoba* behavior is, *"Es, costumbre!"* (It is our custom. This is what we have always done and this is why we do it now.) Beyond this appeal to tradition, Mayos frequently state "the *pariserom* know no shame!" To them this explains why the *pariserom* do not behave properly. Second, the capture and running of the old man strikes Mayos as extremely interesting. For them this character is like Jesus. ("He is not Jesus, but reminds us that Jesus had a body like we do.") Third, Mayos, especially those who are not *pariserom*, frequently remark that the entire ceremony is an attempt by the *pariserom* to usurp and control the powers of God. ("The *pariserom* wish to rule but ultimately only God has the power to rule.") Fourth, Mayos participate in the ceremonial in reciprocation for a *manda* made to a supernatural as the result of alleviation from illness. Some say they are working for *Santo Sewam* (the "Holy Flowers"), by which they mean rewards in heaven. The *mandas* made by the *pariserom* are to the holy image of Christ crucified; they explain, therefore, that they have God's permission to make the Lenten ceremonial. Although the *pariserom* control the ceremonial in which they crucify Jesus, they always emphasize, "but only God commands!"

Myths 2, 3, and 4, presented earlier, establish the relationships between Mary, Jesus, and the *pariserom*. The following myths, which are summarized here very briefly, are considerably more esoteric and explain the creation of the *chapakobam* and the origin of the conflict between God and the Devil. These myths explain the comment "the *chapakobam* know no shame," and reveal the basis of a wider dispute

63. The decorated church crosses will be replaced when Christ arises at 3 a.m. Saturday morning.

64. The *pariserom* surround the coffin.

and of the opposition between death and life. Full versions of these myths are presented in the endnotes.[27]

Myth 5. The *pariserom* have Jesus' permission to make the ceremony. They imitate the dead and enact what happened to Jesus when He appeared and the *pilatom* killed Him. Their masks are like the Devil, very hairy. The Devil is God's enemy. He is the Devil. The *pariserom* are his soldiers. But Jesus arose from the dead and the Devil has retreated to the forest and his soldiers have been killed.

Myth 6. When the world began God began to make animals, hens, etc. His very dear and close friend, the Devil, began to imitate God, but an owl resulted from his attempts at creation. God then created human beings. The Devil also imitated God but his "humans" turned out like himself—bad. The Devil imitated God and did not respect Him. Lacking respect and speaking badly about other people is the sin which God cannot forgive. Speaking badly is a means of falling from grace. Now, the world is in a trial period of 6,000 years to see if God or the Devil will win.

These myths offer a Mayo explanation for the behavior of the *chapakobam* and discuss why they have no shame, usurp power, and ultimately are burned up by God-the-Sun. Individual members of the *parisero* society, by stating "but only God commands," are quick to deny a personal metanymical identity with the Devil. Yet the society itself is clearly identified with an authoritarian type of social structure. As the weeks of Lent progress, the *pariserom* assume more and more power, becoming increasingly overbearing and demanding, while the *chapakobam* do almost anything that interests and pleases them. Ultimately they chase the old man and crucify Jesus. Clearly members of the *parisero* sodality believe they have God's permission to crucify His Son and in fact have made a promise to God to make His ceremony. Some *pariserom* explain that Jesus tired of this world and wished to return to His Father. The *pariserom* provide the

means for His return. They conceive of themselves as instruments of God. A Mayo who has been cured by a saint or God is obligated to repay that service with ceremonial labor. Ceremonial societies are able to recruit members because of the seriousness of these obligations. The *parisero* serves God not only by producing the ceremonial, but also through his own suffering and confession. The idea that participation in Lenten ceremonialism functions as a confession is widely prevalent among Mayos. The wearing of a mask and running the sacred way is spoken of explicitly by the *pariserom* as confession. *Chapakobam* must work while wearing masks that cause them to sweat profusely. *"Tuisi lotila"* (very tired) is an expression commonly heard after a Friday procession. The participants in the Easter ceremonial, especially the *pariserom*, suffer as Jesus did during the last weeks and hours of His life. They confess themselves of their ultimate destruction of Him but also of the transgressions of the preceding year made by all members of the community. Suffering and confession are thought to be purifying and bring about the renewal of life celebrated on Holy Saturday and Easter Sunday—the Resurrection—which is in actuality the resolution of the life-death opposition.

The fourth focus of Mayo comments elaborates upon the old man and, in a general way, upon death and funeral ritual. When asked why the house crosses have crowns of greenery and flowers, a *parisero* replied, "that house cross is Our Father—Old Man-God. It is because the *pariserom* have the old man and the old man has greenery around his head. They are going to throw the old man down and we throw down all the house crosses everywhere." The old man is like Jesus in that he wears the crown of greenery, the crown of thorns, as did Jesus prior to crucifixion. Some Mayos believe that each Easter, when the crown of thorns is placed on the large crucifix, blood runs down

65. The image of Christ is only returned to the cross at the moment of Resurrection, 3 a.m. Saturday morning. The cross from the small Crucifix can be seen tied to the center of the large cross.

Jesus' face. The old man wears a red and green waist band and rope which is used by the *pariserom* to pull him down, and is believed to be used also by the angels to pull a deceased person up into heaven. Thus the waist band and rope of the old man symbolizes the struggle between the *chapakobam*, in this case representing the already deceased who join with the Devil to pull the newly deceased into the earth,[28] and the angels and Jesus who resurrect the deceased and pull them up into Heaven. The "falling" of the old man takes place as he runs around the second Way of the Cross from green bower to green bower. (I never saw him actually knocked to the ground.) He is given water to drink from two painted gourds. The image of San Juan carries water gourds also when he "runs" to Mary to announce that Jesus has arisen. Protecting the old man are eight *madrinas* (godmothers), equal in number to the women who had accompanied Jesus. Some of the godmothers have long mesquite switches which they use to drive away the *chapakobam*, while others hang on to the rope between the old man and the *chapakobam* in order to protect him from their pulling. In between attacks, the old man rests in the little bowers. These are like the forest to which Jesus fled and in which He was ultimately captured by the *pariserom* (as the old man will ultimately be captured on Palm Sunday). The bowered house crosses are like tombs and at night on Good Friday have burning candles placed beside them. (Similarly, when death occurs in a family it is crucial that candles be burned before the house cross.) The symbolic Crucifixion of Jesus takes place within a bower that also houses several boys who wear crowns of greenery and are called the Kings. After the crucifixion, the image of Jesus is placed in the earth tomb that has been constructed in the church. During the funeral prayers for the deceased Christ, the *alawasim* (lowest ranking ritual hosts, another term for the *paskome*) guard this tomb from the *chapakobam*. The *alawasim* carry long cane switches, which they use to drive off the *pariserom*. Four long cane sticks accompany the deceased to the cemetery during traditional Mayo funerals. The *bato achaim* (godfathers) and *bato ayem* (godmothers) of the deceased use these canes to beat away dogs or trespassers who might harm the body. At grave side the canes are placed in the four corners of the grave and removed on the eighth day. These canes are like the switches used by the *alawasim* at the time of the funeral ritual for Jesus, by the godmothers of the old man at the time of the "running," and by the *alawasim* guarding the stations of the cross on the first six Friday processions. In all cases they are protecting sacred objects that symbolize Jesus from the *chapakobam*, who wish to deface, destroy, and control them in order to bestow them on the Devil. All of these objects, personages, and actions represent complex ritual values associated with funerary practices and beliefs about death. Until the the first hint of dawn early Saturday morning heralds the Resurrection, ceremonial organization and activites of all participants focus upon the ritual symbols of death. The Return of Jesus mediates the life-death opposition and the rituals of Holy Saturday and Easter Sunday focus upon symbols referring to life.

In the most general sense, the Jupare Easter ceremonial integrates the individual and the group with the culture through use of meaningful symbols. The individual may participate as child, youth, or adult. At each level the ceremonial serves as a dramatic mechanism to enculturate the individual. The elaborate symbolism and the anomalous roles of the *pariserom* and especially the *chapakobam* heighten participants' awareness of their unique culture and society. In the final resolution of the ceremonial, Mayo customs are emphasized, reaffirming tradition-

al norms and values. For the youthful *pariserom*, their (often) three years of service acts as an initiation ritual. Membership in this all-male sodality intensifies male identity through shared experience and suffering. The ceremony serves, too, to diffuse hostility toward the authority of the elders by "knocking down the old man." During this ritual there is a great deal of pushing and loud, rough laughter that is quite atypical of Mayos. At the group level it would appear that a model of hierarchical and authoritarian social structure is advanced. However, with the defeat of the *pariserom* this principle is replaced with a more egalitarian one as the church authorities assume power and control. Within the context of traditional norms, Mayos place a high value upon equality and individual freedom. The actions of the *pariserom* first offer an alternative structural principle, one that is always threatening to an egalitarian society. Through portrayal of hierarchical social organization that results first in greater power; second, in irrational destruction of the most holy of personages; and third, in the ultimate loss of power, traditional structure of society is reaffirmed as the one supported by supernatural sanction. In terms of present cultural and ecological conditions in the Mayo valley, this egalitarian type of structure offers greater survival value than does a hierarchical, authoritarian one whose leadership has had a history of destruction by the dominant society.

The Easter ceremonial resolves cultural questions concerning the meaning of life and health. Although the *pariserom* are the instruments of Jesus' death, they themselves must die because of their use of extreme authoritarianism and because of their introduction of death. In the end, life, in the person of Jesus as the great curer, returns from the dead just as spring returns and is followed by summer rains. At the moment of *Gloria*, the *pariserom* become human, the *pariserom* organization is defeated, and flowers are thrown. As part of this culminating ritual the earth is whipped, perhaps awakening it for the agricultural year, or, as one of my Mayo friends explained, "in repayment for the innocent ones, such as little children or Jesus, who have suffered without cause."

Without question, the ceremonial is also the archetypal funeral ritual. "Young Man God teaches us all how to die and return to Our Father Old Man God."[29] The ceremonial shows Mayos how to behave when confronted with death and presents the hope for health and life beyond death. The ceremonial introduces a complex array of intensely aesthetic, emotion-laden ritual and symbolism into their materially impoverished environment. The Easter ceremonial, with its dramatic and integral employment of a ritual masking tradition, confronts a crisis and offers a solution to intellectual problems concerned with ultimate meanings.

A reexamination of Myth 1 reveals striking parallels between it and Mayo Lenten ritual. As a narrative about rebirth in pots, the myth refers to pre-Christian funeral rituals. As suggested earlier, oral narratives as well as ritual dramas may represent varieties of mediating roles that afford transition between opposites in dualistic concepts. Information obtained from Mayo ceremonials indicates that sacred narratives and rituals refer to the life-death opposition and provide the means of mediation. The pot filled with medicine and the bones and flesh of the man of knowledge refers to the physical process of rebirth, while the death of Jesus at the hands of the *pariserom* and His Resurrection are mystically achieved through the power of God and the Lenten ritual. For Mayos, ritual and especially prayer are vital entities that provide food for God and the saints. Like Jesus, the man of knowledge is sacrificed. He is chopped up in order that he may be resurrected as a little baby. He fails to be reborn because of the intervention of foreigners, who trick the guard into leaving and then open the pot. The Mayo guard and the foreigners are replaced in the Lenten ritual by the *pariserom*. In other words, those who destroy the man of knowledge are structurally equal to the anomalous *pariserom* who, although burlesquing the ritual, have God's permission to make the ceremony in return for their *mandas*. Both the resurrection pot myth and Easter myth and ritual treat the identical problem of the reality of death through first generating and then mediating the opposition of life and death. Because of human failing with regard to respect, both resolutions seem bound to fail. The baby is destroyed and the powers of the resurrection pot to bring about rebirth are lost forever. Jesus is killed or sacrificed by the *pariserom*, but because His power is greater than theirs He is able to establish eternal mediation upon his return and "teach humans how to die." The following statement by a Mayo *maestro* reintegrates ritual symbolism and ceremonialism and clearly can be understood to embody the major meanings of *parisero* mask symbolism and ritual in particular, together with Mayo Lenten symbolism and behavior in general:

imi santo, kalbariompo, itom yauchiwa Dios, imi muku, nasuk
here on the holy Calvary our Chief God died by means

kuruhta we'ekapo. ime Hudiom intok, imi'irima na kontiak,
of the cross And the *Judios* (*pariserom*) surrounded him

imi'irima me ak. bai kurusim habue ka apo, muku itom yauchiwa
and killed him. Where there are those three crosses our Chief

Itom Achai Yo'owe, te hiba yoko ket weye Itom Achai
Itom Achai, the Elder, died. *Itom Achai*, the Elder always will

Yo'owe te hiabihtenake. hibako aman tetem hunake hume, pariserom
rise the next morning. And always they will go (those *pariserom*)

bwiyata am tattanake.
to the tomb in the ground.

66. Saturday morning.
The image is returned
to the "place of rest"
on the cross.

67. Burning the masks
after the "Baptism" of
the *pariserom* late
Saturday morning.

68. A *maestro* leading
the Easter Sunday
service.

1. The Mayos are a group of Uto-Aztecan speakers living in southern Sonora and northern Sinaloa along the Mayo and Fuerte rivers. Although considerable material has been published on the Yaquis, who live directly north of the Mayos, and on Yaqui ceremonialism, especially their Easter rituals (see Spicer 1940, 1954, 1964, and R. Spicer 1939), rather little besides the work of Ralph Beals (1943, 1945) and Charles Erasmus (1961, 1967) has been printed concerning Mayo ceremonialism. The data reported here were collected during two years' field residence, 1961 and in 1972–73, and during many Easter Week visits up to the Spring of 1986. The field research was financed by a National Science Foundation Grant for Dissertation Improvement, a Canada Council Research Fellowship, and numerous University of Victoria Research Grants. Some of the descriptive material summarized here is considerably elaborated in my doctoral dissertation which has been published (Crumrine 1974b).

2. See Crumrine 1983b and 1986.

3. This is true not only for the Mayo region but also for northwest Mexico in general. At present Rosamond B. Spicer and I are editing a comparative collection of descriptive and analytical articles which focus upon Easter ceremonialism in this general area of North America.

4. See Leach 1961.

5. See Crumrine 1979 and Levi-Strauss 1963.

6. See Crumrine 1974a.

7. Caifás, a Jewish priest who condemned Christ.

8. See Crumrine 1974a, 1976.

9. This voluntary Mayo association includes the *pilatom, capitanes,* and *cabom* (the officers of the organization) and the *chapakobam* or *judios,* the masked soldiers in this army of Pilate.

10. See Crumrine 1969a, 1974b.

11. For a more detailed discussion of Mayo history, cultural ecology, and modern adaptation to mestizo Mexico see Crumrine 1964, 1975, 1977a, 1981a, 1981b, 1983a, and 1987.

12. *Ejido* parcels are lands given in common by the government to peasant farming groups called *ejidos* and worked in common or in the Mayo case parcelled among the individual members or *socios* of the *ejido*.

13. See note 12.

14. The lowest ranking member of the *parisero* sodality. The term *chapakoba,* while recognized by Mayos, is not popularly used. They prefer the term *parisero* which is somewhat confusing as *parisero* is also the general name for the sodality and all its members. They also recognize the Yaqui term *chapayeka* but also use it rather infrequently. *Koba* means head, while the meaning of *chapa* is unclear but seems to refer to a pointed shape like the *chapakari,* a type of house (*kari*) with a pointed sloping roof. In this article, I use the term *chapakoba* when the referent of *parisero* might be unclear and I wish to focus emphasis specifically and

only on the masked members of the *parisero* sodality.

15. There is some, although not very good, evidence that pre-Contact Mayos buried their dead in large jars or pots, thus this sort of "pot burial" seems to have been an actual custom, perhaps acting out, in the actual funeral rituals of that time, the resurrection belief expressed in the myth. See also Crumrine 1974c and 1982.

16. The material in parentheses represents my comments while the translation is free in places and rather close in others.

Myth 1, The Loss of the Resurrection Pot:

Hewi, na hikaila, sabio. sabiotukai, bwan (hewi, hu'u
Yes,   I heard the history of the *sabio* (man of knowledge) (yes, the

sabio). wanai intok huchi . . . huchi usita yaabari (hewi)
sabio) well then   that child he wanted to make.

aap imi si'imeta chukti, si'ime. (hewi) bwe'eru sotopa
   all of him was cut up,   all.   (yes)   A huge pot

patiak.   (hewi) huchi pake bemela tubarek, usi tubarek (hewi)
was closed up.   that is in order to remake new, a child to remake

hummm . . . (hewi, luturia) te como taarua hariwa bu'uruka
(yes, true)   he was as lost, sought   by many,

haria waatia (hewi) te tubuk patiay sotopo (hewi)   aaa pues . . .
sought, they desired him, tightly closed was the pot.   aaa well

hariwa bu'uru nacion huebena nacionim a watia (hewi)
seeking him were lots of people, many nations strongly desired him

no bes ke hu' tuli sabio, tuisi. (hewi) aa . . . pues hariwa
because he was a good sabio, very good.   well, they looked

hariwa (hewi) ka tewa (e'e) kaba a tewa,   (e') no bes
looked (yes) they did not find him, no one found him (no) because

humu patiay (hewi) huchi usita yabar   huchi bemelachi
it was closed tight,   he wished to make a child, this new one

(hewi) huchi bemelachi tekipanoabarayo. (hewi, turi) aa . . .
(yes) again renewed,   he wanted to work. (yes, certainly)

pues antonce wanai intok . . . besa imin hakun taabwi nacion
well then   still another people

a yaaka haria howapa haria   kaita. huu wepulai hiba
looked for him at home, sought but nothing. One

suaiya, (hewi) yorem o'o   (hewi) yoreme. (yoreme) huwara
guarded (yes) a Mayo man (yes) a Mayo (Mayo)

suwaiya wa ka . . . ka etapo (e'e) ka etapo. como aapa ama
he guarded   no not open (no)   not open. as he,

howakam ame (hewi) a suaiya hiba 'a suaiyha. (hewi) kaa . . . be
by the household,   was guarded   to him they guarded. nobody

tau lisensia,   (e'e) a pos wa hente bu'uru ka yauna nacioni
had permission, (no) well many people not one   nation

aa waatia, beha hakun bicha siika o empa me'awak sai,
him wanted, yet no one   had seen in or it would have killed him,

(hewi) beha volkaroabawa kutawi, (ah) naria tai
now the guard wanted to cut wood,   a fire

echaba hikaobicha, (hewi) antonse wanai beha iya'abwi,
he makes   (yes)   thus he went to do it

(hewi) aa pues humu oore, ka tem ne hum maa meebarebwa,
well then he was there, nobody wanted   to   kill him.

(ah) hewi, piyola misimmeatooya, (ah) hikauwa' a wiikbare,
    yes,   piyola wood

(hewi) volkaroabawa, (ah) apo ka mukbarekai yemu oore.
he wanted to cut it,   he had not died, he was there,

apole ili usi belechik ama booka, formaroak. (hewi)
he alone, a little child   rested there, formed.   (yes)

huch ama formaroabe. (hewi) apo wami mukuk. (hewi) muku,
there forming.   (yes)   he then died.   (yes)   dies,

(ah, he . .) no be hu' o etapowa. si ka etapokatek
             it   was opened. If it had not been opened

nuebe mechampo beha huchi usi teeyei, (hewi) hummm. . . . usi
for nine months for each child needs,   (yes)   the child

teeyei nuebe mechampo. (hewi) como an . . nim ili usi ha . . . uil
needs nine   months. (yes)   like . . . .   little child

hamuchim asowa benasi, (hewi, benasi) nuebe metpo (hewi)
women bear children like that (yes, like that) nine months (yes)

huchi usitpeye, (hewi) te beha formaroa lim belep (hewi)
each child requires, (yes) now   formed a little one   (yes)

aa pos etapo waka mukuk (hewi) hummm . . . ka yo'otu, (e')
well   opened that one died (yes)   did not grow up, (no)

mmu'umm ipa'ali lutek. (aaa lutek) ummm . . . hum (umm humm, me?ak)
       lost   (aa, lost)   (umm humm, killed)

a me'ak (aaa . . .) heee . . . (hita me'ak?) pues hu hente (ah)
he was killed   (what killed him?) people killed him

(aapo) yewi, no bes heka ad bwite a'abo, heka me'ak, (he'),
    yes, because the wind blew in on him, the wind killed,

no bes h u'u patiari, (hewi) kaba a bicha, (e'e) mas
because it was closed,   nobody could see him, (no) just

de hu enkargawarihabit,   (hewi) wepulak.
the one who was in charge, guarded him, (yes) just one.

17. Banari is my earlier pseudonym for Jupare, a Mayo ceremonial center located in the Huatabampo Municipio of southern Sonora. Even though the Banari Easter ceremonial has been observed a number of times, no profound changes in the ritual or structure of the ceremonial have been noted.. The number of participants has varied. In 1970 there were a total of 202 *pariserom* and in 1969 it was reported that there were over 300 *pariserom*, although this seems amazingly high. Since that time, the numbers of *pariserom* have run between 100 and 200 persons. Several years ago a new Easter Ceremonial was established at Nobowaxia, nearer Huatabampo. This new ceremonial has drawn some of the former *pariserom* of Jupare and Etchoropo and prevents the Nobowaxia *paskome* from participating at Jupare. Although the numbers of *pariserom* at Nobowaxia are considerably smaller than those at Jupare, the Jupare *pariserom* still number over 100 persons. Thus the new ceremonial has not seriously reduced the participants at Jupare.

18. Mayo often pluralizes with the addition of a final -m, i.e. a *parisero*, but several *pariserom*.

19. In addition to the masked *pariserom*, Mayos have other masked impersonators such as the *paskola*, who wears a round wooden face mask and dances to violin, harp and flute, and drum music, and the *maso* or deer dancer, who wears a deer head and dances to the music and song of several musicians, two or three who play rasps and one who plays a water drum.

20. See Crumrine 1969.

21. See Crumrine 1964.

22. For a description of those groups see Crumrine 1977.

23. For more recent figures on the numbers of members of the *parisero* sodality see note 17.

24. See Crumrine 1969, 1969a, and 1976.

25. See Crumrine 1969b and 1974.

26. For a more comprehensive description see Crumrine 1974b and 1977b: 113–16.

27. In order to retain the social context as well as the development of the explanatory argument, my questions and comments are included in parentheses.

Myth 5. (The Easter ceremony is very interesting. How many *chapakobam* were there?) The *chapakobam* have permission to make the ceremony of *Itom Achai* (Our Father). (Why must the *chapakobam* remain silent?) They must hold a cross in their mouth under the mask. (But on Wednesday, *Tinieblas*, they cry out?) They make the cry of the owl (*tecolote*, Sp.; *mu'u*, Mayo). (Why can they make sound only Wednesday night?) It is the custom. They also make the cry of the crow (*cuervo* Sp.; *koni*, Mayo). (But the *tecolote* is a sign of the dead?) Yes! Yes! It is a bad sign. They aren't the dead. They just copy the song of the *tecolote* and the *cuervo*. (Where did the *chapakobam* live? Aren't there stories about them?) It is a custom, they imitate what happened with *Itom Achai*. They imitate the time when Jesus appeared and the *pilatom* killed him. (But what do the *chapakobam* signify and why the masks? Why do they have this form?) They require it because they have paint. They paint themselves on their body with red paint which symbolized the blood of Christ. (But I still do not understand why they need the masks?)

A long time ago in that time they were like Kaifas. And Kaifas was truly very hairy. Kaifas, when Our Lord was taken prisoner, when they took him prisoner in order to kill him. Kaifas was truly very bearded, very hairy. The masks are like this, are an imitation of this beardedness. (I do not know anything about Kaifas?) Kaifas is God's opposite, contrary (*contra*). He is God's enemy. (He isn't the Devil?) Exactly, he is the Devil. Kaifas is not baptized, not a Christian, he is the Devil, Lucifer. (And does he have soldiers?) Certainly, he has soldiers. (Are the *pariserom* and the *chapakobam* in his army?) Certainly. (Today where is Kaifas?)

Today Kaifas is ashamed because our Lord arose from the dead at Gloria in such a manner giving life to sinners. Kaifas has retreated to the forest. His soldiers have been killed, are dead, but Kaifas still lives. (Is it possible to see Kaifas in the forest?) Of course. (Kaifas is not baptized?) No. (*Itom Achai contra hu'u.*) This one is the opposite of our Father. Kaifas is the Devil, he is dangerous, bad. He does bad things. He tries to gain, to win good men. It's diabolical. (Does Kaifas also have power?)

Certainly. Like God, Kaifas also has power. This is all written in the words of *Itom Achai* in white clay (*masilla blanca*). These words have power. Here is permission from *Itom Achai* to do everything a Christian should do. With permission from *Itom Achai*'s words one may act, without it one may not act. (And the witches are they friends of Kaifas?) Certainly. The witches make people sick and kill them. They are invisible, you cannot see them. They operate by bad thoughts through the mind. They are dangerous. (Do they have bad words?) Certainly. They have words which they use to make people sick, bad words. The *chapakobam* imitate sorcery (as they do all kinds of Mayo behavior) but they do not have the power of a witch. They imitate the story of *Itom Achai*, of his death, burial and resurrection. In the end they ask the pardon of *Itom Achai*. They make the ceremony of *Itom Achai*. They do the passion of *Itom Achai*.

Myth 6. (When I was here last year you told me about an enemy of God. His name was Kaifas. But I still do not know who Kaifas was?) There are two roads, a good one and a bad one. (The *paskola* dancers and entertainers, what road do they take?) If they complete their promise and go to the altar asking forgiveness from God for their joking and bad talk, they are on the good road. But if they don't complete their promise and ask forgiveness, then they are promised to Kaifas.

(A long time ago, were *Itom Achai* and *Kaifas* friends?)

In that time when this world commenced, *Itom Achai* began to make hens (*gallinas*) and all the other things which exist. God made things correctly. The very close, very intimate, friend of *Itom Achai, Kaifas* began to imitate God. (Were they compadres?) No, only very intimate friends. *Kaifas* began to imitate God. When *El Señor* (God) made the hen, the hen saw the world and liked the world. The hen was happy, gay because *El Señor* gave the hen breath. And Lucifer, this *Kaifas*, also began to make a hen. This hen he made of (*barro*) clay. In clay *Kaifas* began to make a hen. Instead of a good hen coming out, a *tecolote* came out. *Kaifas* made an owl (mu'u). *Kaifas* imitated *El Señor*. But this was not yet the sin which *Kaifas* was going to commit againt *El Señor*. This wasn't much. Nothing much because *Kaifas* had equal power with *El Senor*. He controlled equal power to that of God. *Kaifas* was able to use the power, but he used it for bad purposes, for evil. And *El Señor* made the light of day and saw everything as good. In the light of day everything was good. People, men, he made. Because He foresaw them, saw that they were going to live in the world. *Kaifas* also made men, people. But the people *Kaifas* created were just like, were similar to him. They were equal to *Kaifas*. When *Kaifas* made men, they came out equal to him, that is bad.

To turn to the understanding of The Good and The Bad. The Bad is to act in excess. Many, many of the men especially those of *Kaifas* wouldn't do because a man needs to have respect, value for all other people. One can sin with only a few words when they are about another. This danger converges in the tongue, the mouth, when a person talks of another. This is very bad, dangerous. Because to speak much about people who are not at fault, that is to say to speak badly of a person is a sin which God will not pardon. For those who speak badly, it is a means of falling. Well people should speak good words about others. This means our tongue can make us happy. One ought to respect others. One should give respect and tenderness to people, even those whom one doesn't know. In this form one should respect everyone, that is good. It is good to have respect for everyone. That is to say many people go to sacred temples (churches). They go to the church, but they study other books, bad books. They aren't good Christians but bad, dangerous ones. They teach other bad things, dangerous things. The greatest good is to value to appreciate everybody. (Are some of the temples of the devil?) No! *Itom Achai* made the temples.

And God gave permission for 6,000 years of trial. Nobody knows if the world will turn to God or to *Kaifas*. In these 6,000 years the devil will do what he can to gain it. But the wise men even those of Rome don't know what will happen. All this is according to the scriptures. But even the wise men don't know if there will be winds or perhaps nothing. (Where are we now?) We still lack 4,000 years. These things about life and death of Our *Señor* are very sad (Crumrine 1973: 1136–9).

28. Mayos will remark concerning their "contract" with the earth, "the earth will eat us up." This means that while during our lives we live from the earth's nourishment when we die the earth in turn will be nourished by consuming the deceased persons.

29. See Crumrine 1974.

1. It was the Spaniards who first employed the name Tarascans because the people reportedly worshipped a god named Taras or Thare. Another version of the etymology is that the word *tarascue,* meaning father-in-law, was mistakenly employed by the early Spanish colonists. The Aztecs called them *michua-que*—"people from the place of fish" —because of the large lakes in their land, which they in turn called Michoa-cán. At present, Tarascans refer to themselves as *purepecha,* a term that had originally meant "commoner." In pre-Hispanic times some of their number referred to themselves as *Chichimeca,* a word in widespread use in ancient Mexico that was applied to nomadic, warlike hunting groups of diverse ethnic origin. Still others used the names of their lineages, such as Uacusecha—the Eagles (Esser 1984: 31). Because so much confusion exists as to the proper ethnic designation for the people under discussion, I have rather conservatively opted for the use of Tarascan as more generally recognized.

2. In this article and elsewhere, I have attempted to supply the reader of English with a vernacular translation of the many mask characters that appear in Tarascan dances.

69. Blackmen breakfasting. Corupo, Michoacán, January 1, 1988.

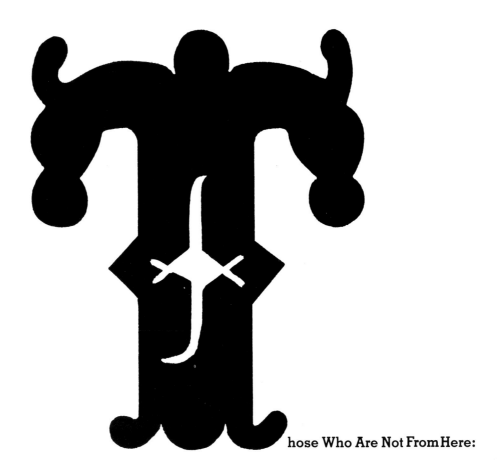

hose Who Are Not From Here:

Blackman Dances of Michoacán

Janet Brody Esser

In the sierra villages of the Tarascan Indians or, as they are alternatively known, *purepecha,*[1] a number of dances are performed in which masks representing the Blackman appear.[2] These dances, usually performed on December 25, January 1, and January 6, are part of the winter ceremonial season, during which officers are confirmed in their *cargos* (offices in a civic-religious ceremonial government) for the coming year.[3]

Blackmen are known in the Tarascan language as *turía* or *turíacha,* which is said by some Tarascans also to mean principal beings who control the air. While the Tarascan word *turí* means "black," it also has the implication of *catrín* (elegant, urbane). *Acha* means "man" or "lord" and *acha turí,* although

literally "black lord," is translated into Spanish as *hombre que no es indígena,* that is to say, a non-Indian. When speaking Spanish, the Blackman characters are referred to as *negros* or *negritos* by Tarascans and non-Tarascans alike. The diminutive form connotes the affection or familiarity felt toward Blackmen, rather than referring to their physical size; in fact, Blackmen are usually danced by grown men whose headdresses contribute additional height.

Tarascans live in villages, towns, and even parts of cities in the mountains of the state of Michoacán in western Mexico. Their forested and lake-studded highland region, which they have occupied since at least the eleventh century, forms part of the nation's central

107

Since nomenclature differs from community to community, I hope, thereby, to avoid confusion as well as to convey equivalent meanings.

3. Masks are danced in conjunction with festivals for patron saints, Carnival, Holy Week, religious pilgrimages, and government-sponsored exhibitions, but performances are most numerous during the winter ceremonial season. Winter ceremonies mark the change of officers in a hierarchy of ritual obligations to images of Catholic saints and are performed on or near Christmas Day, New Year's Day, Epiphany, and Candlemas. The obligations are called *cargos* (literally, burdens); the officers, *cargueros*; and those who pass a certain number of *cargos* become elders (*principales* or *cabildes*). The association of elders and most important officers is known as the *cabildo*. While the *cabildo* with its various posts was originally a Spanish introduction, native adaptation combined this late medieval European town council system with pre-Columbian ceremonial and political offices. For an interesting survey of the similarities and differences between Spain and the New World, see Foster (1960).

4. The origin of the Tarascans remains unknown. While some implements and articles of clothing suggest a relationship to

volcanic axis. In the last two centuries prior to the conquest of Mexico, the Tarascans had forged a powerful tributary empire that included parts of Querétaro, Colima, and Guerrero and dominated the rich region of Michoacán that borders the Pacific.[4]

I have been regularly observing dances of Blackmen in the central portion of what is called the Tarascan *meseta* and in the city of Uruapan since 1970. This article will describe the dances and discuss some of their social and historical implications.[5]

In several villages Blackmen wear dark business suits, white shirts, dark ties, black shoes, and gloves, thus explaining the Tarascan use of the term *catrín* to describe them. In other villages Blackmen wear white embroidered trousers, black vests trimmed with rickrack, and elaborate overtrousers in the manner of Colonial cowboys and militiamen. Most Blackmen wear wigs of black sheepskin to which various adornments are attached. Some wear elaborate ribbon nests in which small plastic animals are placed so as to form miniature *nacimientos* (Nativity scenes). In several villages fringed beards made of decorative cording are attached to the lower edges of the masks. Many varicolored ribbons hang from the back of the headdresses, each two inches in width and, in some cases, reaching almost to the ground. Strings of paste beads, cardboard-backed gilded mirrors, tinsel ropes, and artificial flowers are also used as adornments in the headdresses of Blackmen.

The small, regular features of Blackmen masks have been described as European (that is, Caucasian) in appearance (Beals 1946: 145). However, frequent use of black sheepskin wigs and modeling of nose, cheeks, and lips suggest intentional representation of black Africans. Employment of what have been assumed to be European features is more likely to derive from conventions related to representations

of saints. Except in color, the image of San Martín de Porres, present in almost every Tarascan church, is not unlike those of Caucasian saints.

Masks of Blackmen are painted with either an indigenous lacquer containing *aje* or *axin*—a wax obtained by cooking coccids (Jenkins 1967: 130)—or commercial oil enamels. Faces are painted black, lips red, and eyes white with black or, sometimes, blue irises. Surfaces of masks that are still danced exhibit a high degree of luster as a result of periodic repainting.

Blackmen of Cherán

The sierra town of Cherán is situated on the federal highway leading from the Guadalajara-Mexico City highway to the Pacific coast. The population in 1970 was 7,793 (Martínez de Lejarza 1974: 290) and, in 1980, 10,239 (INEGI 1983: 8). The Centro Nacional Indigenista (Center for Indian Affairs) for the Tarascan region is located at Cherán, where field studies by Mexican and American anthropologists and geographers were undertaken as early as the late 1930s and early 1940s (Beals 1946). Performances by Blackmen in Cherán observed by me from 1970 to the present do not differ materially from those reported about fifty years ago.

As in other *meseta* towns, Blackmen here are associated with the *cargo* of the Santo Niño (Holy Child), who is their patron saint. The *cargo* of the Holy Child is the most prestigious and expensive of all the offices in the *cargo* system of Cherán. The Blackmen are invited to dance by the *carguero* (ritual officer), who will house the image of the Holy Child for one year and give feasts to mark his obligation. The new *carguero* officially assumes his duties on December 26 when the Holy Child is taken from the church and, accompanied by the Blackmen, is brought to his house.[6]

Here Blackmen are impersonated mostly by young, unmarried men.

Ecuador and Peru in South America, many other aspects of their culture exhibit close ties with the nomadic groups that were moving about in northern and central Mexico during the last few centuries before the Spanish Conquest. The Tarascan pre-Hispanic dynasty appears to have been the result of a merger of settled farmers and fishermen with one of these nomadic groups. During the course of several centuries Tarascans established control of a large portion of western Mexico and were successful in keeping their still more powerful rivals, the Mexica (or, as they are more commonly known, the Aztecs) at bay.

5. The period of field research from March 1974 to June 1975 was made possible by grants from the Dickson Foundation of the University of California at Los Angeles and the Social Science Research Council, New York City.

6. Some towns may have more than one *carguero* and more than one image of the infant Jesus. Some of the images reportedly are very old and obviously well carved; others are mass-produced of plaster and sold all over Mexico. Regardless of these differences, the images are treated with extreme reverence, dressed exquisitely, and housed in vitrines together with offerings; they provide the focus of

Recently, a few small boys have also participated as Blackmen, their costumes identical to those worn by the young adults. In Cherán, as elsewhere in the *meseta,* the role of serious (as opposed to comical) mask characters is assumed because a *manda* (religious vow) has been made by the participant or by someone else, usually a parent, on his behalf. This *manda* results from the participant or someone close to him recovering from a serious illness. As such, it lends to Tarascan dances a dimension of gravity quite different from usual masquerades. While the Blackmen exhibit the high spirits appropriate to their youth, it is clear that they are aware at all times of their obligation to perform in reciprocation for restored health.

Blackmen of Cherán may wear ribbons as much as two meters in length. There is much competition among participants as to the number of ribbons worn. Forty years ago a young man was considered wealthy if he could afford to wear as many as twenty-four ribbons (Beals 1946: 145). Today it is not unusual to see double that quantity in use. When Blackmen walk in the street they often hold their ribbons folded over their arms to prevent them from becoming soiled (fig. 71). The dark business suits that Blackmen wear are usually rented, while masks are owned, borrowed, or rented. Although the masks conform to a style recognizable as Cherán's, carvers are known to depict facial features or expressions recognizable by the townspeople as satirical humorous portraits of their own—clearly an inside joke not intended to be shared with strangers (fig. 72).

For the dance, the Blackmen arrange themselves in two files, leaving a clear area in between of from four to twelve feet, depending on available space. The leaders, known as *la letra* and *el segundo,* recite stylized couplets recounting the birth of Jesus. A *maestro* is hired by the *carguero* to rehearse the

performers. The *maestro* is chosen not only for his ability as a director but because he owns a notebook in which he has hand-copied the couplets. His sources include older copies belonging to former *maestros* (the rights to which he has purchased) or published editions sold in shops in Mexico City specializing in religious articles.[7] The *maestro* reads the various parts to his charges, who commit the lines to memory. He also directs the performers' movements and gestures and corrects mistakes during practice sessions and performances. Rehearsals usually begin about three weeks before the first performance. The last week is the most intense and the *carguero* of the Holy Infant must provide meals for the *maestro* and Blackmen on the occasion of each rehearsal. This, of course, entails considerable expense.[8]

The leaders pace between the two files of dancers while reciting the verses, which are in Spanish. They are delivered in a somewhat stilted manner with regularly recurring emphases and stylized gestures. At intervals each Blackman joins his neighbor in the file and performs a slow waltz or sprightly polka. As the Blackmen move, their tinsel and mirror adornments sparkle and flash in the sunlight, creating a dazzling effect (fig. 73).

The Blackmen begin dancing at the home of the *carguero* at about nine p.m. on Christmas Eve and continue until after Midnight Mass, which they attend. They accompany the image of the Holy Child as it is carried through the streets to the church. The Holy Child remains in the *nacimiento* within the church all Christmas Day, where it is visited by the Blackmen. Beginning at ten or eleven on the morning of Christmas Day, the day after Christmas, and on January 1, Blackmen dance at homes of past and present *cargueros.* They also dance at the municipal building in honor of civic officials. Throughout the dancing, with the exception of ceremonies and feasts. Some, but not all, of the images are believed to have curative powers.

7. The published couplets belong to a large genre that includes Everyman, Miracle, and Shepherds plays that go back to the origin of theater in medieval Europe.

8. The number of meals for which a *carguero* is responsible varies with the status of the *cargo*. The most prestigious require the greatest number. Meals consist of breakfasts and dinners; since they are festival meals they are very lavish. Chocolate, sweet wheat bread, various stews, tortillas, beans, rice, and stuffed tamales are traditional. Much more meat, served with elaborate *moles* (chile sauces), especially beef and pork, is consumed than usual. Besides hot chocolate, beverages include *atole* (sweetened cornmeal gruel), bottled sodas and beer, and *charanda*, a local spirit made from sugarcane. As has been noted by several of the authors in this volume, those responsible for festival activities are expected to invest in them a considerable portion of their wealth. Impoverishment, however, is not the result. The elders of the ceremonial system must be applied to for permission to participate. Those without sufficient means are denied.

Midnight Mass, they are accompanied by girls of from ten to fourteen years of age wearing elaborately decorated sombreros. The dancers are given gifts of fruit and sugarcane by each host, which the townspeople explain are foods appropriate for children in a feast that is for the Holy Child (Beals 1946: 138).

Blackmen of San Lorenzo

San Lorenzo is a small, quiet village lying just off a very rough road that connects Highway 37 with Los Reyes. About 2,000 people live here, most of them housed in distinctive and traditional timber structures called *trojes*. Here Blackmen dance every day from Christmas to New Year's Day. Blackmen, together with "white" *viejitos* (little old men), for which the entire *meseta* is famous, appear for the first time on Christmas Eve when they range themselves in rows behind the *nacimiento* in the presbytery of the church. Among the congregation, a few toddlers and even babes in arms are dressed as Blackmen and *viejitos*. Here, also, health and the *manda* determine participation.

On January 1 a colorful public fiesta is held in the afternoon and attended by most of the townspeople. Elegantly dressed *guares* (Tarascan women dressed in the fiesta finery typical of their village) dance together with even more elegantly dressed *maringuillas* (little Marys)—men dressed as women and wearing black masks (fig. 74).[9] Various groups of "old ones," each with its own band, perform simultaneously in front of the church (fig. 75). The *feos* (uglies), those unruly clowns of which there are many, keep order with sticks and dummy rifles and improvise outrageous pantomimes. Groups of Blackmen (and Blackwomen) arrive from the home of their *carguero*, and, remaining separate from the "old ones," each of the dance groups promenades several times around the plaza. The Blackmen

move in tight formation, clapping their hands in unison to a snappy rhythm in accordance with local perceptions of African dance rhythms (fig. 70). After the promenade the Blackmen dance, still clapping hands, while the "uglies" police the plaza.

The Blackmen continue to dance until about four in the afternoon, when several young women, gorgeously attired in traditional finery, emerge from the church carrying large images of the Virgin and Saint Joseph (fig. 76). The portable stands upon which the images rest are smothered in *nochebuenas* (poinsettias) and other flowers. The elders in the ceremonial system, followed by the "old ones" and Blackmen, each group accompanied by its *carguero*, lead the procession (which by now includes most of the townspeople) off to the south edge of town, returning to the plaza from the western periphery of the village about half an hour later (fig. 77).

After the procession the elders, those who have served the community during the previous year by assuming religious *cargos*, are seated on benches just outside the government building (fig. 79). The place of honor is occupied by the *mandón* (commander), or *alkandi*, as this highest-ranking *mayordomo* is locally known. It is he who has custody of the *vara*, symbol of civic self-governance, during the year.[10] The elders and those they invite to be their guests are served traditional festival food: *nakatamales* (steamed maize dough), *pozole* (pork, cabbage, and hominy stew), huge clay jars of *atole negro* (sweetened maize gruel), and enormous rings of homemade sweet white bread. "Uglies" entertain elders and other spectators by performing their antic sketches in the plaza.

Just as the repast nears its end, the Blackmen arrive. Actually these are Blackmen and Blackwomen, sumptuously dressed and engaging in outlandish gestures while speaking only

Through a complex system of compensatory obligations (if I do something for you, you will owe me a favor I can call upon), those with means may actually increase their wealth.

9. San Lorenzo is the only Tarascan town where I have observed men masked as women and real women performing in the same dance. In some towns women have come to take the place of men wearing masks of women; in others, female impersonation by men persists, with and without the aid of masks. The word *guare* is Tarascan for woman but has come to mean an indigenous woman or girl dressed in traditional clothing of the finest quality.

10. The *vara* is a ritual staff of office that is kept in a special place, adorned, exhibited on special occasions, kissed and bowed to, and otherwise treated exactly like a saint's image. When the traditional form of Spanish city government—the *cabildo,* or town council—was introduced in native communities during the sixteenth and seventeenth centuries, the *vara* was the symbol of vested governmental authority. Today, in many Tarascan communities, the *vara* is housed by the highest-ranking *carguero* in the ceremonial organization.

11. Inspired by humanistic teachings of the Renaissance, missionaries

in cooing and gurgling sounds. The black *maringuillas* serve sweet store-bought cookies from their baskets to the elders, while the men pour drinks from the *charanda* (*aguardiente,* sugarcane spirits) bottles hanging from their waists (fig. 81). After the elders' festive meal, Blackmen disperse at dusk to the home of their *mayordomo* where they themselves will dine and dance (fig. 80).

Blackmen of Nuevo San Juan Parangaricutiro

The town of Nuevo San Juan Parangaricutiro was buried by lava in the early 1940s when the volcano Paricutín erupted. The people were resettled on a tract of land about five miles west of Uruapan. The new town, famous as a pilgrimage center focusing on a miraculous image of Jesus, has prospered; its population in 1980 was 6,773 (INEGI 1983: 10). One Blackman is responsible for delivering stores to the incoming *kengyi* (*mayordomo* or steward) of the *hospital* in a ceremony that takes place on December 26.[11] The mask is painted in glossy black oil enamels and has a large retroussé nose and slanting almond-shaped eyes. A black sheepskin wig adorned with mirrors and ribbons of many colors is attached to the top of the mask. The Blackman wears a long-sleeved white shirt, a dark vest with additional woven belts across his chest, white trousers of homespun cotton with embroidered hems, and black overtrousers decorated with mirrors and gilded braid ending in triangular points on the front and back of each leg (fig. 82).

On his back the Blackman carries a wooden construction meant to represent the *huacal* (crate) of the *huacalero* (long-distance trader, or, in Tarascan, *inspikuriri*), a vestige of the merchants who plied their trade in pre-Columbian times. Tied onto the *huacal* are life-size and miniature cups, plates, pitchers, firefans, chocolate beaters, whiskbrooms, and other household necessi-

ties that are presented to the *kengyi,* who is to serve in his post for one year (fig. 83).

Although the *huacal* is quite heavy, the Blackman moves as though it were weightless and dances vigorously with the female relatives of the new steward (fig. 78). He is assisted in the delivery of stores by a Gorilla (in a rubber mask) who carries a replica of a *troje* on his head. The miniature house is a gift and badge of office for the *kengyi* made by *los semaneros,* an association of householders who take turns caring for the chapel of the Virgin that adjoins the *hospital.* In addition to Blackman and Gorilla, a group of masked "uglies" also deliver supplies, all of which are carefully noted by the steward, his wife, and their relatives (fig. 84). The delivery of supplies constitutes the culmination of the day-long ceremony involving "old ones" and "uglies" that accompanies the installation of the steward of the *hospital* (fig. 85). After the supplies have been received, generous quantities of food and drink prepared by relatives of the steward and his wife are served to guests and dancers, who disperse for home shortly after eating.

During the festival of the Lord of the Miracles on September 14 in Nuevo San Juan Parangaricutiro, two Blackmen from the barrio of San Miguel in Uruapan accompany a dance of *Chichimecas*. The *Chichimecas* in Nuevo San Juan Parangaricutiro are impersonated by local residents—men and women—in traditional Tarascan dress who wear headdresses made of feathers and foil. The dancers are said to represent the Indian people of San Juan prior to the arrival of the missionaries. The women carry *sonajas* (rattles), while the men carry bows and sticks. *Chichimecas* also dance on the octave of the Lord of the Miracles (September 21) and again on the fourteenth day of every month when the traveling image of the Lord of the Miracles is received by a new steward. The Blackmen or-

70. Blackmen in procession, clapping their hands as they walk. San Lorenzo, Michoacán, January 1, 1986.

114

71. Blackmen on their
way to the home of the
carguero. Cherán,
Michoacán, January
1, 1984.

introduced the institution of the *hospital* to the New World. The *hospital* was originally a place where devotion to the Virgin, care of the sick and poor, instruction in useful crafts and orderly living, and shelter for the traveler were provided (Ricard 1966: 159). Among Tarascan communities only devotion to the Virgin has survived and the *hospital* in Nuevo San Juan Parangaricutiro houses an image of *La Inmaculada* (the Virgin of the Immaculate Conception) that is believed to possess miraculous power.

ganize the dancers in two files and serve as policemen, brandishing their braided leather whips at both dancers and crowd. They make cooing noises all during the dance and occasionally mumble unintelligible words. The Blackmen also have their own dance, which they perform between the two lines of *Chichimecas.* The Blackmen dance on these occasions, they. say, because of vows they have made to the Lord of the Miracles in return for restoration of health.

Blackmen of San Felipe de los Herreros and Corupo

San Felipe de los Herreros was so named because this was the center of an ironwork industry throughout the Colonial period and the nineteenth century (West 1948: 70). The population at present is about 1,500.

The *carguero* of the Holy Child has the responsibility for the dance of the Blackmen which is performed on Christmas, New Year's Day, and Epiphany. The dance sometimes is performed by children, whose small masks have the effect of making the performers appear to be miniature adults rather than dwarves. Blackmen wear city-style dark suits and are accompanied by a *maringuilla*—a boy dressed in the style of a Tarascan woman but wearing a black mask.

Corupo (population estimated at 1,000) is accessible only by rough and broken road. Blackman dances are performed on January 1 and 2. Blackmen dress much as they do in Cherán, but with more ribbons on the top of their headdresses (fig. 69). Their supernatural patron is a small image of the Holy Child thought to be very effective in working miracles. This image, which is painted to appear Caucasian and is about eight-inches high, is dressed exactly as are the dancers, with headdress, city-style jacket, and a long wide tie. Only a mask is lacking to complete the connection.

Blackmen of Uruapan

The mercantile center of Uruapan has grown rapidly since the beginning of the nineteenth century. The population in 1980 was 122,828 (INEGI 1983: 12). In spite of its large size the city's barrios—vestiges of the nine original wards, each with its own small church and patron saint—have retained something of the rural, tightly knit quality of the villages. Blackman masks of Uruapan are distinctive with their high cheekbones, large aquiline noses, and carved, twisted, and forked beards. Blackmen dance on the day of the patron saint of the participating barrios, at present including San Juan Quemada, San Miguel, and La Magdalena.

In the barrio of La Magdalena, Blackmen accompany the dance of the Children. The children are arranged in two files with girls on one side and boys on the other. One Blackman is associated with each file and weaves his way through the line dancing between the children and carrying a braided leather whip which is held above their heads. The children are dressed very elaborately in what is perhaps an expression of poor people's conception of the way rich children dress. Colonial dress modes are sometimes adopted (fig. 86).

Blackmen are hired by the sponsor of the dance of the Children and have their own dance that they perform in the street before the sponsor's house. The Blackmen guide the children as they move from house to house, helping to keep the children's files straight and preventing onlookers from pressing too close. Occasionally the Blackmen menace children in the crowd and brandish their whips, but clearly they are caretakers of the small dancers.

Masks are painted with black lacquer, an indigenous technique for which Uruapan is justly famous. Attached to the masks are headdresses made of black, curly lambskins hanging almost to the waist. At the juncture of fur and mask, long, broad ribbons of red, green, blue, yellow, and orange are stretched with strands of silver and gold tinsel along the sides. Mirrors set into gilded cardboard stars, cloth flowers, ribbon rosettes, and strands of paste beads cover the top of the head. The Blackmen wear red cummerbunds, with long sashes and red scarves of a diaphanous fabric across the chest. Trousers are of white homespun cotton with wide bands of embroidery at the lower edges. The black overtrousers are trimmed with ribbon rosettes, mirrors, and braid. Shirts are long sleeved and white.

Many of the Blackman masks used in Uruapan are carved by Victoriano Salgado of the barrio of La Magdalena. In addition to masks with carved beards, Sr. Salgado also makes a beardless Blackman. This mask, known as *el negro de la pastorela,* was originally copied from an old mask belonging to Marcelino Báez, whose late brother had danced it in the early 1930s. While this version of the Blackman mask appears' as a black pageboy in the Shepherds' Play, which Salgado hosts each year, it also seems to be related to the type of Blackman found in the *meseta* village. Before the Revolution of 1910, Blackmen in Uruapan also wore black masks without beards and dressed in black city-style suits. They danced on the day of María Magdalena and again on Christmas Eve when they recited *relatos* in the Shepherds' Play.

Jesús Escobar, a candlemaker of the barrio of San Miguel, dances as a Blackman in the barrio of La Magdalena and in the village of Nuevo San Juan Parangaricutiro. He and his friends also perform during the festival of San Miguel, for which he serves as one of the captains or organizers. It is Sr. Escobar who, together with a friend, oversees the dance of *Chichimecas* in Nuevo San Juan Parangaricutiro. Es-

cobar owns the mask that he wears, which he calculates was made at least fifty years ago. He reported that formerly no more than two Blackmen danced on any one occasion in Uruapan and always in conjunction with the dance of the Children.

Blackmen of Zacán

The population of Zacán is about 2,000 at present. San Pedro Zacán used to be famous in the Tarascan region for its dance of Blackmen. Since 1953, however, when the last *maestro* died at the age of eighty-five, the dance has not been performed. Zacán, located about ten miles from the epicenter of seismic activity, suffered severely when the volcano Paricutín erupted. (While the *cargo* system was never fully resumed after this catastrophe, the dance of Old Ones was retained. This dance is performed each January 7 and, except for the fact that masks and wigs are white, is structured very similarly to the Blackman dance of Cherán.)

Blackmen of Zacán danced on January 6 at the homes of past and present *cargueros*; their meals were provided by the four co-stewards of the Holy Child. There were usually thirty Blackmen, elegant in dress and dignified in manner. They too recited couplets relating the story of the Nativity that had been taught to them by the *maestro.*

Blackmen wore wigs of black sheepskin meant to represent the hair of black Africans (and in fact were exhorted by the *maestro* to "move their bodies like Africans"). A silk sash across the chest served to keep their long ribbons in place while they danced. In all respects but in the elaboration of details, their adornments resembled those still worn in Cherán and Corupo. After a hiatus of thirty-five years, a decision was made in 1987 by those responsible for the care of one of the Holy Child images to resume the dance of the Blackman in Zacán.

72. Blackman outside
carguero's house.
Cherán, Michoacán,
January 1, 1984.

73. Blackmen dancing
at the home of the
principal *carguero*.
Cherán, Michoacán,
January 1, 1984.

74. Women in festive, traditional dress together with masked male dancer impersonating *maringuilla*. San Lorenzo, Michoacán, January 1, 1986.

12. A number of important works have been published in the last few decades that make clear the vital and lasting contributions made by black Africans in Spanish-speaking America. Elsewhere (Esser 1984), I have assembled an extensive bibliography on this subject. Here, in addition to the citations in the body of the text, I would like to call special attention to Herskovitz (1970), Mörner (1967), and Rout (1976).

13. The work of the great Mexican ethnohistorian González Aguirre Beltrán suggests that in sixteenth-century Mexico there were times when blacks actually outnumbered whites in the population. This was the same century that saw the native population of Mexico decline from about twenty-two million to about a million and a half! (See Borah and Cook 1963.)

Blackmen of Charapan

The sierra village of Charapan lies seventeen miles from the Uruapan-Carapan highway. Approaches to the village are all but impossible for ordinary vehicles. In 1970 the population was 3,299 (Martínez de Lejarza 1974: 299) and, in 1980, 6,524 (INEGI 1983: 8). Charapan used to perform Blackmen dances. Dancers were called *turí uarari* (black dancers) and always performed on the sixth of January. Blackmen wore city-style suits and dressed much as the Blackmen of Cherán, with many strands of beads and black masks. A local *maestro* of the Old Ones dance (which is performed each year) reported that *turí uarari* means *gente extraña* (foreigners), rather than "Africans." He interpreted the pursed mouths often represented on Blackman masks as *chiflando* (blowing) and said that this referred to *el aire*—a spiritual force that the Blackmen, as principal beings, controlled.

Blackmen of Nahuatzen, Aranza, Sevina, and Paricutín

The population of Nahuatzen was 5,770 in 1980 (INEGI 1983: 10) and that of Aranza is estimated at about 1,000. Nahuatzen and Aranza were still dancing Blackman in the early 1940s (Beals 1946: 145). A photograph taken by mask collector Donald Cordry before 1940 (Toor 1947: Plate 84) shows two Nahuatzen Blackmen dressed much as do those from Cherán. Sevina, a village of about two thousand, reportedly also used to have Blackman dances.

In 1940 the population of Paricutín was 733 (West 1948: 19). In 1943 the eruption of the volcano destroyed the town and its people were relocated at Caltzontzin, six miles east of Uruapan. *Turisha uarani* danced on the occasion of the day of the patron saint, wearing citified clothes and masks (Beals 1946: 156).

The Role of Black Africans in Colonial Mexico

Tarascan villagers and barrio dwellers clearly invest a good deal of wealth and talent in producing dances of Blackmen. What can the motivation be for so much effort in a region where there are few, if any, persons identifiable as black? Surprisingly, research indicates that there were sizeable populations of blacks residing on the fringes of the Tarascan area all during the viceregal epoch. Blacks labored in numerous occupations, many of these requiring skill and even exercise of authority over the Indians. Tarascans worked with blacks and served under black command. They experienced blacks during the Colonial period as stewards, builders, traders, tailors, artisans, cowboys, and soldiers, because those indeed were some of the capacities in which black Africans served the New World.[12] It is my contention that these experiences fused with Tarascan pre-Columbian religious imagery to produce the mythic Blackman of contemporary Tarascan dances.

During the three centuries of the Spanish viceroyalty, at least 250,000 African slaves were introduced into Mexico (Aguirre Beltrán 1952: 162). As the indigenous population sickened and died from the twin scourges of harsh treatment and Old World viral diseases, Africans were imported in greater numbers.[13] In addition to the manual skills Africans brought with them from their homeland, they also brought a talent for political organization, which they employed in the many *palenques* (settlements) they founded as *cimarrones* (insurgent slaves). They also brought with them a love of pageantry drawn from their own rich ceremonial past. Black brotherhoods dedicated to the Virgin Mary flourished throughout Mexico and were famous for their use of elegant and exotic costumes.

In the Iberian world, the institution

14. See Gage (1958: 73) for a vivid description of blacks in service to wealthy families in early seventeenth-century Mexico City. See Carrera Stampa (1954) for a thorough discussion of the guild system in Mexico and work performed by blacks.
15. Government merchants transported luxury goods such as cacao, marine shell, tropical feathers, and *copal* from the subjugated hot lowlands to the mountainous center of Tarascan power (Gorenstein and Pollard 1983: 106).
16. This work, known officially as Ms. C. IV. 5 de El Escorial, consists of testimony taken from surviving Tarascan nobles in the 1530s by a Franciscan missionary named Jerónimo de Alcalá. The manuscript and illustrations, executed by native artists, provide one of the few sources for information about pre-Hispanic Tarascan beliefs and ceremonies. It resides now in the library of the Escorial, the palace built by King Philip II of Spain in the sixteenth century. Several publications of this work are in existence. The latest, and in many ways the best in my opinion, is Miranda (1980).
17. The process of *mestizaje* (racial mixing) commenced with arrival of people from the Old World and persists into the present.

of slavery had ancient roots, and reliance upon black African labor had been intense since the introduction of plantation crops in the fifteenth century. Many blacks came to Mexico not from Africa but from Lisbon or Seville. These *ladinos,* as Hispanicized, Christianized blacks were known, served their absentee white masters as stewards of the haciendas, dispensing food and goods to Indian servants (Chevalier 1963: 70). Blacks worked as *calpixques* (overseers) of gangs of Indians in the silver mines. They served as captains over groups of Indians on cattle ranches and as militiamen fought against the *Chichimeca* on the northern frontier. They were smiths and leather workers, muleteam drivers and long-distance traders. They also worked as guards in the infamous *obrajes* (workshops where woolen cloth was made), to which unfortunate Indians were consigned.

In towns and cities occupied by Spaniards, of which a number were located in Michoacán, blacks worked as artisans, tradesmen, and especially as servants of the wealthy, who dressed them in extravagant livery. The imagery that emerges from contemporary Tarascan dances of Blackmen—footmen to the image of the Holy Child, custodians of richly dressed children, overseers of *Chichimecas,* smartly attired devotees of the Virgin, exotic foreigners—all derive from actual events experienced by Tarascans in the Colonial epoch.[14]

The Significance of the Color Black Among Pre-Conquest Tarascans

But what of the autochthonous world view of the Tarascans? As descendants of a group of powerful lineages who held dominion over much of western Mexico, the Tarascans were heirs to a rich cosmology. As was common in other of the ancient Mexican peoples' world views, each of the cardinal directions was associated with certain col-

ors, deities, plants, and birds. Among the Tarascans the so-called gods of the left hand held dominion over the south, by which was meant the rich tropical lowlands of the Pacific littoral, source of exotic trade goods (Seler 1960: 139).[15] The supreme god Tiripenie Curicaueri was black as well, and so were his brothers, the Tiripemencha. The Tarascan ruler Tariacuri and all his nobles painted themselves black with soot in their honor. In the *Relación de Michoacán,*[16] a manuscript compiled in the early sixteenth century, we are told, "and they held it a great honor to go about thus blackened" (Miranda 1980: 103–4). Priests blackened themselves in order to see visions and obtain power and also as a sign of penance. Warriors blackened themselves before going into battle to make themselves more valiant.

In a pre-Hispanic Tarascan ceremony intended to encourage the rainy season to commence, two individuals of high status impersonated clouds in the colors of the world directions—white, yellow, red, and black in turn. "When they represent the black cloud they dress in black and likewise for each of the other colors" (Miranda 1980: 11). Also, at the ceremony for the installation of a new ruler, it was customary for all his subjects to blacken themselves (Miranda 1980: 281).

At the time of the struggle for independence from Spain, according to conservative estimates, there were in Mexico 1,860,000 persons of African and part-African descent (Rosenblat 1954, 2: 36). In 1940, 115 years later, an estimated one hundred and twenty thousand persons were recorded to be of part-African descent.[17] The black was a stranger in a land to which he had been brought against his will. As a slave, a man who was treated as a thing, deprived of liberty and any but the most grudgingly conceded rights, he nevertheless applied his skills to the task of building a New World. Some of those skills had

75. "Old ones" with light-colored masks and horsehair wigs perform in front of church. San Lorenzo, Michoacán, January 1, 1986.

76. Women emerge from the church carrying heavy, flower-adorned stands with images of saints. Light-faced *maringuillas* with their *carguero* accompany them. San Lorenzo, Michoacán, January 1, 1986.

77. Elders in procession behind the saints' images. The *alkandi* carries the *vara* of his office. San Lorenzo, Michoacán, January 1, 1986.

78. In the courtyard of the *hospital* the Blackman, *huacal* on his back, performs a vigorous stepdance with relatives of the *mayordomo*. Nuevo San Juan Parangaricutiro, Michoacán, December 26, 1985.

79. Members of the
cabildo, some with
varas, are seated on a
bench near the town
hall. San Lorenzo,
Michoacán, January
1, 1986.

been brought from his African home, and others he had acquired in Europe and America.

In pre-Columbian times the color black was associated with the extraordinary; with godhead, power, and lavish display of riches. According to a Tarascan origin myth, Curicaueri's brother gods and Curicaueri himself had founded lineages in the lake region of Michoacán. The gods were referred to as "celestial engenderers," but they were also called "our Grandfathers." In addition to being the ultimate owners and distributors of wealth, the gods of the Tarascans were also conceptualized as ancestors—the founders of the Tarascan people. When rulers and elders dressed themselves in ritual finery and undertook to dance, they affirmed an identification and sense of community with those progenitors. Since the ancestor-gods were associated with the cardinal color black, the dancer blackened himself. In other words, the Tarascan dancer was a god-impersonator. In the tumultuous period immediately following the Spanish Conquest, black Africans were experienced by the Indians as having control over people and goods. It is suggested that these convergences allowed the Tarascans to continue their association of blackness with power and wealth, display and authority, now transferred to splendid masks whose presence honors village elders and their images of saints.

The Blackman is experienced and expressed by the Tarascan as "other." His clothing is that of women, saints, and the urban rich. The indigenous non-Tarascan populace that occupied the hot country and coastal lands in pre-Conquest times saw their numbers drastically reduced in the sixteenth century; blacks took their place. Tarascan dealings with these lands had been mercantile. Now the riches from these regions were worked and transported by blacks. Hot-landers had been of

80. Toward evening Blackmen proceed to the home of their *carguero* for dancing and a festive meal. San Lorenzo, Michoacán, January 1, 1986.

134

81. Blackmen carrying
bottles of liquor, cups,
and baskets of sweets
arrive, still clapping in
unison, to serve the
elders. San Lorenzo,
Michoacán, January
1, 1986.

82. The Blackman, *huacal* on his back, emerges from dressing house, the location of which has been kept secret. Nuevo San Juan Parangaricutiro, Michoacán, December 26, 1985.

83. A view of the
household supplies
carried by the
Blackman on his
huacal. Nuevo San
Juan Parangaricutiro,
Michoacán, December
26, 1985.

84. The "uglies" take
the miniature *troje*
from the Blackman's
assistant. Nuevo San
Juan Parangaricutiro,
Michoacán, December
26, 1985.

85. The Blackman
arrives to join the
"weeklies" and the
"uglies." Nuevo San
Juan Parangaricutiro,
Michoacán, December
26, 1985.

diverse linguistic stocks—they too had been "other." But the goods which the contemporary Blackman carries are intended for the Tarascans themselves, and his gorgeous dress honors their elders.

Black Africans occupied an interstice between Indians and Spaniards. Because his position was ambiguous—because he moved in both the Indian and the Spanish worlds while belonging to neither—the space the black came to occupy in the Tarascan world view was a sacred space, the place of myth. Even his names—Blackman, Cityman, Foreigner, Lord, Principal Being—express the many levels of meaning that his representation encompasses. The black African was neither Spanish nor Indian. Refuge afforded by the *palenques* was temporary. While he could not blend into the population, his descendants could and did. It is indeed an irony that "those who came from Africa are now most visible in historical documentation" (Bowser 1975: 363).

But as the Blackman the African *has* survived. Blackman masked dances in the villages of the sierra Tarascans are monuments to the presence of black Africans and to the vital role that they played in viceregal Michoacán. But now the Blackman has been transformed into an idealized village leader. He remains, together with the "old ones" and the "uglies," among the most important of Tarascan self-portraits.

86. A Blackman accompanies a dance of Children as they exit from the barrio church. Barrio de la Magdalena, Uruapan, Michoacán, July 23, 1981. Mask by Victoriano Salgado.

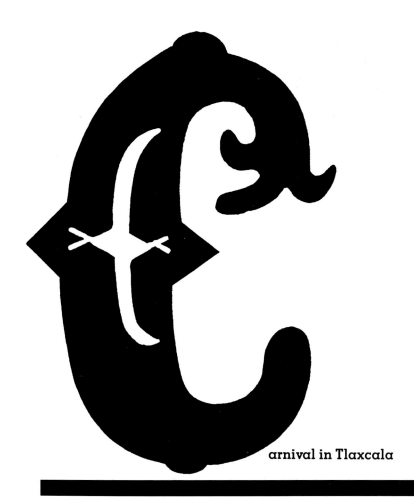

arnival in Tlaxcala

Ruth D. Lechuga

Notes

1. As reported by Sahagún, for the pre-Conquest Aztecs the year began on February 2 with the first twenty days dedicated to the *Tlaloques* (rain gods) and to Chalchihuitlicue, goddess of water. Today in central Mexico farmers begin to cultivate their cornfields by the middle of February, but must wait to sow until the first rains arrive, usually some time in March. Because of its crucial importance there are many rites to

Though pre-Christian in origin and preserving certain traits of European folk culture, Carnival today usually is performed by Westerners as an elaborate masquerade. As such, it is an explosion of profane rejoicing wherein participants express a lust for life before entering the time of introspection and fasting appropriate to Lent. People dress in disguise in order to abandon themselves to the pleasure of these days without being recognized.

Carnival among the indigenous people of Mexico, however, is quite different. The period of Carnival, Lent, and Holy Week, representing one single group of celebrations beginning usually in February, is profoundly religious in nature. These festivities take place at the beginning of the agricultural cycle; thus, rain-petitioning ceremonies constitute an important theme in many of the celebrations. Another important element, deeply rooted in indigenous culture, involves purification by means of fasting and sacrifice (Sahagún 1955, 1:95–97).[1]

In the course of centuries of domination and catechization, another component was incorporated into the Carnival celebrations. Indians have always been very keen observers and have made use of every means at their disposal to express themselves. Thus, they adopted the European custom of wearing disguises during Carnival in order to make fun of their oppressors with impunity.[2]

While the Carnival festivities in the state of Tlaxcala, in central Mexico,

144

87. Dancers assemble
at the house of the
person responsible for
the group. Here the
maringuillas are
enacted by very
young girls. San
Lucas Cuauhtelulpan,
Tlaxcala, 1978.

ensure proper rainfall. For example, in Quintana Roo Maya Indians celebrate a special ceremony conducted by the *h'men* (indigenous priest). This ceremony is called *cha-chaac,* which means the summoning of the *chaacs,* or rain gods (Sodi Morales 1976: 45). Another example of a ceremony related to the fecundity of the earth occurs in Capuluhac, state of Mexico, where during Carnival men wearing masks representing black Africans actually plow the earth, guiding two oxen in circles in front of the churchyard. Purification rites were also customary among the pre-Conquest Aztecs. Prior to each ceremony the people, and especially the priests, fasted. Water was used for purification. According to Fray Diego Durán (1967, 2: 209), people were born of water, enabled to live thanks to water, and with water able to wash away their sins. Elsewhere (1967, 2: 211) he reports that, having fasted, everyone went to wash early in the morning and afterward ate *tzoalli,* a paste of amaranth seeds shaped into images of gods and thought to represent their flesh. The ablutions served both as confession and purification. Today in many places in Mexico purification rites are observed during Carnival and Holy Week. In the Tzotzil village of

include all these elements,[3] there are distinct dances whose names and plots, as well as the costumes of the dancers, vary from village to village. In each community there are usually several groups, all of them performing the same type of dance. There is a general sequence of events which is the same in all the villages:

1. Each group assembles at the house of the person in charge. Each dancer arrives fully dressed (fig. 87).

2. Dancers, musicians, guests, and casual visitors are invited to eat a meal in this house.

3. The group dances in the courtyard or in front of the house of the person in charge. Each group is accompanied by its own band.

4. Each group dances from house to house wherever they are asked to do so. The owner of the house gives them some money to help defray expenses.

5. In the late afternoon each group organizes itself to begin the parade in which all the groups of the town take part, each one followed by its band of musicians.

6. The parade leads to the main plaza or, sometimes, to inside the churchyard. Every group has its assigned space and there they dance to the music of their band. The dancing is accompanied by skyrockets, fireworks, and so on. This is called *el remate* (the conclusion) and takes place during the last day of the festivities.

The dates of the celebration have differed from village to village during past years for several reasons. On Carnival Sunday in Tlaxcala City a dance contest sponsored by the state government is held. Many groups attend this event and therefore cannot dance on this day in their own villages. In the past in Panotla, in the state of Tlaxcala, groups used to dance on Carnival Tuesday, the first Thursday of Lent, and the following Tuesday, called the *octava* (the

eighth day after the festival day). Because the inhabitants of Panotla work at regular jobs during the week in the cities of Tlaxcala and Puebla it is necessary for them to change their schedules and dance on Carnival Sunday. Therefore the following three Sundays are substituted for the Tuesdays and Thursdays of the older pattern. It is the same in other villages. In any event, whether due to demands made by employment or to the custom of celebrating the *octava,* it is remarkable how many villages in Tlaxcala are engaged in Carnival dances during the actual Lenten period.

In each village there exists a system of organization in order to fulfill the commitments of the fiesta. This system is slightly different in each place. In Panotla people dance for their own amusement. There is no sense of compulsion; participation is not considered a religious obligation. Even so, there used to be four dance groups and now there are six. Some young men prefer merely to watch or play soccer, but most of them dance willingly each year. There is a board of directors which is in charge of paying the musicians and providing for the meals during the four Sundays. Each year this board of directors is reconstituted. In addition, there is an agent, a person of economic substance, who takes care of transportation and other arrangements for the group whenever they dance outside the village. Each member of the group pays for his own costume and that of his female partner.

In San Lucas Cuauhtelulpan there are three *encabezados* (headmen or leaders)—the president, the secretary, and the treasurer. They are in charge of directing the dance and offering the meals for the community. Here, too, people dance voluntarily, for pleasure, but the *encabezados,* once they are appointed, regard their obligations as solemn vows.

In San Cosme Mazotecochco there are

88. A new board of directors is appointed to officiate during the festivities of the following year. San Bernardino Contla, Tlaxcala, 1963.

89. The two "women" photographed here are actually male dancers. Today, real women assume these roles. San Bernardino Contla, Tlaxcala,

90. This mask is
meant to represent
Ché Guevara and
was madé in San
Pablo Apetatitlán,
Tlaxcala, 1977.

91. The masks at
either end are made
of leather; the three in
the center are molds,
all by Francisco Pérez.
The central mold, used
to make masks of old
men, shows wrinkles.
Amaxac de Guerrero,

92. A group of very
elegantly attired
catrines, uniformly
dressed, with their
female partners. In
this town *catrines* do
not carry umbrellas.
All of these masks
were made by the
Reyes family. Panotla
Tlaxcala, 1977.

San Juan Chamula, Chiapas, this is accomplished by running barefoot over burning straw (Sodi Morales 1976: 78). On Holy Saturday in Jesús María, Nayarít, Cora Indians bathe in the river at the conclusion of their Holy Week ceremonies in order to wash away their sins (Benítez 1970, 3: 519).

2. It is the Carnival dancers from Tlaxcala themselves who relate that they mean to make fun of the rich landowners of the nineteenth century. In other carnivals one may also observe similar burlesquing, as in Nezquipayac, state of Mexico, where two dancers dressed as priests in an attempt to hear a mock confession from a big rag doll and end by destroying it. Many female characters, usually enacted by men dressed in city-style gowns and carrying handbags (which Indian women do not use), ridicule urban women. In the Mixtec town of Juxtlahuaca, Oaxaca, the *macho* dance mocks the urban family (Brown 1978: 15). Esser (1984: 179–238) relates that the *feos* (uglies) in the Tarascan mountain towns act as ceremonial clowns.

3. Tlaxcala is the smallest state of the Mexican federation with an area of 3,914 square kilometers. It is located in central Mexico on the high plateau and is dominated by the volcano Malinche. Rainfall

93. The six newly appointed *fiscales* enter the churchyard in order to kneel and pray in front of the church door. Amaxac de Guerrero, Tlaxcala, 1966.

twenty *encargados* (persons charged with the functioning of the group, including teaching and rehearsals), with obligations similar to those of the *encabezados.* All the *encargados,* as well as the dancers, sign a contract in the presence of the municipal president. Each person chooses the years in which he wishes to participate. This constitutes a very formal obligation; should a person not comply, a large fine will be levied against him. Dancers rehearse once a week, beginning with the end of December and continuing until Carnival. The *encargados* assume responsibility for teaching. My informant had agreed to perform for eight years because, as he said, things went well with him and, therefore, he felt obligated to give something in return to his community. This is a clear example of the way that the fiesta system with its many duties functions as a system of balances in the economy of indigenous groups.

In Amaxac de Guerrero there are six dance groups, one for each of the town's districts. Each group has a board of directors, consisting of one *fiscal* (clerk), one *mayor* (mayor), one *merino* (judge), one *escribano* (scrivener), four *topiles* (policemen), and four *tequilma* (tribute laborers). The board of directors pays for the musicians, meals, and so on (fig. 88). The groups dance on Sunday, Monday, and Tuesday of Carnival. On the last day *el remate,* the culmination of the festivities, takes place, and afterward the new board of directors is elected. These new appointees must appear with their group of dancers for the first time at the *octava* of Carnival Sunday (first Sunday of Lent) and then again on the three days of Carnival the following year. There is a similar organization in each village.

All the groups are called *camadas* (literally, a brood of young animals or a gang of rogues) or *huehues* (old men), and most of them have an additional name identifying the character

represented. Until 1960 almost all the female characters were enacted by men (fig. 89). Today some villages still observe this custom, but many have changed to include women participants, usually girls or young women. In San Lucas Cuauhtelulpan, these girls are called *maringuillas* (little Marys). All male characters in the villages where dances take place use masks, irrespective of the name of the dance or the rest of the costume. Actual female participants do not use masks, and in some villages men dressed as women are unmasked too, a situation that has existed since anyone remembers. In other towns men dressed as women do use masks.

Without exception the masks present images of Caucasians and are of the same general type throughout Tlaxcala, regardless of the dance for which they are intended. The masks are dear to the dancers, who take good care of them and treat them with respect bordering on veneration, and sometimes the same ones are used for twenty or thirty years.

At present there are two workshops that produce most of the finely executed masks. One is run by Sr. Carlos Reyes and his sons in San Pablo Apetatitlán, Tlaxcala, and the other belongs to the Méndez family in the nearby city of Puebla. A few fine masks also are produced by a mask maker residing in Cholula, Puebla. Each of these craftsmen also is a sculptor who carves fine images of saints. Sr. Reyes originally is from Cholula, where a venerable tradition of image sculpting survives. The Reyes family uses a hard wood called *ayacahuite* (pine) for their carefully wrought carvings. For coloring they use a special technique that consists of applying fine oil pigments, like those used by painters, over a layer of Spanish white and, while this paint is still fresh, rubbing the surface with a chicken's crop. This process imparts a smooth look to the painting, imitating the ap-

154

94. The ribbon dance
is performed in
several villages as the
culmination of the
fiesta. Santa Cruz
Techachalco, Tlaxcala,
1978.

95. *Catrines* in full
dress, including um-
brellas. The mask on
the left was made by
Eladio Hernández;

that in the center by
the Reyes family in
San Pablo Apetatitlán;
and the small bearded
mask was probably

made of papier-mâché.
Amaxac de Guerrero,
Tlaxcala, 1977.

is scarce and although there are a few rivers the land is mostly arid. The villages discussed in this article are located in the southern and central parts of the state and are Nahuatl in origin. Of the inhabitants, approximately 26,000 are bilingual—Nahuatl and Spanish—speakers (PRI-IEPES 1977–82: 5.7 and Scheffler 1986: 153). In spite of the short supply of land and scarcity of rain, agriculture is the main occupation of Tlaxcalans. Many, however, also work in the factories of nearby Tlaxcala City and Puebla.

4. Wax masks with beards made of horse or cow hair are traditionally made in Santa María Astahuacán, which lies within the Federal District and in neighboring Chimalhuacán, in the state of Mexico. These masks are used during Carnival throughout a large area extending from the Guadalupe shrine in northern Mexico City to Texcoco and nearby villages in the state of Mexico. Masks from Santa María Astahuacán and Chimalhuacán are very similar in appearance, and it is not possible from discussions with the people of Panotla to know for certain the origin of any particular mask.

96. While the *fiscales* pray at the church door, the dancers, left in the street, also kneel to pray for rain. The three masks in the foreground are leather and were made by Francisco Pérez. Amaxac de Guerrero, Tlaxcala, 1971.

pearance of human skin. This method, widely employed until some twenty years ago, is now reserved for masks made to special order. For the others, synthetic oil colors or automotive paints are used. The oldest known masks from this region were made of a softwood called *tzompantle* or *colorín* (coral tree). The Museo Nacional de Artes e Industrias Populares in Mexico City possesses some masks of *colorín* dating from 1920 that were made in Tepeyanco, Tlaxcala.

Tlaxcala masks have imported glass eyes and artificial eyelashes. Since about 1960 most of them have been made with movable eyelids that close upon pulling a string. Nearly all the faces exhibit one or more beauty spots. Masks representing famous characters are introduced according to the fashion of the moment. There have been masks of Jorge Negrete, a well-known singer, and Cantinflas, a beloved comedian. Since 1975 bearded masks representing Ché Guevara have become quite popular (fig. 90). These representations are executed in a highly stylized manner so that only the owner really knows whom his mask portrays. I have seen a very old mask from Papalotla with a short beard that had the face of a saint. Since these mask makers were also sculptors of saints' images, the resemblance is understandable.

In the past there were local mask makers in many of the villages. The oldest masks that are remembered by the townspeople of Panotla (and their memory goes back to the turn of the century) were carved by Julian Aro, now deceased. In the town of Huejotzingo, Puebla, where leather masks traditionally are used, people say that "up there in Tlaxcala" masks are made of *tzompantli*. Huejotzingo had some influence over the city of Tlaxcala, and around 1930 some leather masks began to be made in Panotla. People of this village are very responsive to changes in fashion. Once, somebody brought

them wax masks from the outskirts of Mexico City; but as such masks are very fragile, this fad did not last.[4] Finally around 1960, dancers discovered Carlos Reyes, and now all masks used in Panotla are carved by him. The dance group would not permit a dancer to appear in a less elaborated mask.

In Amaxac de Guerrero, Tlaxcala, two mask makers are still making masks. Eladio Hernández works only part-time at this trade. In addition he carves all kinds of figures in wood, makes objects of cast iron, and cares for his fruit trees and cornfield. He uses softwoods as well as some varieties of hardwoods including *ayacahuite* (pine), willow, and ash, all of which must be carved while still green. He uses oil paint and covers the wood with varnish, ignoring the special treatment used by Sr. Reyes. Masks by this sculptor are very well carved and extremely expressive. It is only by examining the backs of the masks that one can observe that these are not as finely finished as the ones made by Sr. Reyes. When I visited Sr. Hernández for the first time he had in his possession a mask that had not been accepted by the dancer who had ordered it because it was too wide and did not fit the measurements of his face. In other places in Tlaxcala I heard the same complaint. Measurements are considered very important. If the size is incorrect, the dancer may reject the mask. Therefore, mask makers usually measure the face of the person who orders the mask.

The other mask maker in Amaxac de Guerrero is Francisco Pérez, who is now ninety-seven years old and still works part time. (As his son also is now making many masks, it seems likely that the tradition will continue.) Sr. Pérez began making masks in 1928. Originally he was a barber, but an associate of his in the town of Atlixco, Puebla, taught him to make leather masks, which he calls *de suela* (of the sole). He makes his own molds using

158

97. *Paragüeros* or *charros*. The figure on the left wears a leather mask from Huejotzingo, Puebla; the other two wear wooden masks made by the Méndez family in Puebla City. The capes worn by these dancers are rather simple. In other towns, such as Papalotla and Mazotecochco, these would be considered old-fashioned, as this style has not been used by them for at least ten years. Acuitlapilco, Tlaxcala, 1978.

baked clay covered with concrete. The leather is cut to the desired size, split, sewn under the chin, soaked, and then beaten over the mold until it takes on the right shape (fig. 91). Some masks have beards attached, made of *ixtle* (agave fiber) or of horse or cow tail. Since 1960 Sr. Pérez has made wooden masks too, using the soft *colorín* wood. He uses synthetic paint and describes himself as "not a sculptor" and self-taught.

There used to be mask makers in many other villages, too, but when they died people who could not afford the very expensive masks made by Sr. Reyes and his sons had to find substitutes. Some buy leather masks from Huejotzingo, Puebla, while others use the very well made papier-mâché masks lined with cloth that are made in Huamantla, Tlaxcala. A few dancers buy papier-mâché masks from Celaya, Guanajuato, or cloth or plastic masks, but they are in the minority. The mask is still the prized possession of each dancer, who usually will make any sacrifice to own a fine one.

The dances and their associated costumes in the state of Tlaxcala can be placed in one of two major divisions. In the southern region, between Tlaxcala City and nearby Puebla, the groups are called *charros* (equestrians) or *paragüeros* (those whose headdresses resemble umbrellas). Toward the north, between Tlaxcala City and Apizaco, we find the designation *catrines* (city dandies). There are few exceptions to this rule.

The *catrines*, also called *huehues* or *enmascarados* (masked ones), are dressed very elegantly in tuxedo or frock coats, ceremonial shirts, top hats, and gloves. In most of the villages they carry large umbrellas. The elegance displayed in Panotla is extraordinary. Hats are adorned with rosettes made of ribbons; a gilded fringe hangs over the forehead of the masks, and a paper flower is held in one corner of the

mouth. An embroidered cloth, worn under the hat, covers the shoulders (fig. 92).

Each group of *catrines* is headed by a *fiscal* dressed in white who carries a banner. Each dancer has his female partner. In the past, as noted, these were men dressed as women, wearing the typical costume of the region and covering the lower part of the face with a kerchief. Between the late 1950s and the middle 1970s, village after village changed to use actual women to impersonate female roles. Now some dances include groups of women all dressed identically in very elegant, stylized costumes. In other villages, women wear their everyday garments; some even wear trousers. The women continue the practice of covering the lower part of their faces with kerchiefs. Some of the male dancers regard the change as unfortunate. Formerly they were able to make rough jokes with the men who were impersonating women. Now, in order not to give offense, they have abandoned this custom.

In Amaxac de Guerrero each of the six groups of *catrines* enters the town center headed by its *fiscal*. When two *fiscales* meet, each lifts the other in turn, rotating him toward each of the four cardinal points. On Sunday, the *fiscales* of the previous year, together with the next year's newly elected *fiscales*, enter the churchyard and kneel in front of the closed church door (fig. 93). Outside the churchyard, in the adjacent streets, all the dancers kneel, too, while the music stops. When the *fiscales* have finished praying and rise, the dancers also stand. Simultaneously, each of the six groups of musicians commences to play while everyone begins to dance, first in the streets, and later at the house of the *fiscal*.

In San Juan Totolac and some other nearby villages the dancers dress in white. It is as if the whole *camada* has adopted the outfit of the *fiscal*. During *el remate* in San Juan Totolac and in

98. A very richly embroidered cape representative of current usage. All of the empty spaces between the embroidered motifs are filled with sequins. San Cosme Mazotecochco, Tlaxcala, 1978.

99. *Paragüero*, dancing with a doll in his arms. It is no longer customary for male characters to carry dolls in Tlaxcala dances. Acapetlahuaya, Tlaxcala, 1963.

5. Even if the external form of the ritual has changed, the ceremony that petitions rain through the use of sympathetic magic strongly suggests a pre-Hispanic root. Now, as in the past, rain is of central importance to a rural society that relies completely on rainfall for success-ful harvests. Rain-fall has been scanty in Tlaxcala since prehistoric times. Prior to the arrival of Europeans the solar year was divided into eigh-teen periods of "months," four of which were dedi-cated to Tlaloc, the chief rain god (third month) and to his assistants, the *tlaloques* (first, sixth, and sixteenth months) (Sahagún 1955, 1: 96, 99, 103, 119). The thirteenth month was dedicat-ed to "the mountain tops, where clouds are formed" (1955, 1: 115) and the second, fourth, and eighth months hon-ored the agricultur-al deity Xipe Totec and other deities of maize (1955, 1: 97, 100, 106). The first two months, both dedicated to gods of rain and earth, were celebrated between February 2 and March 13, exactly the time when Carnival occurs. Today rain-petitioning ceremo-nies take place all over Mexico, both among groups that were evangelized early in the Colo-nial period as well as among those that still retain non-Catholic beliefs, as do, for example, the Huichols of Jalisco and Nayarít (Lumholtz 1904, 2: 6–13).

Santa Cruz Techachalco the *danza de listones* (ribbon dance) is performed. This involves braiding, while dancing, ribbons of different colors around a central pole (fig. 94). According to Fran-cisco Xavier Clavijero (1974: 178), an eighteenth-century historian, the dance is of pre-Hispanic origin. Most other authors, however, consider it to be a version of the European maypole dance (Warman and Warman 1971: 744). It is still performed in Spain (Timón Tiemblo 1979: 36). As the dance was already tra-ditional by Clavijero's time, it may have been introduced from Europe early in the Colonial period.

The *catrines* raise their umbrellas while dancing (fig. 95). When asked why the dancers use umbrellas, they reply, "because it rains so little here." And again when asked about the ori-gin and antiquity of the dance, a vari-ety of answers follows. The dancers from Panotla and their directors allege that in their village Carnival originat-ed during the French intervention and that the *catrines* are meant as a paro-dy of the elites of that time. In another village, San Lucas Cuauhtelulpan, it is believed that the celebration dates from the time of Herod. Francisco Pérez, the ninety-seven-year-old mask maker from Amaxac de Guerrero, estimates from what his predecessors have re-ported that the dance has existed for at least two hundred years. The other mask maker, Eladio Hernández, ex-plains: "It is related to the New Testa-ment. The masked characters are the Jewish people who persecuted Jesus Christ (See Editor's note, page 63). When they went out to kill Him every-one put on a mask so he would not be recognized. The costume which they now wear is meant to make fun of the wealthy landowners. Years ago they used to also dress as priests, as the gov-ernor, and other well-known dignitar-ies. Until very recently, the clergy did not approve of their dancing and for that reason the church remains closed

during Carnival."

All of the above information suggests that Carnival is a very ancient celebra-tion, with petitioning of rain as its cen-tral theme. Over many years the dance has changed as innovations were in-troduced. The custom of alluding to contemporary events and characters permits us, on occasion, to observe nineteenth-century costumes used with masks that include representations of the recently famous and/or notorious. Although the ribbon dance goes back at least to the sixteenth century, when it was brought to Mexico by the Span-iards, the dance as a form of sym-pathetic magic used to petition rain strongly suggests a pre-Hispanic root.[5] It is important to note that in Tlaxcala both dancers and their audience are perfectly aware of the significance of their dance. Their explanation for why they dance with umbrellas opened, performing as they do an action that demonstrates fulfillment of their wish, manifests a belief in sympathetic mag-ic. Roman Catholic religious sentiment is also expressed when, as part of the dance sequence, the same dancers kneel in the street outside the church-yard to pray for rain. Inclusion of Cath-olic practice in the dance sequence persists in spite of the clergy's opposi-tion to these unorthodox celebrations (fig. 96).

The *charros* or *paragüeros* in the southern part of the state of Tlaxcala dress in dark suits, including vests and neckties, and chaps made of chamois and tied with handwoven ribbons. A large cloth completely covered with embroidery and sequins is knotted over the shoulders like the pre-Hispanic *tilma* (a large cloak worn by the men of this region prior to the Conquest). The dancer covers his face with a mask and wears a hat lined with cloth, usu-ally velvet. A framework with an enor-mous cascade of feathers emerges from the top of the hat, forming a kind of umbrella above the head of the danc-

er. Each headdress is composed of forty-eight brightly colored ostrich feathers (figs. 97, 98). In most villages several colors are used; in San Cosme Mazotecochco all the plumes are of one color.

In addition to these personages there is a group of costumed couples sometimes referred to as *vasarios* (vassals). Their dress differs from village to village, but is the same for everyone in the group. The female characters used to be enacted by men, each of whom covered his face with a mask. In Papalotla since 1985, real women without masks have been substituted for female impersonators. A doll is carried in a box by a boy and each time a special tune is played it is taken out and displayed to the spectators by one of the women. During the 1960s more than one doll occasionally was used, and sometimes even a *paragüero* carried a doll (fig. 99). In Papalotla since 1977, in addition to a very large group of *paragüeros* with their *vasarios*, the dance has included two *cuerudos* (men wearing cowhide) or *chivarandos* (men who use trousers of cowhide) dressed in large sombreros (usually made of cardboard), city-style jackets, and chaps of cowhide. They wear small wooden hobby horses which they appear to be riding. In Xametla a whole group of *cuerudos* dances around a man who carries a big *torito* (a framework with bull's head attached) adorned with colored paper (fig. 100).

In Tepeyanco, the dance group is called a *cuadrilla* (court dance) or *locos* (crazy ones), and performers are extremely elegant in appearance. There are only two *paragüeros* in the group; the rest of the men dress like eighteenth-century Spanish grandees in black velvet coats and trousers, embroidered in bright colors, and hats adorned with feathers. All of the women are impersonated by men, who attempt to move as gracefully as women. They wear finely carved masks with feminine fea-

tures, big wigs, and contemporary white dresses that alter with changing fashions (fig. 101). One older tradition is still observed in Tepeyanco: During *el remate,* members of the *cuadrilla* pronounce flattering sentences to women in the indigenous Nahuatl language.

An important rite in the *paragüero* dance is the presentation of a doll to the spectators by "women" and *vasarios.* Dancing, they carry the doll in their arms as though it were a child, displaying it to the audience while singing lullabies (fig. 102).

During the same dance there is a special sequence in which only the *paragüeros* participate. It is called *la culebra* (the serpent) and is always performed even if, as in Tepeyanco, there are only two *paragüeros.* Each *paragüero* carries a big whip made of *ixtle* fiber. During the sequence they form two lines and to the music of a special tune each dancer tries to whip the dancer facing him on his legs. The other must jump in order to avoid the blow (fig. 103). At the end of the sequence the performers place their whips on the floor, thus forming the image of a group of serpents, and then dance around them. Only the *paragüeros* take part in this particular dance; the rest of the *camada* are only spectators at that moment.

Ever since pre-Hispanic times the serpent has symbolized lightning and rain in indigenous Mexico. Rain refers to the fertility of the earth, while the doll-child refers to the fertility of women. Both references combine here to signify the continuity of life. Thus dances of *paragüeros,* like those of *catrines,* are, on one level, rain-petitioning ceremonies.

It is important to emphasize that the seriousness with which dancers participate in dances and the economic sacrifice made by both dancers and festival officers demonstrate the importance of Carnival within Tlaxcalan culture. Many citizens of Tlaxcala must live far from their place of origin in order to earn

100. A *torito* (center) and two *cuerudos* or *chivarandos* dressed in sheepskin trousers. The little wooden horses pass between the legs of the dancers. Xametla, Tlaxcala, 1977.

101. The costumes worn by the male *locos* are very old and are cherished by the group because of their beautiful embroidery. The dresses worn by the "women" will be altered to reflect changes in fashion. Tepeyanco, Tlaxcala, 1964.

their livings. There they work hard all year in order to earn the money to spend upon their return for Carnival.

Importations have enriched these celebrations over the centuries. Spaniards introduced the system of festival organization that is still in use. The ribbon dance was likely an early importation. Many of the tunes played to accompany dances were composed for eighteenth-century court dances. The attire of the male *locos* from Tepeyanco is reminiscent of that worn by eighteenth-century Spanish nobles. The ridicule of nineteenth-century hacienda owners (oppressors of the Indians) is today joined with masks representing famous actors, singers, and popular heroes, revealing the ever-changing face of a tradition whose essential nature remains the same over the years.

In Tepeyanco, as well as in San Sebastian Atlahuapa, *el remate* ends with the killing of a rooster. A cock is suspended on a string stretched high up between two poles while the *paragüeros* dance under it, striking it with their whips until it is dead. There are similar ceremonies in other parts of Mexico. Spaniards of the sixteenth century introduced gamecock fighting to New Spain, which they in turn had adopted from the Arabs. On the other hand, investigator Vicente Mendoza (1976) believes that the custom of striking the rooster represents the survival of a pre-Hispanic rite of fertilizing the earth by sprinkling it with the blood of sacrificial gladiators. Fray Bernardino de Sahagún, a sixteenth-century chronicler, described the festivities, which took place during the first and second months of the Aztec year: "They killed many slaves in honor of the water deities; first they slashed them, fighting with the captives who had been tied to a stone, like a millstone and at the moment they won the fight, they took the slaves to the shrine called Yopico, where their hearts were cut out. When these captives were killed, their own-

ers, who had captured them, gloriously decked out with plumes and dancing in front of them, showed their bravery" (Sahagún 1955, 1: 97). The description of plumes certainly fits well with the dress of the *paragüeros,* and one could find similarities between the rich capes worn by these dancers and the pre-Hispanic *tilma* that was profusely adorned when worn by a brave warrior who had taken captives (Kingsborough 1964,[1]: illustrations 65, 66). But on the other hand, ostrich feathers are not of New World origin. European noblemen wore feathers on their hats also and the capes of the *paragüeros* might as well have their counterpart in the Spanish *mantón de Manila* (a large, heavy cape worn like an overcoat). Therefore, in spite of the assurance of Mendoza that we have here another ceremony of fructification of the earth transformed over the centuries, most probably what is represented is another example of the syncretistic evolution of cultures.

It is clear that many elements from many epochs have fused and are still coalescing in the different versions of Tlaxcala's Carnival. For this reason, Carnival continues to be a vital, pulsating, and relevant celebration, one that represents an essential and integral part of the culture of today's participants.

102. A group of *vasarios* presenting the doll. In the background is one of the *paragüeros* from the same group of dancers. San Cosme Mazotecochco, Tlaxcala, 1978.

103. *Paragüeros* performing the Serpent dance. The dancers lift their capes with one hand to get them out of their way. Papalotla, Tlaxcala, 1971.

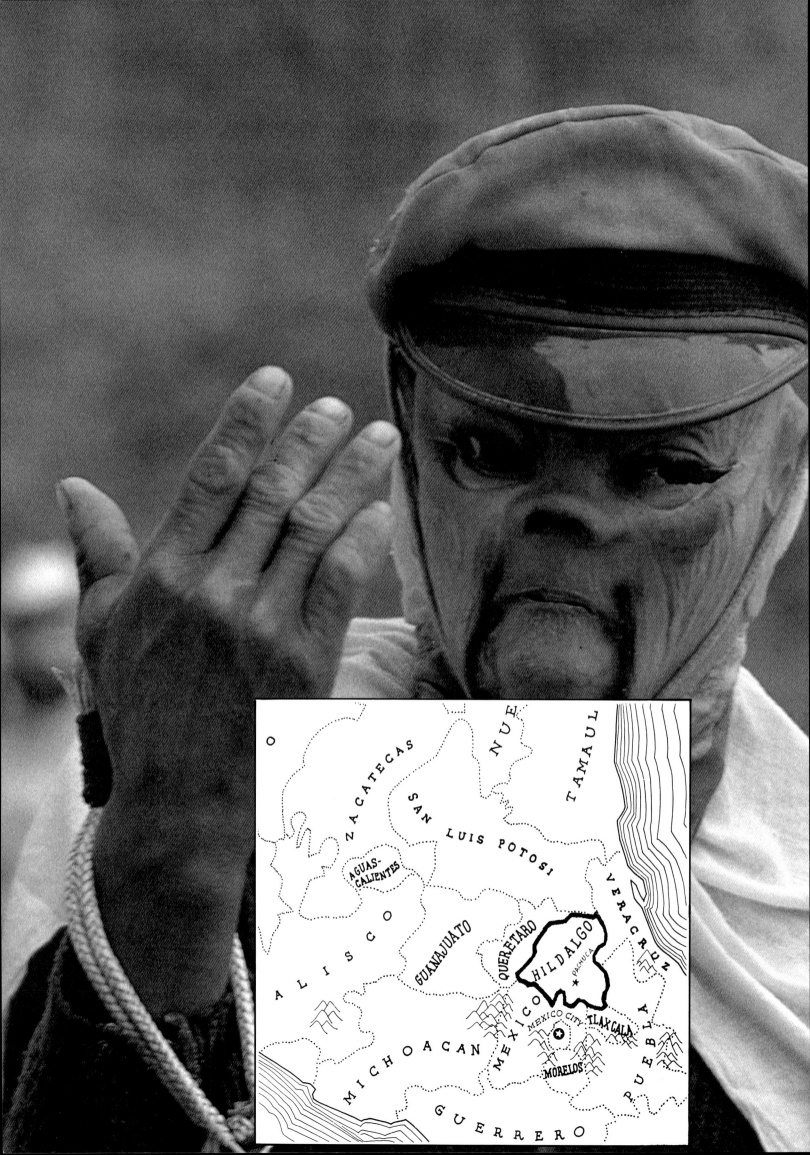

Sierra Otomí Carnival Dances

James Dow

Notes

1. Hñąhñų is the native name for Indians who speak the Otomí language. The phoneme indicated by the letters *hñ* is a silent nasal, spoken like an English *ng* but without voicing; *ą* and *ų* are nasalized *a* and *u*. Natives have decided that Hñąhñų is the proper name for their people.

2. *Gente de razón* can be translated as "intelligent or educated people." It implies that the Indian is culturally inferior to the Spanish-speaking mestizo.

The Hñąhñų[1] Indian people, also known as the Sierra Otomíes, live about ninety miles northeast of Mexico City in the state of Hidalgo, where the mountainous terrain has isolated them from the cultural changes emanating from the more urbanized areas of Mexico. Today they maintain a vital local culture, conserving many traditional Mesoamerican Indian traits and religious rituals, some of which include the use of masks.

These rituals are best viewed within the context of the lives of the Hñąhñų people. Two classes, the mestizos and the Hñąhñų Indians, live in the *municipios*, political divisions of the state similar to small counties in the United States. The *municipio* of Tenango de Doria, which had a population of 13,438 in 1980, contains one large town called Tenango de Doria, four Indian pueblos, and thirty-nine smaller hamlets called *rancherías* and *ranchos*. The mestizos, who are called *gente de razón*,[2] are inheritors of Spanish Colonial culture. They speak Spanish and live in the municipal capital or in one of a small number of hamlets, where they own considerable land. While they are not rich, nor even well-off by U.S. standards, they constitute a sort of rural upper class. Their children look forward to entering the small-scale businesses of the *municipio* or making their way in the larger towns and cities of the central plateau.

The other class consists of the Indians, most of whom still speak Otomí, their traditional Hñąhñų language. They live in the municipal capital as a

poor class, in Indian villages as the only class, and in hamlets. They tend to be traditional subsistence farmers living on small plots of their own land. Their culture is rich in Indian tradition, and they have extensive knowledge of farming techniques and of the plants and animals found in the region.

` The typical Indian family grows corn, beans, and other foods for its own use. Men go to the fields to work while women stay at home preparing meals and tending to children. A picture of pastoral serenity, however, does not accurately describe the daily routine. Many eventful things happen every day in the typical Indian village. Agriculture itself can be a challenge. Men examine the fields carefully to determine when they must wage war against marauding *tlacuaches* (maize-eating opossums), and other pests or weeds. Many local concerns arise from a variety of problems such as the damages done by the livestock of careless neighbors. The time when the maize should be bent and harvested must be accurately determined. Excitement and the pleasure of symbolic expression are provided by religious rituals.

The Ritual Context of Masked Dances
The ritual life of the municipal capital Tenango de Doria differs from that of the Indian villages and hamlets,[3] primarily due to the presence of the powerful mestizo class in the town, which is intolerant of the traditional Indian civil-religious hierarchy. In predominantly Indian towns, this hierarchy would put authority in the hands of the Indian leaders. Thus, the public religious rituals of Tenango de Doria do not have the political impact that they would have in an Indian village. Yet the town has a rich ritual life that, while less politically influential, is even more expressive because it serves to release some of the tensions created by conflicts between the Indian and mestizo classes.

The ritual expression of the relationship between the two classes occurs primarily in one of the two fiesta periods, the Easter period. The other, the fiesta of Saint Augustine, held in August, is primarily an Indian affair. The full panoply of ritual activity during the Easter period is not seen every year, but natives object if it is not played out fully at least once every four years. During the Carnival week, held every year before the Easter festival, masked dancers are seen. At no other time is this the case.

Since Hñähñu masks exist only in the context of Carnival, to describe their use is to describe the Carnival dances. We will first observe the dances as performed in and around the municipal capital of Tenango de Doria; later their symbolic interpretation and relationship to the rituals of other Indian cultures in the sierra will be discussed. Class divisions are an important background to understanding the Carnival dances. Two complementary interpretations will be discussed. First, the dances are rites of reversal in which Indians ridicule mestizos and symbolically link them to creatures of the underworld. Second, they are survivals of pre-Columbian Flaying-of-Man ceremonies (Boilés 1969: 44–57, 1971; Williams 1963: 292).

Carnival in Tenango de Doria
The Carnival celebration begins the Sunday before Ash Wednesday and lasts until the following Sunday. During this time groups of masked dancers circulate on the trails and streets, dancing and asking for gifts at houses. They are accompanied by local musicians who play guitars, violins, flutes, and drums. It is a time of fun and frivolity, especially for the young Indian men who do the dancing.

In the morning musicians go to a public place and begin the dance. Hearing the music, the young male costumed revelers join them, and when

3. For a full description of the civil-religious hierarchies and other types of oratorio celebrations, see Dow (1974).

104. A whimsical papier-mâché face mask representing a Caucasian with a beard. The mask is worn by a boy. Tenango de Doria, 1968.

a goodly group has gathered, they troop off to entertain the rest of the village. Arriving at a house, their leader, the *capitán,* asks for money from the owner. Their dancing is comic and delights the occupants of the house, who may also provide some drink to enliven the dancers' spirits. The music is fast and wild and the dancers shriek as they reel about. The dancers are called "old people," *viejos* in Spanish or *humdǿ* in Hñąhñų. The dancers are not divided into special categories or special groups.

The mood is one of comic gaiety. Men, some boys (fig. 104), and very rarely women or girls do the dancing and plan and create their own costumes well in advance to create a personal comic effect. The dancer's costume at times mocks an aspect of his own personality but more often makes a wry comment on mestizo society. Comic effects are created with ordinary clothing. Capes are created with towels; pants are worn inside out. The identity of the dancer is completely disguised to the casual observer by face mask, bandana, and costume, but friends know each other and boast of their comic effects. One dancer friend once asked me if I noticed him in his "wild man" costume (fig. 106) made up of an old felt hat, a dark green face mask, animal skins, and a toy rifle. I told him that while I had enjoyed the performance I had not recognized him at the time. Later I remembered that he prided himself on being a good hunter, and I realized that his costume secretly revealed himself to those who knew what to look for.

The costumes can be roughly grouped into six categories: "ladies" (fig. 105), "military figures" (fig. 107), "tough guys" (fig. 108), "*ranchero*" characters, "old people," and "wild men." These categories are similar to those found in other sierra Indian dances, as described later. One might find a bishop with a monkey face (fig. 109), a buxom veiled

"woman" with a white face, a helmeted wrestler, a caped Hitler (fig. 110), a bearded Spaniard, an old man with a twisted face, a green-faced monster, a moustached *charro* (fig. 112), or a revolutionary soldier. The face masks most often are made of papier-mâché and purchased in the market place. Others are homemade, and some are ancient wooden masks that often depict bearded Spaniards (fig. 111). If a young man wants to dance and cannot find or afford the right face mask, he simply hides his face behind a plain cloth mask (fig. 113).

In Tenango in 1969 one large group of dancers circulated every day. Their *capitán* was an older man respected around the town. He called himself the "Master of Carnival" and collected the money, which went to pay the musicians and to provide occasional drinks for the dancers. In Damo, a nearby hamlet, a much smaller group circulated. Hamlet musicians, decidedly not as accomplished as the Tenango ones, played traditional dance tunes like "The Flea" and the more modern *huapangos.*[4]

The boys in Damo said the face masks cost from six to twenty-five pesos apiece. Several still used the old wooden masks made locally. These relics showed only traces of white paint on what was a traditional Caucasian face. One morning they were especially excited because of a rumor that a young woman was going to dance with them; however, she did not appear. As usual, the atmosphere of revelry was a little too rough. The drinking might get heavy, lewd language and gestures might be used, and women are reluctant to associate themselves in public with these particularly male excesses.

Carnival in Other Parts of the Sierra Norte de Puebla

In other parts of the Sierra Norte de Puebla and the nearby Huasteca in the state of Veracruz, similar masked dances

4. *Huapangos* are modern country dance tunes indigenous to the Sierra Norte de Puebla, the southern Huasteca, and adjacent Gulf Coast regions.

are held during Carnival. The Tenango celebrations, in fact, do not seem as highly structured as others further to the north, although one can recognize in the Tenango performances characters such as "old people," "ladies," and "savages." Boilés reports that the Hñąhñ̨ų of El Zapote open their Carnival season with the erection of an altar to the Lord of the Underworld, also known as Lord of the Dead, Chief of the Judases, or Ra Zitų (Eater of the Dead) (Boilés 1969: 47–48). There are distinct groups of dancers in El Zapote. The first to appear during Carnival week are the "old people," played by men at least twenty-five years of age. They dance with another group called "ladies" (damas), played by boys of at least twelve. The ladies' masks and costumes mock mestizo women. Two other groups, the "savages" (mecos) and the "Comanches" (comanches), appear during the last days of the week. The "savages," imitating fierce Chichimeca warriors, and the Comanches, or "wild men," do their begging and attack the "old people" in mock battle. The "savages" are played by little boys of at least seven, and the comanches by men between eighteen and twenty-five. The comanches wear skirts, carry bows, and cover their heads entirely with red cloth masks. For a headdress they make a crown of turkey wingfeathers (Boilés 1969: 54). Several special characters, Lord of the Underworld, Jaguar, and Grand Lord, make their appearance at certain points in the revelry.

In the nearby Nahua-speaking village of Tizal in the Huasteca, the dances are similar to the Tenango ones. There are no special groups, and all the dancers are called "savages" (Provost 1974, 1981). The costuming is also similar to that in Tenango.

Among the Tepehua of Pisaflores the dancers are divided into "old people," "ladies," "devils" (diablos), and "comanches." The "old people" and "ladies" dance in a group. The "devils" dance in a group. The "devils"

receive offerings from families who have lost a member to murder (Williams García 1963: 246).

The dancers among the Totonacs of Mecapalapa are divided into "old people" and "colored folk" (Afro-mestizos) (Inchón 1973: 431–43). The "old people" are subdivided into the dance roles of "old people proper," "ladies," "devils," and "comanches." The "colored folk," who are part of another dance complex, are divided into "mistresses" (malinches), "cats" (gatos), and "bulls" (toros). The dancers of the "old people" complex perform in a manner similar to what has been described. The "mistresses" are men dressed as Indian women. They are humorously attacked by the "cats" and "bulls," who place their tails between their legs to simulate the phallus.

In spite of linguistic and historical differences, there is a strong similarity between the Sierra Norte de Puebla and Huastec dances. They are all performed by perambulating bands of men dancing for money; they are humorous and satirical; and the communities welcome the diversion.

Carnival Dances as Rites of Reversal

The Carnival dances are rites of reversal, rituals in which the normal social order is reversed. Authority, propriety, and beauty are mocked, and rebellion, wantonness, and ugliness reign. Men dress up as women. The humor of the dances lies in this reversal. Provost (1981) sees reversal as the most important function in the Huasteca festivals.

An important symbolic reversal occurs in the status of the mestizo, as generals, landowners, and bishops are ridiculed. The beautiful, light-skinned mestizo ladies are made to look like bawds. We also see a reversal of the Indian parental roles in the "old people." Respected fathers and grandfathers become wanton. Normal sexual decorum is also torn down, while the dancers delight in lewd gestures.

105. A "lady" dancer.
The dancer is a young
man. Tenango de
Doria, 1968.

106. A typical "wild
man" with a rubber
face mask. Tenango
de Doria, 1968.

107. An aggressive
"general" commands
the photographer.
Tenango de Doria,
1968.

108. "Wrestlers" dance
with others. Tenango
de Doria, 1968.

109. Two "ladies" and
a monkey-bishop
dance in line. Tenango
de Doria, 1968.

110. A caped "Hitler"
dances. Tenango de
Doria, 1968.

111. An antique "old man" mask with faded white paint and a beard. Tenango de Doria, 1968.

112. A flamboyant
charro holds down the
center of the dancing
line. Tenango de
Doria, 1968.

In Tenango the mockery of mestizos relieves the tensions of Indian-mestizo opposition and prepares the way for the ritual integration of the two groups in the coming Easter festival. During the Easter festival they jointly participate in the same rituals during which they ritually apologize for their transgressions (Dow 1974).

Like all rites of reversal, the dances have a therapeutic and cathartic value (Wallace 1966: 203–6; Gluckman 1956; Norbeck 1961, 1963). Conflicts and frustrations hovering on the brink of social disruption are released. The young male dancers belong to one of the most pressured age groups in the Indian communities, since they do not have the independence of their own land and family and are expected to help support their parents' household. However, the whole community seems to delight in this tearing down of the social order, especially in the rebellious satire of the most repressive relationships, those between Indian and mestizo.

Synthesis and Syncretism

Two earlier religious traditions have merged in the modern Carnival celebrations, the Spanish *Carnaval* (Foster 1966: 172–78) and the pre-Columbian festival of Flaying of Man (Tlacaxipehualiztli in Aztec or Antsayoh, meaning "flaying of dogs," in Hñąhñų) (Boilés 1971). Of the two, the pre-Columbian precursor contributes far more symbolism. In the past, both were rites of reversal.

Flaying of Man was held at the same time of year as the modern Carnival. Its purpose was to celebrate the clearing of the fields before burning to make them fertile for the new planting. The Aztecs made it into one of their grisly rites of human sacrifice by dressing a person in the skin of a flayed human victim, which symbolized the old crop residue.[5] This person perambulated from house to house receiving gifts. He

also represented Xipe-Totec, god of fertility. Besides this person with the old, dead skin, there were characters similar to those found in the sierra and Huasteca carnivals of today. The modern "ladies" are similar to prostitutes that danced in the Aztec festival (Boilés 1971: 1961). During Tlacaxipehualiztli the Aztecs held ritual battles with captives. Archers shot captives to symbolize the fecundation of the soil. The modern "*comanches*" with their bows and arrows are reminders of the Aztec archers, and the "savages" represent the captive foreign figures.

The ancient and modern festivals have complex symbolic links that are subject to various interpretations. However, it seems clear that the Carnival dances are modern survivors of ancient festivals aimed at celebrating the revitalization of the fields. They serve as releases from repressive social relations, much as spring is a release from the bondage of winter. They mock the mestizo class and prepare the way for the Easter festival that symbolically reintegrates Indians and mestizos.

5. Williams García (1963: 292) reports that one of the images constructed for the Carnival in the Hñąhñų town of El Zapote was called *yonxitzá*, which is probably *yon xizą*, meaning dry (*yon*) leaves (*xizą*). A reference to clearing fields can be seen. *Xi* means "skin of" and *zą* means branches. Therefore *xizą* means "leaves."

113. A "lady" with a plain cloth face mask dances with a bearded Caucasian. Tenango de Doria, 1968.

114. The *capitán* with
his four *voladores*.
Cuetzalan, 1969.

GUANAJUATO

QUERETARO

HILDAGO

VERACRUZ

CUETZALAN

MICHOACAN

MEXICO

MEXICO CITY

TLAXCALA

PUEBLA

MORELOS

PUEBLA

GUERRERO

OAXACA

Some Dances of the Nahuas and

Otomíes of the

Sierra Norte de Puebla, Mexico

Ted J. J. Leyenaar

As the name *Sierra*—a saw-toothed mountain range—suggests, the Sierra Norte de Puebla is a mountainous region forming part of the great Sierra Madre Oriental. The Nahua Indians, sometimes called "the Aztecs of today," along with three other indigenous groups, live in this area at approximately 800 to 1,800 meters above sea level. Depending on altitude the climate is more or less subtropical, and there are a great many plantations— mostly coffee and citrus fruit—with banana plantations in the lower lying regions.

The weather throughout the Sierra Norte de Puebla is typified by rain and wind, usually brought by northerlies— the infamous *nortes*—which come from the United States and Canada, pass-

ing over the Gulf of Mexico before assailing the Sierras. Apart from the wind and rain, cold and mist can last for days, and in such conditions the daytime temperature can drop to below fifty degrees (F). (In my experience one never suffers from the cold so much as in regions known as tropical or subtropical, where methods of house building tend to ignore the existence of cold.) The worst periods are autumn and winter when the *nortes* strike, and there is seldom any respite. In this so-called dry season, when most of Mexico enjoys a great deal of sunshine and even suffers from lack of rain, the Sierra Norte de Puebla and its people are shrouded in a veil of rain and mist. It is thus one of the few areas in Mexico where enough rain falls to permit two harvests

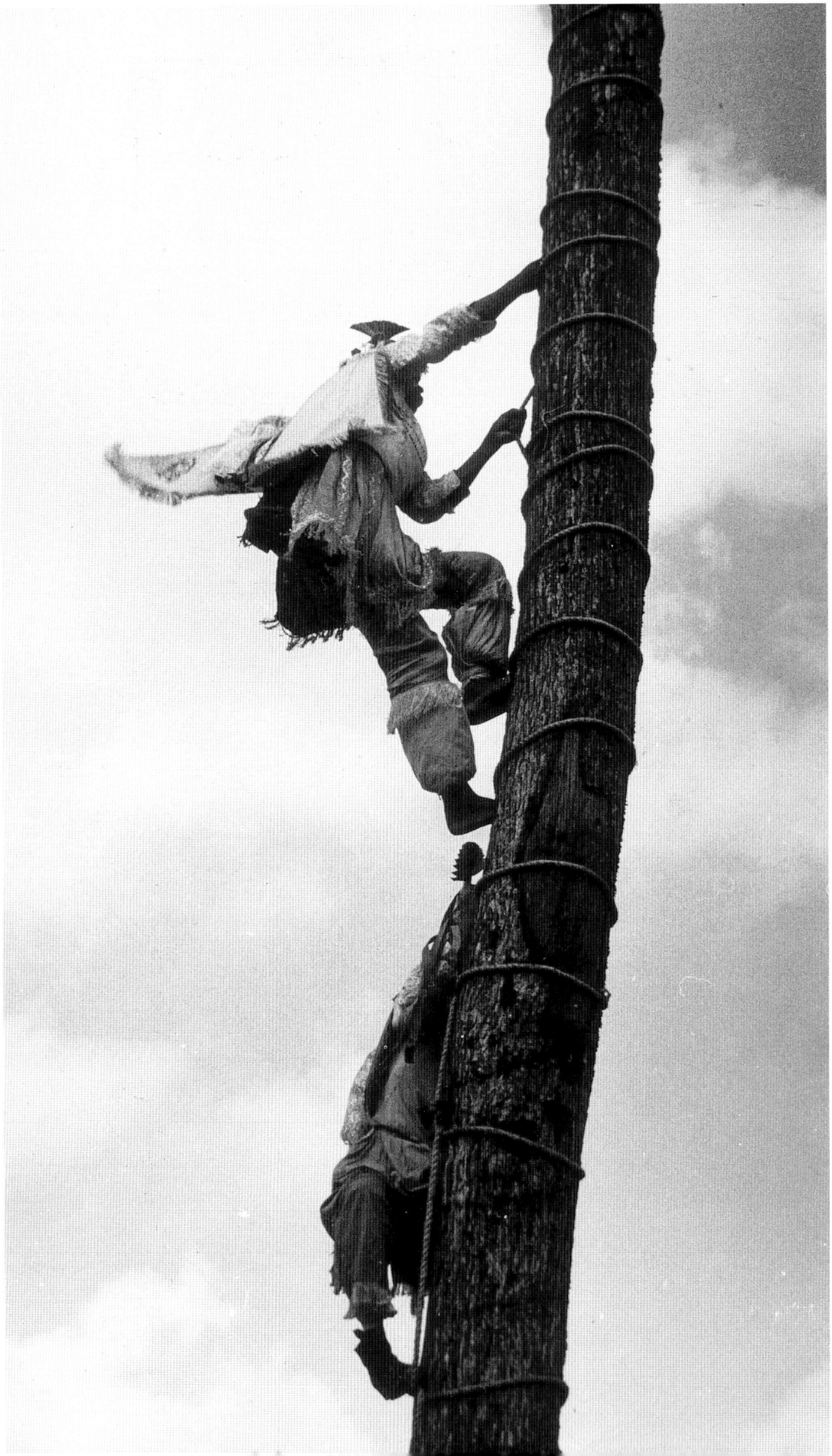

a year without irrigation. Although this area may not correspond to the popular image of "sunny Mexico," it is precisely here that, because of the large number of indigenous people, many customs from the pre-Hispanic period have survived. This fact is demonstrated by several of the dances performed in the area.

La Danza de los Voladores

One of the most popular dances in the Sierra is *la danza de los voladores,* the "Flying-Pole Dance," or the "Dance of the Flying Men." This dance—or rather this event—is performed not only by the Nahuas but by the Otomíes and Totonacs in the Sierra Norte, and by the lowland Totonacs in the neighboring state of Veracruz, as well.

In Cuetzalan the community's patron saint, St. Francis of Assisi, whose name day falls on October 4, is venerated exuberantly by both Indians and mestizos of the region. In pre-Hispanic days a Lord of the Mountains was worshipped during the twenty-day period known as *Quecholli,* from September 20 to October 10. In the Sierra Norte de Puebla, Archangel Michael, venerated on September 29, and St. Francis of Assisi have been assimilated into this autochthonous celebration. The people living in and around Cuetzalan honor St. Francis for several days with all kinds of ceremonies, including dance performances. The pine tree pole is carefully selected and ritually "planted" in the square in front of the church. A small cylindrical platform called a *tecomate* is fixed to the pole, and a rectangular frame attached. In the 1970s— the period in which my family and I spent part of each year in Mexico collecting ethnographical material for the Rijksmuseum voor Volkenkunde in Leiden, The Netherlands—the ladder used by the five *voladores* to reach the platform was made either of lianas or thick ropes (fig. 115).ᐧ Prior to their ascent the *voladores* dance in front of

and inside the church to entreat the blessings of the saints. From there they make their way, dancing, to the pole (*el palo volador*—the flying pole), dancing around it before climbing. The musical accompaniment of bamboo flute and drum is provided by the *capitán,* the leader of the other *voladores,* who plays both instruments at the same time. Each of the other four *voladores* of Cuetzalan crouches at one side of the frame. Each attaches to his waist one of the ropes which is wound around the pole just under the *tecomate.* While the *voladores* make their preparations the *capitán* plays the flute and drum while dancing, bending over backwards at times to greet the Winds of the Four Quarters (fig. 116). This seems a typically pre-Hispanic element.

At a sign from the *capitán,* the *voladores* plunge earthwards with arms outspread, like inverted crosses (fig. 114). Other activities cease, spectators fall silent, and in a breathless hush the four *voladores* begin their flight (fig. 118). The frame begins to turn around the pole while the ropes unwind from it, and the men fly to earth in ever-widening circles to land at last on their feet after a somersault. When the *capitán* in his turn has also landed safely, the *voladores,* dancing, again enter the church to honor the saint and thank him for their safety.

In pre-Hispanic days thirteen gyrations were made before the four *voladores* landed. Even old Colonial sources (Clavijero 1958: II: 163, 282; Torquemada 1976: III, Pt. 10, Chap. 38) indicated the link between the four *voladores,* each circling the pole thirteen times, and the Mesoamerican era of fifty-two years (4 x 13 = 52). In the pre-Hispanic *Códice Fernández Leal,* four *voladores* are shown, each dressed in a bird mask (eagle's headdress) (fig. 119). The eighteenth-century *Clavijero* also provided a sketch of *voladores,* in which the four flyers are completely disguised as birds (fig. 120). Nowadays the

115. *Voladores* climbing the pole. Cuetzalan, 1972.

voladores' dance costume generally consists of imitation silk breeches, usually coming to below the knee, with *mascadas*—triangular colored scarves or shawls—secured crosswise over the chest. This dance outfit is worn over the *traje indio,* the typical dress of Mexican peasants consisting of a cotton tunic shirt and trousers (*calzón*). A small *maxtlatl*—Aztec loin cloth—hangs from the waist as a reminder of pre-Hispanic times. On his head each dancer wears a small conical crown from which many colored ribbons dangle.

While this is, generally speaking, the outfit worn by the Nahua and Totonac *voladores,* the Otomí *volador* of Pahuatlán flies in a bird disguise (fig. 121). After the bird costume virtually had fallen into disuse by the beginning of the twentieth century, it was revived, possibly due to the influence of North American anthropologists. In Pahuatlán the *voladores* have replaced the square frame with a six-sided one (fig. 122). so that six *voladores,* rather than four, can fly. Thus the number fifty-two no longer is significant here, although it appears to have been so in the 1940s (Toor: 320).

At other festivals the Nahua and Totonac *voladores* do not always circle the pole thirteen times before landing. During the *feria primaveral*—the spring fair held in Huauchinango to coincide with the third Friday in Lent—we saw *voladores* making more than thirteen revolutions around immensely high cement poles (fig. 123). The members of one of the two groups in Huauchinango were dressed in bird disguise while here, in contrast to the more sober, eagle-like Otomí *voladores* (fig. 119), we encountered Nahua flyers dressed in white, perhaps in imitation of the heron (fig. 124).

La danza de los voladores is a cosmic event, as one can see not only from the greetings to the four world directions but also from the way in which the *voladores* hurtle downwards. They must, as it were, recreate the link between heaven and earth, the *palo volador* acting as a bridge between upper and lower worlds. It is interesting that in the humorous drawing from the sixteenth-century Codex Durán, the *voladores* are portrayed as angels (fig. 125). Clearly, this dance is a peculiarly indigenous affair with its roots firmly in the pre-Hispanic era. In this aspect it is the antithesis of the dance of the Blacks.

La Danza de los Negritos

The dance of the "little" Blacks performed in the Sierra Norte de Puebla derives its name from the black Africans brought in as slaves by the Spaniards. Dancers dress in black velvet or flannel trousers, richly decorated with beautiful embroidery as are the *mascadas,* or shawls, worn over their tunic-shirts. The entire dance costume is worn over *camisa* and *calzón,* as with the *voladores.* The sombreros worn by the dancers are decorated with mirrored glass filaments and strings of beads. The dance steps are *zapateado,* or tap, in which the dancers wear *botines* (boots) rather than *huaraches* (sandals), thus enabling them to tap with their heels more effectively. Each dancer holds a pair of castanets and a whip, and the troupe is composed of at least twelve men including, usually, two masked buffoons (fig. 126) who often have the task of focusing the audience's attention. These buffoons are the only masked figures among the *negritos* dances of the Sierra Norte de Puebla, in contrast to the Blackmen dancers of the Tarascans (see Esser 1981: 5 ff).

In the Sierra Norte de Puebla the *negrito* dancers often carry a pole which they place upright in front of the church; they then dance around the pole, taking turns to wind ribbons off or onto the pole. It is not inconceivable that the dance of the "little" blacks was based on the European Maypole dance. The use of castanets and violin, some-

116. The *capitán,* fluting and drumming, salutes the four winds. Cuetzalan, 1972.

117. *Santiagueros* with
Santiago on a horse.
Pilate (left) and
Sabarius (right). San
Andrés Tzicuilan,
1975.

118. *Voladores* "flying"
to the ground.
Cuetzalan, 1972.

119. *Voladores. Códice Fernández Leal.*

120. Eighteenth-cen-
tury drawing of flyers
dressed as birds.
Clavijero.

121. Otomí *volador* in bird disguise. Pahuatlán, Janurary 29, 1976.

122. Six-sided frame
of the *palo volador*.
Pahuatlán, January
29, 1976.

times combined with the guitar—all musical instruments unknown to the Indians before the Spaniards arrived—has given this dance much more of a mestizo character than that possessed by the *voladores'* dance described above.

Malinche

Among the *negritos,* as well as in other dances, the *Malinche* figure, usually called *Maringuilla,* fills an important role (fig. 126). The *Malinche* is a complex figure based on the Indian mistress of Hernán Cortés, conqueror of Mexico. The Spaniards called her *Doña Marina,* but the Indian name for her was *Malintzin,* the hispanicized form of which is *Malinche.* Although sometimes regarded as a traitor to her people, she was the mother of the first mestizo, Don Martín, the son she bore to Cortés. The *Malinche* character that participates most frequently in the dances, for example those performed by the *acatlaxqui* (reed throwers) (fig. 127), is usually portrayed either by teenager or adult males dressed in women's clothing. This disguise is meant to symbolize the treacherous, dark side of human nature. *Malinche* carries a wooden snake or a gourd containing a snake (fig. 127). The snake escapes during the dance, is chased, recaptured, and finally killed, at which point all the dancers sing of having been freed from evil. (The snake act is not always performed. In practice, the dance performance may be spread out over several days, often far apart; and the killing of the snake takes place at the finale.)

La Danza de los Santiagos or Santiagueros

One can very easily discern this mingling of two cultures in a frequently performed dance devoted to portraying the entire *conquista,* or Conquest. In this event, in which long speeches have to be learned by dancers coming to town from other locations, it is not the Spaniards' conquest of Mexico that occupies central place but rather the *reconquista*—the winning back of Spain from the Moors by Christian forces. The monks and colonists introduced the story of the struggle between Moors and Christians, so closely connected with the history of Spain. On the one hand, the church could demonstrate the triumphant might of Christendom, while on the other those Indian dancers who represented the Christians could imagine themselves to be the victors, a psychological advantage, perhaps, for a people who only a short while before had been beaten by the Spaniards and reduced to a subordinate state. For this and many reasons, the Conquest theme has enjoyed great success from the time of its introduction. In nearly all regions of Mexico, and certainly in those with relatively large Indian populations, a dance based on the *conquista* theme is performed at major ceremonies.

The dance of St. James, or rather the dance of St. James' devotees, is one of the *conquista* dances often performed in the Sierra Norte de Puebla. Santiago was the patron saint of Spain and of the Spanish soldiers who invoked his name repeatedly as they went into battle. The saint made a deep impression on the Indians, who soon adopted him as one of their own patrons. In the process he also lent his name to one of the most popular dances in Mexico. Although for us the word "dance" immediately suggests music and dance steps, the *conquista* dance also includes mock battles and dialogues, which may be lengthy. A remarkable aspect of the dance is that the Moors are sometimes replaced by Roman soldiers led by Sabarius, Pilate's general. In such cases *Sabario* and *Pilato* both appear as characters in the dance. This occurs in the Sierra Norte de Puebla, where the *santiagos* or *santiagueros* always make their appearance at festivals held in honor of patron saints as,

123. Two *palos voladores*. Huauchinango, 1976.

124. The bird-flyer. Huauchinango, 1976.

125. *Voladores* as angels. Codex Durán (after Mompradé de Gutiérrez, 1977).

for example, those of St. Andrew on November 30, St. Michael, Archangel, on September 29, St. Francis of Assisi on October 4, and on the day of the Immaculate Conception of the Virgin, December 8. The *santiago* character has a white horse made of wood, which he wears round his waist so that he appears to be riding (fig. 117). *Santiago*, in contrast to *Pilato, Sabario*, or the soldiers, never wears a mask. His dance costume, consisting mainly of red imitation silk with yellow trim, again is worn over the Mexican peasant's tunic-shirt and trousers. The most striking elements in *Sabario's* dance costume are the headdress, mask, shield, and festive sash, the *xochipayo*. *Sabario's* headdress, which often hangs down his back, is fastened to the back of his head by a cord (fig. 117). The headdress is an elongated triangle made of a wooden frame covered with glued paper, to which elements such as fiberglass plumes, gold-paper stars, ribbons, and real feathers are attached. The wooden mask is often worn on the forehead rather than the face (fig. 117). The mask is easily recognized by the distinctive slits—two for the eyes and one for the mouth, and two holes for the nostrils. Eyes, eyebrows, moustache, and chin are painted in gold on a red background (fig. 129). The mask's lower edges are surrounded by a beard made from a semicircle of white cotton yarn trimmed on the underside with a wide pleated strip of cotton cloth and a small pleated band of colored imitation silk on the upper side.

Pilato may also wear a bearded mask, but the beard is much smaller than that of the *Sabario* figure. It may be that representations of beards emphasize the European origins of the *santiagueros*, since beards have rarely been fashionable among indigenous males. *Sabario's* red-painted wooden shield—he is the only figure to carry a shield—bears the superimposed image of a golden sun with silver rays, with

the most striking element hanging from the middle (fig. 129). This is a piece of hand woven material that reminds one of the belts worn in the days before Columbus, just as the apron represents a memory of the pre-Hispanic loin cloth. When the *Santiago* dance ends to the sound of flute and drum, *Santiago Caballero*—Santiago on his horse—defeats his adversaries: Pilate, Sabarius, and all the heathens are converted to Christianity, and all's well that ends well.

La Danza de los Quetzales

This brief survey of dances from the Sierra Norte de Puebla would be incomplete without the dance of the *Quetzales*, though no masked characters figure in this dance. The dance of the *Quetzales* is one of the main dances—if not *the* diagnostic dance—of the Cuetzalan region, which together with the area around Huauchinango is most thickly populated with Nahuas. The dance, pre-Hispanic in origin, in which the dancers greet the four world quarters, is supposedly named in honor of the quetzal bird whose long tail feathers are thought to be symbolized in the dancers' large headdresses (fig. 128). Although this seems a plausible explanation the source of the name of the dance can also be found in the name of the small town itself—Cuetzalan—which in earlier documents had been spelled Quetzal(l)an. Thus, the title may mean the dance "from Quetzalan." This seems the more plausible explanation, as the dance is found only in and around Cuetzalan. It is also true, however, that the quetzal bird gave its name to Cuetzalan, as the town's emblem—past and present—shows. It is displayed, for instance, on the occasion of the crowning of *La Reina de los Huipiles*—the queen of the Indian women's traditional costume (fig. 131).

The dance of the *quetzales* is accompanied by one man playing flute and

127. *Acatlaxqui* dancers with *Malinche* in front of the basilica of Guadalupe. Mexico, D. F., 1975.

126. *Negritos* with two buffoons and *Malinche*. San Andrés Tzicuilan, 1969.

128. *Quetzal* dancers
on their way to
church. San Andrés
Tzicuilan, 1969.

129. A bearded *Sa-
bario* mask made by
Sr. Pablo Huerta.
Cuetzalan, 1977.
Rijksmuseum voor
Volkenkunde, Leiden.

130. *Santiagueros* with
the *xochipayo*, the
ceremonial sash.
Quetzal dancers in
background. Zacati-
pan, December 8,
1975.

131. Use of quetzal
bird and bunch of
quetzal feathers as an
indication of Cuetza-
lan/Quetzallan equi-
valency. Cuetzalan,
October 4, 1972.

132. *Quetzal* dancer in church doorway. San Andrés Tzicuilan, 1969.

drum together. Each dance group consists of ten to twelve males and may even include young boys. During the dance each performer usually carries a handkerchief and always carries a rattle made of two gourds filled with seeds and fastened to a stick. Decorations made from colored metallic paper are glued to the gourds, and the same decorations adorn the dancers' head-dresses—the most striking part of the dance costume (fig. 132). This head-dress, the *corona de quetzal,* consists of a large wheel with a piece cut out for the conical headpiece. The spokes, about sixty in number, are made of *ocote* (pine wood) or *taro* (bamboo). Ribbons of colored metallic paper are woven between the spokes and wound around the ends, and chicken feathers are stuck on with beeswax. The total effect is one of rays or plumage, and in spite of the considerable size of the headdress the dancer manages to move around with great adroitness.

As usual the dance costume is worn over tunic-shirt and trousers. It consists of two colored *mascadas* crossed over the chest and a pair of imitation silk breeches. The breeches, usually red in color, are trimmed on the back of the legs in deep yellow. As a reminder of pre-Hispanic times the quetzal dancer wears a short apron round the waist as a kind of *maxtlatl.* This apron matches the breeches in material and ornamentation. The costume, musical accompaniment on flute and drum played by one man, and the greetings to the four world quarters bears a great resemblance to the *danza de los voladores.* It is also patently obvious that the roots of these dances lie in pre-Hispanic times.

In the Sierra Norte de Puebla the dances give a clear demonstration that Mexican culture is a mestizo culture. This mingling of two cultural patterns, one from southern Europe and the other from indigenous Mexico, adds an extra dimension to present-day Mexican society.

Notes

1. In pre-Hispanic times, Nahuatl speakers comprised one of the most numerous and influential ethnic groups. The Mexica (also known as Aztecs), founders of the great city of Tenochtitlán (now Mexico City), were Nahuatl speakers. The Aztecs dominated a vast tributary empire which embraced an enormous part of central Mexico. After conquest by the Spaniards in 1521, many Nahuatl speakers continued to dwell in their pre-Conquest locations. Today we find approximately 1,500,000 persons in Mexico who still speak this indigenous language. In Guerrero approximately 130,000 Nahuatl speakers continue to draw upon their ancient heritage, which they bring to their twentieth-century experiences to form a complex syncretic culture.

ask Making in Guerrero

Ruth D. Lechuga

Of the four ethnic groups living within the state of Guerrero—the Mixtecs and Amuzgos, who also live in adjacent Oaxaca, and the Tlapanecs and Nahuatls of central Guerrero—the last constitutes the largest and most vigorous indigenous group of the region, and its members are important carriers of modern Nahuatl culture.[1]

An outstanding feature of Nahuatl culture is the performance of a great variety of dances, many of which are shared by neighboring Tlapanecs and Mixtecs, who adapt them to their own use. During the last fifty years many indigenous groups have been assimilated by the general Mexican culture, but even in these mestizo towns many dances are still performed. The tradition has survived even where Spanish is sub-

stituted for the indigenous language.

Among the many early Colonial dances performed are a number of local interpretations of the Moors and Christians cycle (fig. 133). These include dances of santiagos (followers of Saint James), *moros y cristianos* (Moors and Christians), or simply *moros. Moros* may be further differentiated as *moros chinos* (curly-haired Moors) or *moros cabezones* (big-headed Moors), according to the type of headdress used. In some places they are called *retos* (challenges), which in turn may be Challenges of Saint James or Challenges of Moors. The Twelve Peers of France is another variation in the cycle. Related to the Moors and Christians cycle is a group of dances that reenact the conquest of Mexico, but with Indians in

place of Moors as the heathens to be defeated. These are called *el cortés* or *el marqués* (the marquis), referring to the leader of the conquerors, Hernán Cortés; or *la malinche,* after the Indian woman who was Cortés's mistress and interpreter. Other related dances are *los gachupines,* a contemptuous name for Spaniards, and *el tenochtle,* referring to an inhabitant of Tenochtitlán (now Mexico City) at the time of the Conquest. Morality plays featuring such characters as devils, angels, saints, death, and sin are very popular in the state of Guerrero and were also introduced early in the Colonial era (fig. 134).

Other dances are pre-Hispanic in origin, although additional features have been added from time to time. Such is the case with the "Old Ones," important representations everywhere in Mexico, which are enacted in Guerrero and called *huehues* (fig. 135). Dancers in the role of animals are ubiquitous. The *tigre,* really a jaguar, is the central character in many dance sequences (fig. 136).[2] In Guerrero dances he is usually accompanied by a dog, deer, coyote, or vultures. Other animal dances include fish, alligators (fig. 137), turtles, birds, goats (fig. 138), donkeys, mules, bulls, and many more. The dances abound with references to daily life: the *tlacololeros* (farmers) plow the fields (fig. 139), the *tecuanis* hunt the jaguar, the *vaqueros* (cowboys) drive the bulls, and so on; inventiveness and creativity appear to be limitless.

Some dances display a keen sense of humor as well as a critical attitude toward society, as in the case of the *mecos* (savages) performed in Mochitlán.[3] *Mecos* wear red masks with black stripes and feather headdresses. In the course of the dance a white-faced and a red-faced priest fight over the souls of the "savages." The red-faced priest wins (fig. 140). In many of the current dances a character called the *huetzquistle*[4] accompanies the group. While dancing slightly apart, he entertains the audience and at the same time maintains the open space needed by the dancers. He sometimes plays a native drum, the *teponaxtle.* His role is half-serious, half-comical, and, to a great extent, sacred (fig. 141).

Within the social and ritual life of each village, dances and their associated masks play an important role that is independent of their dramatic content. There is a fixed schedule for performances by dance groups. Each dancer usually dresses in the house of the person in charge of the group who may, at the same time, be the *maestro* (teacher) of the dance. This leader usually blesses his charges with *copal* (incense), which he has burning on his home altar. All pray for a short time and then march through the village streets led by the *maestro,* who often also plays the music (fig. 142). The next stop is the church to beseech the saint's permission before initiating other activities.

Whenever the saint's image is carried through the streets, dancers, together with the whole population of the town, form part of the procession. Flower offerings, flags, candles, and incense burners are carried by the paraders (fig. 143). Sometimes a huge floral ornament intended for the church portal is paraded prior to its installation.

In Mochitlán no images of saints are carried in the procession. Instead, the floral frontispiece for the church is carried together with a huge palm mat adorned with flower garlands. Also included in the parade are carts carrying allegorical figures. Women carrying plates heaped with food emerge dancing from the house of the *mayordomo*—the man in charge of feeding the whole village for the duration of the fiesta. All the dance groups join in this parade (fig. 144). When the parade is over, everyone assembles at the *mayordomo's* house to eat, dance, and play music (fig. 145). During the rest of the day the dancers perform at the church-

2. The jaguar has been a powerful divinity since the time of the ancient Olmecs, at least one thousand years before Christ.

3. *Mecos* is a contraction of *chichimeca,* the term for hunting groups who came from the northern part of Mexico in pre-Hispanic times.

4. No precise translation of *huetzquistle* is known. María Teresa Sepúlveda Herrera (1982: 53) employs the term *hueyquistle,* which she translates as "old." All of my informants in Guerrero pronounce the word as *huetzquistle,* however.

133. An angel, Saint James, and a Moor in a dance of *Santiagos.* Mochitlán, 1976.

yard (fig. 146), in the main plaza, and throughout the streets of the village.

Civic celebrations as well as saints' days are occasions for fiestas. The Sixteenth of September, anniversary of Mexico's independence, is usually commemorated with parades of schoolchildren. These sometimes include carts with allegorical figures representing *la patria* (the fatherland) or *la raza* (the Indian race). Occasionally mock battles between "Mexicans" and "Spaniards" are enacted. In the town of Chapa these battles are performed, but in addition there are two other groups of masked actors. One represents the *toreros* (bullfighters)—many of whom wear devil masks—who fight against a wooden bull's head fixed to the waist of one of the dancers (fig. 147). The other group is called the *mercaderes* (merchants), masked characters who parade through the village streets on foot or mounted on donkeys (fig. 148). Baldomero Mendoza, a mask maker from Chapa, believes that this performance dates from the time of the Mexican Revolution (1910), when merchants were frequently attacked by robbers. It is also possible that these *mercaderes* refer to even earlier times, when mule drivers carried Chinese goods from Acapulco to Mexico City, or more remote ones still, when Aztec traders traversed the country on fixed routes.

In the town of Teloloapan the highlight of the Sixteenth of September celebration is the *mojiganga de los diablos* (mummery of devils). In other villages of the same region devils also appear for Sixteenth of September celebrations, but in Teloloapan the local authorities take an exceptionally active role, organizing an annual contest with rewards for the best disguise. As a result of this competition, devil masks have become increasingly elaborate and intricately adorned. New ones are worn each year. Mask maker Fidel de la Fuente, Jr. carves the masks, but

each dancer innovates his ornaments to suit his own taste and in hopes of winning a prize (fig. 149).

Clearly, the use of masks is widespread in Guerrero. It is an art form that is very much alive and likely to remain so as long as it continues to form part of people's customs and activities. The masks used in all these dances in Guerrero are as varied as the characters they represent. In many cases they are works of strong plastic expression. Not all of them are made of wood. In some instances, the *tigre* and other animal impersonators wear leather masks, and in Acatlán, a village near the important town of Chilapa, several people are engaged in making masks of papier mâché.

The mask maker occupies an important niche in his village. Usually he invests only part of his time in carving masks, but his services are no less significant. The splendor of a dance depends upon his ability, and his knowledge is manifold. Besides his technical skills, he must be capable of imparting a distinctive face, based on the tradition of his village, to each of the characters taking part in a given dance. He knows exactly what each character should wear and which accoutrements—such as swords, crosses, or the little horse worn tied to the waist of Saint James—are appropriate. In many instances the mask maker bequeaths his art to a son or grandson, who learns from childhood simply by observing his mentor at work (fig. 150). If for some reason a village is left without a mask maker, it will be considered a serious loss and may even, in some instances, modify the whole structure of the fiesta system.

Some craftsmen, in addition to carving the masks needed for dances within their village, make commercial, usually fantastic masks that differ radically from those used traditionally. This type of work probably has always existed throughout Mexico to serve the sou-

5. The late Donald Cordry was a close personal friend of mine and it is not my intention to detract from his memory. But for the sake of future work on the subject it is necessary to distinguish between real dance masks and those decorative sculptures that are sometimes mistaken for them.

venir market. During the last ten or twelve years, however, manufacture of masks for an alien clientele has developed into a sizeable industry in the state of Guerrero, resulting in the production of a great number of rather odd masks. Dealers encourage production of these pieces because they command high prices from those avid collectors who seek that which is different and rare.

But the practice of collecting masks without documentation appears limited to the uninitiated collector. Nowadays any serious buyer will want to know where a mask comes from and in which dance it is used. Dealers, however, take great pains to make their merchandise look old and well worn and will invent names of dances and even of villages in which the masks have supposedly been stored for a long time. In some instances, the collector himself will unconsciously suggest certain motifs to the dealer because these fulfill his expectation of finding a particular symbolism. When he receives the mask for which he was longing—perhaps custom-made for him—he will take it as proof of his theory.

It must be emphasized that many of these pieces are impressive works of art, reflecting extraordinarily high levels of craftsmanship and creativity. In the fine contemporary handling of paint on *amate* bark paper, a new commercial invention in Guerrero, one is tempted to associate the images and patterns that emerge with pre-Hispanic codices. But *amate* bark paper painting is no more an example of the continuity of codex painting than are these souvenir masks part of indigenous tradition. Beautiful as they may be, these commercial pieces are meaningless to their producers and to members of the communities in which they are made.

When Donald Cordry's book, *Mexican Masks,* was published in 1980—the first publication to attempt a serious discussion of Mexican masks—the poten-

tial danger of mask misrepresentation became public.[5] Some of the fantastic masks and hitherto unknown dances discussed in the Cordry book raised serious questions of authenticity. The Museo Nacional de Artes e Industrias Populares in Mexico City decided that it was necessary to investigate Cordry's claims, and I was commissioned to do the work. Nearly thirty years of observation of fiestas in Guerrero had shown me a fundamentally constant employment of dance patterns and types of masks. Cordry's findings seemed to contradict that research.

In the course of my investigations I talked with mask makers from Guerrero and showed them pictures of masks in the Cordry book and asked them to identify them. The area that includes Ostotitlán, Apaxtla, Campo Morado, and La Parota had been, according to Cordry, one of the most prodigious mask-making regions in the past. I first visited Ostotitlán and Apaxtla. Some very ornate bearded masks, as well as face masks of alligators, were said by Cordry to have been made there some fifteen to forty years ago. I talked to many people, including an eighty-six-year-old carpenter from Ostotitlán who had made many masks in the past and remembered seeing dances as long ago as when he was ten years old. He stated firmly that he had never made or seen anything as intricately carved as the example in the Cordry book (1980: 200, Plate 247). Further, many dances that continue to be performed in both villages are the usual ones such as Nativity plays, jaguar dances, and Challenges of the Twelve Peers of France that do not employ the type of masks that Cordry represented.

According to Cordry, La Parota was a very productive place, where, besides masks of silver, big masks of dwarves were made for a rain-petitioning dance (1980: 139, Plate 188). A group of masks described as "harvest celebration" masks also were said to

134. Devils' dance.
Devils with "women"
(men masked as
women). Petlacapa
(near Tlapa), 1980.

have come from there (1980: 204–5, Plates 252–56). I have been to two places in Guerrero, each called La Parota, and neither of them is near Campo Morado. Both are very small settlements, smaller even than villages. No dances are performed there; they have neither churches nor patron saints' days to celebrate. If they want to participate in a fiesta, they must travel to a nearby town.

After some rather fruitless attempts I finally had my first bit of luck, which in turn suggested to me the method to use in the future. I had known mask maker Baldomero Mendoza of Chapa since 1976. He has always carved decorative masks for sale, as well as dance masks used in his village. He, together with his son-in-law Santiago Martínez Delgado, makes the masks used in the Independence Day celebration, the Fishermen's dance, and other dances. The version of the Fishermen's dance as performed in Chapa features a Mermaid with mask and fishtail and an alligator step-in mask for the so-called *caimán,* who uses a face mask too (fig. 151). Another masked personality participating in the dance (not shown in Cordry) is the "old fisherman." The dance is performed in Chapa on Monday of Holy Week. When I showed Cordry's book to Sr. Mendoza, he identified some masks as his own work. One of the masks he identified is the so-called *terroncillo* in the Cowboys dance (1980: 239, Plate 294), which Cordry mistakenly placed in the village of Zacatlanzillo. Sr. Mendoza told me that because he had made it originally for himself, he hardened the horsehair on top to improve its appearance (photo, 225).

The masks described above were made by Sr. Mendoza for use in his own village. Others were commissioned by a dealer from Iguala. Looking at an illustration of a devil mask (1980: 141, Plate 189), Sr. Mendoza exclaimed, "What have they done to my mask? When I delivered it, it was new and

135. Performance of
huehues. Mochitlán,
1963.

136. A *tigre* and his hunter in the dance of *los maizos*. Mochitlán, 1962.

137. Fishermen's dance. The man on the right has an alligator fixed to his waist; the other is a fisherman. Mochitlán, 1964.

Two masks collected by Donald Cordry. The so-called "*terroncillo*" mask of the Cowboy dance (top) and the Devil mask, both made by Baldomero Mendoza. Courtesy University of Texas Press, Austin.

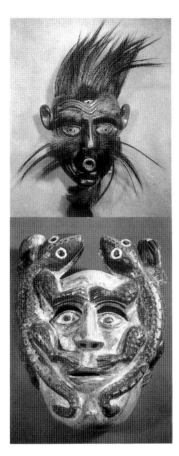

138. A goat from the *chivos* (goats) dance. Atzacoaloyan, 1963.

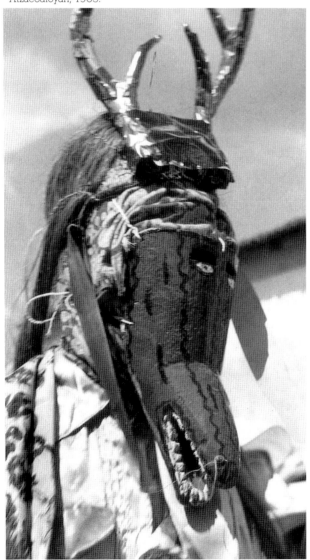

nicely finished. Why did they rub the paint off?" To him, as an honest craftsman, careful workmanship was of the utmost importance; he found it incomprehensible that a mask should be of greater worth if it appeared to be old and very used (photo, left).

Sr. Mendoza was very pleased to be shown two carvings of tall, multifaced casques that he had done some years ago (1980: 42, Plate 50). He did not believe that he would ever make anything like that again, because, he said, such big tree trunks are no longer found. He explained that on the rear of the pieces he had repeated the same faces that appear on the front. He could not have known this had he not been the creator of these works.

Santiago Martínez Delgado, Sr. Mendoza's son-in-law, has carved many distinctive devil masks used in Chapa during Mexico's independence celebration. Cordry mistakenly attributed some of this work to the late nineteenth century, though the evidence points clearly to the young carver (1980: 130, Plate 181). At the time of my visit, Santiago had been working in the United States for about three years. Nevertheless his sons, wife, and father-in-law were all firm in asserting that these devil masks were Santiago's work. Many times, on separate occasions, we looked together at Cordry's book, page by page, and each time they identified the same masks as Baldomero's and Santiago's work. Those discussed above were but a few outstanding examples selected from the many masks they pointed out to me.

Tixtla, a town located near Chilpancingo, the state capital, has traditionally provided surrounding villages, and even the capital, with dance masks. In 1945 Donald Cordry met Tixtla's mask maker, Nolberto Abrajám, and considered him to be one of the ablest indigenous wood carvers. In his book he shows him together with his son Ruperto, both since deceased (1980: 103,

139. A performance of *tlacololero*. *Tlacolol* means the preparation of the fields on the mountain side. Mochitlán, 1976.

140. A dance of *mecos*. Mochitlán, 1962.

141. *Maromeros* dance
(tight rope dancers).
Dancers are joined by
two clowning *huetz-
quistles*. Acatlán,
1970.

Figures 144–45). In 1970 Ruperto told me that he made masks both for decoration and for use in dances. The masks of both father and son have always been distinctively and delicately carved. At present, Ruperto's son Ernesto and his grandson Adelfo are both mask makers. All four generations of these mask makers appear in Cordry's book.

A mask with female features and blue wings framing the face, supposedly representing an angel (1980: 236, Plate 291), is the work of the youngest mask maker in the family, Adelfo, but is attributed by Cordry to the state of Puebla. While Adelfo stated that the mask was meant as "pure fantasy," Cordry attributed it to the *pastorela* dance. The features of this mask are actually very similar in style to Ruperto's work. Adelfo is very proud to have learned the trade from his grandfather and tries to make masks that conform as closely as possible to the family's traditional style.

The harvest celebration masks (1980: 204–5, Plates 252–56), claimed by Cordry to have been made by members of the Bahena family around the turn of the century and worn in autumnal dances, are in truth the work of Adelfo's father, Ernesto, who made the set at the request of a well-known dealer who had asked him to invent something "different." Never before had Ernesto seen any masks that were similar, nor did he know of any dance related to them.

Ernesto's father Ruperto was the carver of a Moor mask (1980: 232, Plate 284) wrongly identified in Cordry's book as coming from Mochitlán. But he made fantasy masks too, as he himself had told me. One of these is illustrated by Cordry (1980: 156, Plate 201) and was recognized as Ruperto's work by his son and grandson. ·Adelfo's great-grandfather Nolberto was greatly admired by Cordry. A very carefully carved mask of a so-called horned serpent and a step-in figure were both his

142. José Colasillo,
maestro of the
machitos dance (little
mule drivers), leading
his pupils through the
streets. Zitlala, 1981.

work (1980: 194, Plate 241). His great-grandson Adelfo again described these as fantasy masks and said they were never intended for use by a dancer, though Cordry's information has them used in a rain-petitioning dance. But Nolberto, able mask maker that he was, also made a splendid set of masks that performed in both *los manueles* and the *los mudos* (the mute ones) dances (1980: 246, Plate 305).

One of the most puzzling issues raised by Cordry has to do with masks coming from Guerrero (but never actually seen in earlier times) said to have been made by a hypothetical mask maker named José Rodríguez (1980: 175, Plate 219). One day a man named Jesús Blanco, from Quechultenango, came to our museum (Museo Nacional de Artes e Industrias Populares) saying that he was the creator of all the so-called Rodríguez masks and that he could deliver any number of them, either unpainted, painted, or with a patina that would make them look old (fig. 152). With him was Aurelio Anota, who was introduced as a co-worker. Aurelio is from the nearby village of Tepexicotlán.

When I went to visit Jesús, I found that he was well known as a mask maker in Quechultenango, as were his father and some of his brothers. On that occasion he was unable to produce any "Rodríguez" masks. At a later date, Aurelio Anota revealed that it was his brother, Cecilio, also from the village of Tepexicotlán, who carved fantasy masks of the "Rodríguez" type at the request of a dealer from Mexico City. A brother of Jesús Blanco's had introduced him to this dealer. The Anota family did not paint the masks but delivered them to Jesús Blanco to finish. I was informed later by a friend, Bernhard Hanreich, that still another mask maker, this one from Mazatlán, Guerrero, a small village very near Tepexicotlán, also carved sculptures of this type.

Cecilio Anota makes not only "Rodríguez" masks but also others that supposedly come from Jaleaca and are said to date from the mid-nineteenth century (1980: title page, facing Plate 1). Jaleaca is located in a completely different part of Guerrero than the region of Tlapa where Rodríguez was supposed to work. Nevertheless, Cordry thought that Rodríguez was influenced by this hypothetical earlier Jaleaca carver.

Jesús Blanco had lived for two years in the city of Iguala, where he painted and "aged" many masks that had been carved by other craftsmen. This may explain why Cordry claimed some of the pieces in his book as having been made by him, even if he had only supplied the finishing touches. Blanco did make, though, some excellent bearded sculptures (1980: 48, Plate 60).

Jesús' brother Rodolfo, in turn, is the creator of the dual-faced death masks illustrated by Cordry (1980: 40, Plate 47). I have no information about other dual masks from Guerrero, but Miguel Cruz López from Pinotepa de Don Luís, in the state of Oaxaca (shown in the book carving a twin mask; 1980: 135, Plate 186), told me that he had made such masks on request and that they were not used in dances.

In a recent publication about crafts made of wood, Manuel Gutiérrez Casillas discusses in some detail San Francisco Ozomatlán, a Nahuatl village in Guerrero (1981: 76–79). He reports that the villagers perform the *tecuani* dance, the dance of Seven Vices, the Mute Ones, the Fishermen dance, and the Mule dance. In addition to masks made for these dances, many decorative masks are produced in San Francisco Ozomatlán. The author reports that the decorative masks are not used for dances but are made exclusively for commercial purposes. Some of them are very large and are carved in the form of helmet masks with three faces (1981: 79). A helmet mask illustrated in Cor-

143. Festival procession. Tlapa, 1966.

144. Dancing with
food signals an
invitation to the home
of the *mayordomo*.

145. Dancers eating
at the house of the
mayordomo. Mochit-
lán, 1964.

146. Dancing at the
churchyard. Dance of
los manueles. Mochit-
lán, 1976.

147. A finely carved bullhead, ready to attach to any "bull-fighter." Chapa, 1976.

148. A group of
mercaderes (mer-
chants) parading for
Mexican Independence
Day. Chapa, 1976.

149. Devils performing
for the jury on a
specially prepared
platform in the central
plaza. Teloloapan,
1976.

dry's book is carved in the same style as that discussed by Manuel Gutiérrez (Cordry 1980: 190, Plates 236–37). Manuel Gutiérrez comments:

> The masks include many symbolic elements such as serpents, eagles, bats, lizards, and frogs. There are figures with wings, saints, old ones, skulls, and a mixture of Christian and indigenous symbols. The production of these masks began some ten years ago and is increasing due to enormous demand. It provides an income for approximately 110 persons counting craftsmen and intermediaries (1981: 79).

Once carved, the surface of the mask is covered with a mixture of Spanish white and glue, painted with commercial oil pigment, and then patined to make it look old (1981: 79). Some masks in Cordry's book exhibit the same facial expressions, profusion of additional elements, and elaborately carved beards and in other ways are similar to masks illustrated by Gutiérrez as coming from San Francisco Ozomatlán (1981: 77).

One object of my inquiry concerned the hammered metal masks. Thanks to Jesús Blanco, I finally found the workshop, on the outskirts of the city of Iguala, where these were made. Upon entering the workshop I saw many copper ornaments like those illustrated in the Cordry book (1980: 113, Plate 158) and said to be from Xochipala. By applying heat and different acids to the copper, either a bright surface or a green, oxidized one may be achieved, depending on the customer's desire (fig. 153). The craftsmen in this workshop were Máximo Juárez Grande, Javier Juárez Ortega, and Isaías Olvera. They used to make gold jewelry, always an important craft in Iguala. When the cost of gold rose these artisans began to make metal masks. At first they were very reluctant to discuss their craft with me, but at my second visit they told me bluntly that all of the metal masks sold as old ones had been made in their workshop. Dealers had brought them a book with pictures of wooden masks

from which they were encouraged to copy freely in order to produce the metal ones. They never painted the copper masks. Again, it was Jesús Blanco who lined them with cloth, painted them, and gave them special treatment to make them look old (1980: 113, Plate 157). They reported that on one occasion a dealer had brought them some sheets of silver and ordered a set of masks to be made from them. Trying to test the truthfulness of their information, I asked if they had dated any of these silver masks. They replied that they had done so with only one, the date reading 1902. This date matches the one supplied by Cordry. I do not believe they could have had this information had they not been the creators of the masks.

It is necessary to point out that absolutely all of the masks recognized by the carvers I visited were represented by the dealers who sold them to Cordry as coming from villages other than, and usually very far from, the actual villages of their origin. It is well known that Cordry was unable to travel for many years and had to rely on the information that was brought to him. It seems clear to me that the desire to make large profits may have motivated some mask dealers to stoop to deception. *Mexican Masks* by Donald Cordry indicates how much investigation still has to be done. My inquiry represents just a beginning. As Cordry himself stated, "Thus I hope that, by making people more aware of the richness and complexity of the Mexican mask culture, this work will engender further studies of this uniquely beautiful art form" (1980: 6).

150. Mask maker José Antonio Gabriel and son at work. Temalacatzingo, 1975.

151. Alligator and
mermaid, Fishermen's
dance. Chapa, 1981.

152. Jesús Blanco
with an unpainted
"Rodríguez" mask.
Quechultenango, 1981.

153. Workshop with craftsmen hammering metal masks. One mask is almost complete, while another, on the floor, has been roughly chiseled. The features on a third mask have been sketched prior to commencement of work. Iguala, 1981.

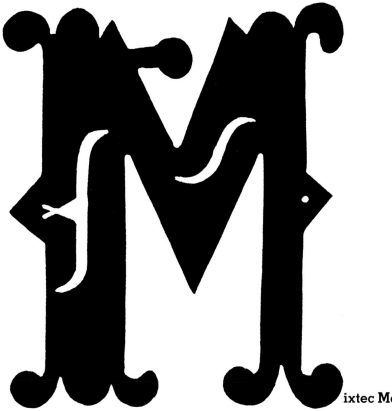

Mixtec Masking Traditions:
Juxtlahuaca, Oaxaca

Betty Ann Brown

Two children stand in a doorway in silent anticipation. One steps out to look down the wide, dusty street. Suddenly, the quiet is shattered by exploding fireworks and tinny, rhythmic music. A procession comes into view, and the child knows it includes not only the honored elders of his village but also the priest from a far-off city and, above all, the figures of Saint James and the Virgin Mary. As the child turns to draw his sister out with him, he thinks of his father, who is one of the six men carrying the Saint James statue. "It is an honor and an offering," thinks the child, and he nods in unspoken approval as he reaches for his sister's hand. But this serious mood is suddenly transformed into merriment: a masked clown grabs

the boy and whirls him in the air, laughing and joking in a squeaky falsetto. The clown returns the boy to the doorway and shakes a plastic doll at the sister in mock admonition. His antics transform the otherwise solemn ceremony in honor of the village's patron saint into one of laughter and entertainment (fig. 155).

The masked clown is a pivotal character whose humorous behavior is just as important to the fiesta as the prayers spoken when the procession pauses at a street-side altar. Of his whole absurdly funny costume, it is the mask that most directly identifies him and signals his clown role. The black wooden mask with its long, unruly goat's-hair beard transforms him from a familiar neigh-

Notes

Note: For a shorter version of this article see Brown (1983).

1. See Dahlgren de Jordan (1954), Ravicz and Romney (1967), and Romney and Romney (1966) for the most comprehensive published treatments of the Mixtec peoples.

bor to a fiesta character. Centuries before, the clown's ancestors also used masks to transform everyday reality into something special and magical. This essay discusses the clown, his masked companions at this and other fiestas, and their antecedents in Indian and European cultures.

The clown and the children are Mixtec Indians. They live in the eastern half of the state of Oaxaca, Mexico, in a valley surrounded by tall, arid mountains.[1] (Some Mixtecs also live in the adjoining states of Puebla and Guerrero.) Although the mountains have isolated the Mixtecs into relatively small villages, there has always been extensive communication between the valley communities, and the Mixtecs share many cultural characteristics. Most Mixtecs today, like their ancestors, are farmers. Their main crops continue to be corn, beans, squash, tomatoes, and chile peppers. Other foods are purchased at the village open-air markets or at local stores. These stores are often simply the front rooms of homes, which have been redesigned to include shelves laden with canned goods and soda pops and a counter tended by a family member. For special purchases, the Mixtecs take busses along winding and often unpaved mountain roads to the nearest city. These cities are industrialized and populated with people who, in lifestyle at least, share less and less with their traditional Mixtec neighbors.

Most of the city-dwellers are mestizos, or people of mixed European and Indian descent. There are mestizos in the Mixtec villages as well. The mestizos can be distinguished from the Mixtecs economically and visually. Instead of farming, they often work in salaried jobs. Mestizos typically hold village positions such as telegraphist and pharmacist. Mestizo men and women both wear European-style clothing. Although the younger Mixtec men are today adopting European clothing, the older ones still wear the white cotton shirts and pants characteristic of the Mexican Indian male. Mixtec women wear skirts of handwoven wool and white cotton blouses with embroidered yokes. While many mestizo houses are made with cement blocks, Mixtec homes are often adobe, the same material Mixtecs of hundreds of years ago used to build their homes.

The Ancient Mixtecs

The ancient Mixtecs were renowned craftsmen. The largest collection of ancient Mixtec arts was spectacularly uncovered when Mexican archaeologist Alfonso Caso found Tomb 7 at the site of Monte Albán (Caso 1969). Although Monte Albán was originally built and inhabited by the Zapotec Indians of Oaxaca (Bernal 1965), Caso's discoveries proved that Mixtecs later re-used some of the Zapotec buildings. Tomb 7 once a Zapotec burial place, was later used to house the remains of a Mixtec noble. And with this noble were buried delicate lost-wax-cast gold pieces (one piece—a death's head pectoral—illustrates the contact between the Mixtecs and Zapotecs by including dates in both of their calendrical systems), jewelry of all sorts of precious stone, intricately carved bones, tiny cups of rock crystal, and brightly polychromed ceramic vessels.

The paintings on the Tomb 7 ceramics are in the same style as the ancient Mixtec books, called codices, which record the religion and history of pre-European times (Caso 1965). Elaborate ceremonies and their priestly participants are illustrated with Mixtec dates for these events indicated by hieroglyphic notations. Events of the genealogical and political history of the Mixtec ruling class are also dated. Codex Nuttall, for example, records the numerous conquests of the Mixtec ruler named 8 Deer-Jaguar Claw. The locale of each conquest is illustrated with what is called a "place sign," such as a hill drawn with a visual clue

2. Codex Nuttall, now in the British Museum, was published in 1902 by Zelia Nuttall. This edition has been reissued by Dover Publications (1975). Smith (1973) is the authoritative source on the analysis of Mixtec place signs, such as those in Codex Nuttall.
3. See Cancian (1965) and Smith (1977) on the economics of fiesta-sponsoring organizations in other parts of Middle America.
4. Ricard's *La conquête spirituelle du Méxique* (1933) is the classic work on the religious conquest of Mexico. Jorge Klor de Alva (University of California, Santa Cruz) has recently finished a dissertation that reconsiders Ricard's work.
5. This is made especially clear on pages v, v through xxx, and 85 through 146 of Romney and Romney's book (1966).

indicating which particular hill is indicated.[2] One of 8 Deer's conquests is a hill on which a stone mask is tied (fig. 156). This mask is turquoise with a large red dot on the cheek. Drawn in profile, it has a flat horizontal forehead line and broad overall proportions. Above the mask is a spear indicating that Hill-of-the-Mask had already been conquered by 8 Deer. Although 8 Deer's conquests in the eleventh century united much of the Mixtec region, the unification was only temporary (Clark 1912; Spores 1967: 67). When the Aztec imperialist extension of the late fifteenth century brought them to Oaxaca, they found the Mixtecs organized into what may be considered "city-states," which were only unified by the family ties of the ruling class.

The Spanish Conquest of the Mixtecs occurred in the sixteenth century. Although the Spanish Colonial bureaucracy set up a state government in the capital of Oaxaca City, each Mixtec village retained a local political hierarchy. The village hierarchy became two-fold, with a secular government reflecting Spanish prototypes and a religious government incorporating much of the native system. The religious governments of today include neighborhood chapel societies and religious fraternities (*cofradías*) dedicated to serving the village patron saint. Such organizations sponsor the Mixtec fiestas in which masked dancers appear.[3]

Mexican Fiestas
Mixtec fiestas are syncretic. That is, they combine aspects of both the native religion and the Catholicism introduced by the Spanish conquerors. Soon after the military conquest came Franciscan, Augustinian, and Dominican friars, who effected a religious conquest of the indigenous populations of Mexico.[4] The friars soon realized that one of the most popular and successful ways of carrying out the conversion of so many thousands of people was through dramatic

reenactments of the major aspects of religious mystery. The religious dramas were often embodied in major events of Spanish history, particularly the *reconquista* (the wars between the Spanish Christians and the invading Moors, who were not ousted from the Iberian Peninsula until 1492). Fray Motolinia gives us a description of such a religious-historical dance drama during the 1538 Easter celebrations in Tlaxcala, a Nahuatl-speaking Indian town in central Mexico. In this case, the event reenacted was not the *reconquista* per se but a battle in which the Spanish Christians won Jerusalem from the Moors (Foster 1950: 111).

We do not have a comparable account of Colonial Mixtec ceremonies, and little has been written on contemporary Mixtec fiestas. Romney and Romney's discussion in *The Mixtecans of Juxtlahuaca* is the most comprehensive yet published, though only a brief chapter in a book more specifically aimed at understanding Mixtec child-rearing practices.[5] However, there is a growing body of literature on both Mexican fiestas in general and on Mexican masks.

Beginning with the pioneering work of Frances Toor, whose *A Treasury of Mexican Folkways* was first published in 1947, and continuing to the recent work of Bricker and Esser, fiestas have been considered among the most important aspects of Middle American native culture. Toor dedicated a large portion of her book to analyzing the content and function of fiestas, as well as to describing various fiesta songs and dances. Toor examined festival arts from all over Mexico, and the spectacular *The Ephemeral and Eternal in Mexican Folk Art* (1971) continues this tradition, as does Frederico Santiago's *Fiestas in Mexico* (1978), which lists major regional celebrations. In contrast, other recent scholars, such as Victoria Bricker, have focused on more detailed analysis of a single region.

154. The *rubios* mask, 1980.

155. The *mahoma* clowns entertain the children of Juxtla- huaca, 1980.

156. Hill-of-the-Mask
in the ancient Mixtec
book Codex Nuttall.

157. A Juxtlahuaca
diablo dancer, 1980.

Bricker's *Ritual Humor in Highland Chiapas* (1973) describes clowns from the state immediately east of Oaxaca, and her analysis gives important insight into the function and meaning of the masked clown character. While Bricker discusses the function of various festival components, other scholars have analyzed the economic structure of the fiesta system. In this light, Cancian (1965) has studied the Maya Indians of Zinacantán, and Smith, those of nearby western Guatemala. The material culture of the fiestas, and particularly the dance masks, has been described by Cordry (1973, 1980) and Moya Rubio (1974, 1978), among others.

Whatever the approach, from description of the fiesta, to analysis of its function, to interpretation of its economic basis, all scholars have agreed that Mexican fiestas of today, although ostensibly Catholic, also embody elements from the pre-European past. Little has been written on pre-European Mixtec ceremonies. (Jill Furst [1977, 1978] has analyzed rituals in the Mixtec Codex Vienna, and Nancy Troicke [1979] has dealt with Mixtec arrow ceremonies.) Even less is known of the fifteenth- and sixteenth-century traditions of mainland Spain.[6] Study of Mixtec masking traditions can therefore shed light on the ceremonial traditions of both the donor cultures—Spain and Indian America—as well as on the dramatic changes that have happened since these two cultures came into contact (see Foster 1960). To develop this study, we must return to the children in the doorway in the town of Juxtlahuaca. What was the meaning of the procession they witnessed? And who was that masked man who teased and cajoled them? To answer these questions, we will look at two types of Mixtec festivals, those dedicated to patron saints and those celebrated during Carnival.

The Santiago Fiesta of Juxtlahuaca

The saint carried by the six men, including the children's father, is Saint James, or Santiago as he is known in Mexico and Spain. Santiago is in fact the patron saint of Spain. His remains are buried in Santiago de Compostela, a major pilgrimage site in the northwestern part of that country, and it is Santiago himself who is believed to have appeared on a white horse to lead the Spanish armies in their victories during the *reconquista.* The Spaniards actually considered the conquest of Mexico an extension of the peninsular *reconquista,* and it is probably for that reason that they elected Santiago as patron of many Mexican villages, Juxtlahuaca included.

Santiago is particularly honored on July 25 of the Catholic calendar, around which date the fiesta occurs. The Juxtlahuaca Santiago festival lasts nine days, but it is anticipated by months of preparation and work. Among the hardest workers are the dancers, who perform in four groups: *chareos,* the *chilolos,* the *diablos* (devils), and the clowns.

Since Santiago led the Spanish armies of the *reconquista,* part of the fiesta honoring him reenacts this victory over the Moorish worshippers of Islam. The dancers who represent the Spanish Catholics on one side and the infidel Moors on the other are all called *chareos* (or Moors and Christians, as it is called elsewhere in Mexico) (fig. 159).[7] The *chareos* perform a line dance of mock combat. The Spaniards wear satin costumes of red and white and are led by a performer representing Santiago himself. The Moors wear varicolored outfits highlighted by long decorative capes and are led by a figure known as *mahoma* (Mohammed). The *chareos* present an elaborate dance drama that includes not only complex speeches delivered by each of the characters but also exciting imitation of battles in which the swords they carry are loudly struck together. Each of the *chareos* characters is known by his outfit and role, but to make the distinction between the "good" Christians and the

6. Very (1962) and Caro Baroja (1966) are among the very few sources on Spanish festivals.
7. See Thompson in Fraser and Cole (1969).

8. Kurath (1949, 1956) and Bode (1961) discuss the Moors and Christians in other areas of Latin America.
9. See Miller, Varner, and Brown (1975) for a discussion of possible meanings of such tusks.
10. Cordry (1980: 226) is in error when he states that the *chilolos* appear only in Juxtlahuaca. I have documented *chilolo* performances in several Mixtec towns, including, for example, Santa Rosa Caxtlahuaca, San Miguel Tlacotepec, and Tecomaxtlahuaca.

11. Similar black-faced clowns appear throughout Middle America. See Griffith (1972: 185), Blaffer (1972), and Miller, Varner, and Brown (1975).

"pagan" opponents clearer, the Moors also wear face masks of silky black fringe. Probably originally derived from ritual face pieces of African royalty (such as those still worn by the Yoruba of Nigeria),[8] the black fringe mask is today interpreted by the Mixtecs as symbolic of the fact that the Moors "have not yet seen the true light of Christianity."

Like the *chareos*, the *chilolos* is a line dance of mock combat (fig. 158). However, while the *chareos* is a direct import from Spain, the *chilolos* appears to be much more native in origin. The *chilolos* performers wear less obviously European costumes (the numerous bells tied to their ankles seem particularly native) and dance to the Indian flute and drum rather than to the brass band music that accompanies the *chareos*. In addition, the *chilolos* wear bright red wooden masks that have the flat top line and broad overall proportions of pre-Hispanic Mixtec masks (fig. 160). Other unusual characteristics of the *chilolos* masks are the black pupils, which project from the eyes so much that they are almost separate spheres and the two boomeranglike projections below the nose, which may represent either moustaches or tusks.[9] All of the Juxtlahuacan *chilolos* masks are alike, and indeed the same kind of red mask is used for line dances in numerous other Mixtec towns.[10] The *chilolos* mask is a fixed form that might have endured for centuries. Unfortunately, the Mixtec term *chilolos* eludes translation, so the exact significance of this mask remains a mystery.

In contrast, the *diablos* (devils) dancers of Juxtlahuaca are quite easily understood. The *diablos* wear cowboy-like outfits with hairy leather chaps and vests (fig. 157). They carry whips which they snap vigorously as they dance through the town. And, above all, they wear devil masks. These masks are as varied as human imagination. Some employ the traditional European image of the devil with fierce red face, pointed

ears, prominent fangs, and curling animal horns. Others are purple, orange, or brown with humorous expressions and exaggerated features. Unlike the *chilolos* masks, the *diablos* masks simply are wood and paint and have much more solemn expressions.

The *diablos* perform an animated version of the *jarabe* folk dance which, like their devil identity, has been imported from Spain. They do not enact a serious dance drama like the *chareos*, nor do they perform a set line dance like the *chilolos*. They appear in large groups of single or paired dancers and anyone who can buy or rent a mask and costume can be a *diablo*. It takes little training or preparation to do so. The *diablos* seem to be only partially integrated into the conservative structure of the Juxtlahuaca fiesta. This is evident in the variation of the mask forms and the laissez-faire quality of their performance. Further, while Mixtecan *chilolos* are always adult males, both young boys and women are increasingly being allowed to perform as *diablos*.

The humorous role of the *diablos* is shared with the fourth type of dancers to appear at the Juxtlahuaca Santiago fiestas: the clowns. The black-faced clowns of the Mixtecs are members of a pan-Mexico family of characters who all perform similar tasks.[11] The Juxtlahuacan black-faced clown is called *mahoma*, and this name, ridiculing the name of the most serious captain of the Moors, indicates one of his tasks: the *mahoma* clown provides comic relief for the intense and complex drama of the *chareos*. He does so by humorously mocking the other *chareos* performers, imitating their movements and exaggerating the litany of their speeches. But he has further duties as well. He acts as an emcee for the *chareos* by clearing and keeping clean the dance area and by making sure that the dancers are in step and properly attired. After eight hours of performance, feathers droop and costumes unravel: it is

158. The *chilolos*
dancers of Juxtlahuaca,
1980. (Note the *viejo*
clown following them.)

the *mahoma* clown's duty to repair these so that the show goes on. He also engages and entertains the audience in a very direct way, which is of course what he was doing when we first met him with the children.

While the role of the *mahoma* clown is performed by an adult, that of the second clown who appears at the Juxtlahuaca patron saint festival is performed by a young boy. The second clown is called *latu nucaca* in the Mixtec language, or *el viejito* (the little old one) in Spanish. His mask is white, with a curling black moustache and bright red cheeks boldly painted on it (fig. 161). The *viejito* clown accompanies the *chilolos* dancers. His role is not as well developed as that of the *mahoma* clown and he appears to be a minor member of the *chilolos* cast. Interestingly enough, when the *chilolos* dance is performed by the mestizos of Juxtlahuaca, increasing numbers of the line dancers themselves are also children, indicating perhaps that as the meaning and value of the *chilolos* dance fades, its participants are younger and younger. A parallel might be seen in our Halloween, which originated as a major religious festival and is now essentially a children's game.

The *chareos*, *chilolos*, and clowns all accompany the processions of the Santiago festival. The processions wind their way through the whole town of Juxtlahuaca. They usually begin at the Mixtec neighborhood chapel, go past the large open courtyard that acts as the Mixtec community center, move through the mestizo part of town, and then return to the community center. Crowds gather along this ceremonial circuit, and all are impressed with the beauty and display of the processions. Along the way, the processions stop at four altars constructed of satin, ribbons, and flowers which frame religious images. At each altar, the Catholic priest says a short prayer honoring Santiago and blessing the Mixtec commu-

nity. The Mixtecs, carrying the large wooden images of Santiago and the Virgin Mary, lower their effigies for a moment and the *chareos* and *chilolos* quiet their musical performances in respect. But the respect is directed not only at the priest and his words. The most highly honored earthly figure in the processions is that year's *mayordomo*.

Mixtec *mayordomos* are men who have somehow accumulated abundant excess wealth and choose to redistribute it ritually through the mechanism of the fiesta (fig. 162). They organize and produce all the fiesta activities. This includes feeding and paying for the costumes and the musicians of the *chareos* and *chilolos*. The performers practice for months in advance, which keeps them away from their cornfields, and they are reimbursed by foodstuffs collected or given by the *mayordomo*. In addition, throughout the nine days of the fiesta itself, not only the dancers but also their audiences are well fed on holiday foods, such as hot chocolate (*champurrada*) and barbecued turkey (*mole*). That is a lot of food and a costly expense, as most of the people of Juxtlahuaca and hundreds of outsiders from as far away as California and Texas attend the Santiago fiesta. The *mayordomo* is assisted by chosen members of the *cofradía* (the religious fraternity that serves the patron saint), but the *cofradía* members' financial and temporal burden is only a fraction of the *mayordomo*'s. The *mayordomo* is the host of the fiesta in a very real sense. Because his offerings are for religious ends (that is, for adoration of the saint), he gains marked esteem in the eyes of his whole community. The *mayordomo* walks slowly in the procession, and he carries a small ceramic dish lined with flowers. A tiny silver sculpture of Santiago on horseback is placed in the center of the dish. This sculpture is the sacred material focus of the entire fiesta experience, and it is the *mayor-*

domo's duty to guard the minute Santiago for a year. After the procession passes through Juxtlahuaca, it returns to the Mixtec community center. The *mayordomo* places the Santiago figure on a flower-wreathed altar, rich foods are brought out and served, and the dancers commence again.

The Carnival Celebrations of Juxtlahuaca

Carnival is the period of celebration before Lent, and it is the only other time that masked dancers appear in the village of Juxtlahuaca. In contrast to the highly structured patron saint fiesta, which is supported by the *mayordomo* and the *cofradía* organization, Carnival festivities are supported by each of the individual neighborhood chapels in Juxtlahuaca. The Carnival performances do not follow a ceremonial circuit (marked by processions), nor do they focus on the community center. Instead, they appear, seemingly spontaneously, on street corners, in the open plazas, and wandering from house to house. There are four types of Carnival dancers: the *chilolos del ardilla,* the *rubios,* the *macho* troupe, and the *mascaritas gritonas.*

The *chilolos del ardilla* (the *chilolos* of the Squirrel) are similar to the *chilolos* who appear during the July Santiago fiesta. As then, the Carnival *chilolos* dance to the music of the flute and drum. Their costumes are similar, except that while the July *chilolos* wear short, knee-length pants, those of Carnival wear full-length trousers. They are accompanied by two clowns. One is called the *mahoma del ardilla* (Mohammed of the Squirrel): he wears a hairy black-faced mask and carries a stuffed squirrel. He also carries a gun and a hunting bag and has a second stuffed squirrel around the rim of his hat. The second clown, called the *tigre* or the *tecuani* (jaguar in both Spanish and Aztec languages) wears a spotted jaguar suit and a dramatic feline mask

(fig. 163). While the *chilolos* perform their mock combat line dance, the *mahoma* and *tigre* clowns enact a spoof of hunting, with the *tigre* as the ultimate victim.

The *rubios* (blonds) line dance is also accompanied by an animal side act. The six *rubios* wear brown masks with large twisted mouths, which may actually represent mouths and moustaches combined into a horizontal S-curve (fig. 154). The *rubios'* masks have the same flat forehead line and broad overall proportions as both the ancient masks of the Mixtecs and the *chilolos* masks of today. Also like the *chilolos* masks, those of the *rubios* are in fixed, unvarying forms throughout the village area surrounding Juxtlahuaca. The *rubios* wear cowboy outfits consisting of chaps, vests, and characteristic cowboy hats, reminding us that mounted cowherds traveled throughout Mexico as well as the western United States (fig. 164). Logically enough, the *rubios* includes a bull dancer. The bull is represented by a man in a *rubios* outfit (minus the mask) who carries a cane armature over which is stretched a cowhide. The armature represents the bulky shoulders of the bull, and his head is identified by two curving bull horns.

While both the Carnival *chilolos* and the *rubios* perform simple parodies of hunting, the *macho* troupe enacts a complex story line. The story is a Mixtec version of "Beauty and the Beast" (fig. 165). Beauty is represented by a man wearing a gorgeous woman's mask, and the Beast is represented by a man with a wild, hairy mask which identifies him as the *macho* (fig. 166). The *macho* troupe involves up to a dozen masked characters who go from house to house to perform. At each house they are served drinks (such as tequila and its less-refined cousin, mescal) and food (such as *pan dulce* or sweet rolls). Generally, more drinks are consumed than food, so that each ensuing performance is increasingly inebriated and hilarious. The audience includes not only the members of the visited households, but also a growing crowd of onlookers, who likewise partake of the refreshments. Their response becomes increasingly uproarious.

Beauty is portrayed as the daughter of a highly respected Mixtec man called *el tuno* (his name is taken from that of the prickly pear cactus and refers to his prickly personality). Both *el tuno* and his wife wear masks with wrinkled pink skin and thick white hair. Beauty's mother, like Beauty herself, is performed by a male dancer, so that both characters are female impersonators. Ritual female impersonation is found all over Mexico today and has numerous antecedents in the pre-Hispanic past, as Fray Sahagún's accounts of Aztec ceremonies make clear.[12] Female impersonation was also an important aspect of the European theatrical tradition: Shakespeare's female characters were portrayed by men. In Juxtlahuaca, the mother wears dark, conservative European clothing, and the Beauty wears elaborate and colorful Mixtec Indian attire.[13] Beauty embodies all the enviable qualities of a proper Mixtec woman.

Beauty's behavior illustrates adherence to Mixtec mores as well. When she meets the *macho,* she meekly obeys her parents' orders not to associate with such an undesirable character. The *macho* is a wild beast from "outside" (he is comparable to the "bush spirits" of African masquerades)[14] who must be tamed by society. But before he is tamed there are several humorous encounters. The usually reserved Mixtecs are entertained by dancers who break every tabu, yelling obscenities, speaking of sex quite explicitly, and, in short, enacting numerous deeds which are funny precisely because they are behavioral reversals. Even the honored Catholic Church is mocked, as a priest character is silly and ineffectual in dealing with the *macho.* The final taming

is done by Beauty's father, *el tuno,* who appears as the righteous authority figure in this dance drama. Afterwards Beauty and the *macho* marry amidst much song and dance and live happily ever after . . . until they move on to the next house and the next more riotous performance of the *macho* troupe.

The *macho* performance depicts the taming of the wild male spirit by society (it is implied that Beauty never had such rebellious tendencies), so that marriage and the ensuing community integration is possible. It illustrates proper behavior directly in the roles of *el tuno* and Beauty and indirectly in the humorous antics of the characters who reverse expectations. In ritually defining behavioral standards, the performance of the *macho* troupe exerts a covert form of social control. The fourth Carnival dance of Juxtlahuaca likewise exerts social control. But while the *macho* troupe does so by providing role models, the *mascaritas gritonas* (the tiny, screaming masks) do so by openly ridiculing individuals who violate societal norms.

The *mascaritas gritonas* is performed by just the young men who, like the *macho,* are kind of wild and have a lot of steam to let off. They let this steam off by first investigating all gossip stories in town and then publicly airing such tales, much to the chagrin of the individuals involved. The *mascaritas gritonas* are protected against retaliation by their costumes, which fully hide their identities. The *mascaritas gritonas* wear long black robes and pointed hoods. Such hoods are still worn by the *penitentes* of Sevilla, Spain, and were adopted from them by the Ku Klux Klan for similar anonymity. But the *mascaritas gritonas* are not as ominous in appearance as the KKK members, as their robes are covered with brilliant appliqué stars and moons and adorned with multicolored ribbons which flutter around them as they run through the streets teasing and telling tales in high,

12. According to Sahagún, priests impersonated women by wearing female attire during several Aztec ceremonies, most notably *Ochpaniztli* (Sahagún 1951: 110–117) and *Tititl* (Sahagún 1951: 143–146). Bishop Zúmarraga bemoaned the continued existence of dances employing masked female impersonators in 1544 (Ravicz 1970: 75).
13. See Esser (1983) for a discussion of similar "Beauties" in Tarascan masked dances.
14. See Leon Siroto in Fraser and Cole (1972).

159 'A Moor in the
textile procession's
dancers' version of
the well-known Moors
and Christians dance
ceremony, 1980.

160 'A doll whisperer
in a boat, 1980.

161. The *viejito* (little old man) clown of Juxtlahuaca, 1980.

258

162. The Juxtlahuaca *mayordomo* carrying the Santiago sculpture during the fiesta procession, 1976.

163. The *tigre* mask, 1980.

disguised falsetto voices. The *mascaritas gritonas* seem to be a Carnival form imported directly from Spain, where related characters "keep people in line" in similarly small, conservative villages.

Social control, whether explicit (as the *mascaritas gritonas*) or implicit (as the *macho* troupe), and entertainment are only two of the many functions of the Mixtec masked characters who perform in Juxtlahuaca. Although most of these maskers appear on the surface to be Spanish-derived, many have roots in the pre-Hispanic past as well. Above all, the maskers and the fiestas in which they appear serve to integrate the communities and to illustrate and validate the regional identities of the Mixtecs.

The children are delighted by the black-faced clown and entertained by the *chareos* and *chilolos*. They respect both their father, who carries the Santiago statue as an offering, and the *mayordomo,* who serves the entire village by financing and overseeing the celebration. The children feel a deep sense of community pride as they witness the beauty and spectacle of the fiesta. They run to join the crowds following the procession, and continue to the street-side altar that is an oasis of brilliant color in the otherwise dusty street. Once again, the fiesta transforms their lives.

164. The *rubios* dancers performing in their cowboy outfits, 1980.

165. Beauty standing
behind her parents,
1980.

164. The *rubios* dancers performing in their cowboy outfits, 1980.

165. Beauty standing
behind her parents,
1980.

166. The *macho* riding
a stick horse, 1980.

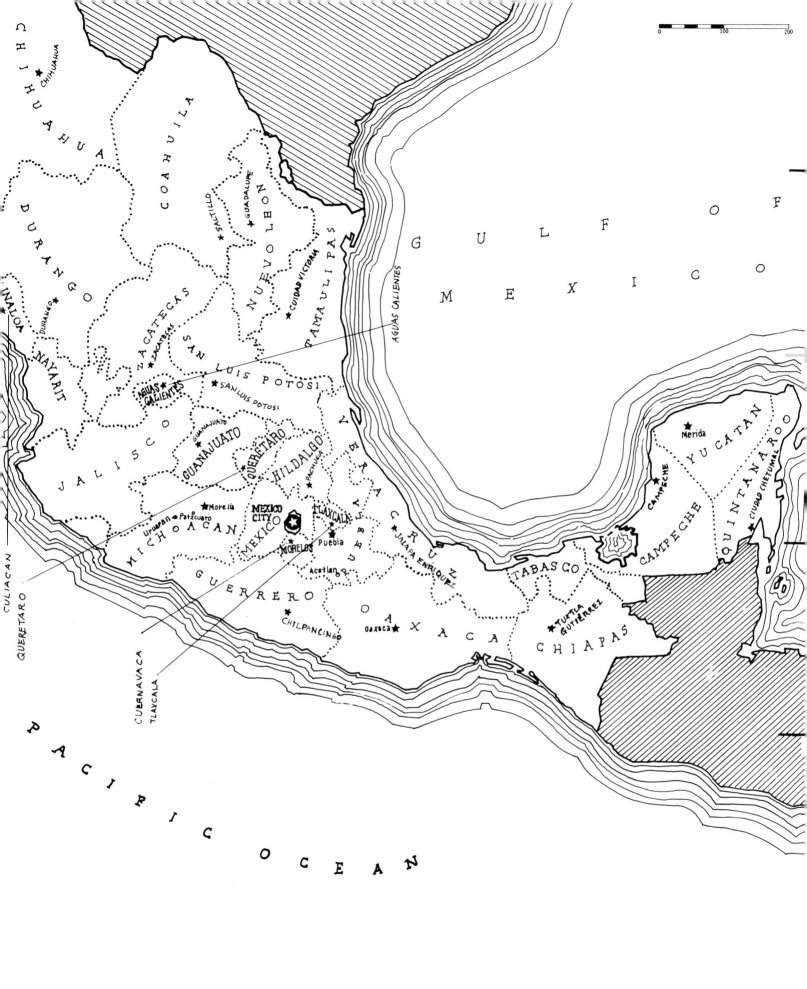

Behind the Mask

in Mexico

The federal republic of Mexico is a vast and varied country about one-fourth the size of the continental United States. Within the boundaries of its thirty-one states are mountains, deserts, tropical rain forests, and temperate plateaus. While Spanish is the national language, more than thirty indigenous language groups have survived from the hundreds that existed prior to the arrival of Europeans. Today's Mexico is a pluralistic society comprised of many different ethnic groups speaking fifty-six separate languages.

More than ninety per cent of Mexicans today are Roman Catholics. The first Catholic missions were established shortly after the Conquest by friars who undertook the formidable task of converting huge numbers of indigenous people to Christianity. During the ensuing centuries religious systems evolved in many communities that reflected both European Catholic and pre-Hispanic American Indian traditions. Black Africans, brought to Mexico in substantial numbers during the Colonial period, also left their imprint on religious expression.

Masks were important in ceremonies and rituals for thousands of years before Europeans colonized Mexico. Soon after their arrival in 1524, friars introduced European-style masked dramas as an aid to religious instruction. Colonists, too, continued to don masks and costumes, as they had at home, to celebrate victories and holy days. Native people everywhere emulated the colonists' use of masks. Today, all over Mexico, masked dances are performed in many cities, towns, and villages. Participants may be farmers, artisans, mill workers, or even bank clerks, but, for the most part, all are people of modest means.

Masked dances are usually associated with important holidays. These include Christmas, New Year's Day, and other Catholic holidays such as Three Kings Day, Candlemas, Carnival (just before Lent begins), and Holy Week. Corpus Christi, which often coincides with the beginning of the rainy (and planting) season in Mexico, and the Days of the Dead at the beginning of November are also occasions for important mask use. Masks are often used in celebrations for a community's patron saint. Pilgrimages to sacred shrines, secular holidays, and government-sponsored exhibitions may all warrant the use of masks. But most importantly, masks are used to honor the community and celebrate its most cherished values. Masked festivals provide an alternate route to power for those for whom the more usual political and economic routes are inaccessible.

Masks not only refer to face coverings but by extension also include costumes, headdresses, and accoutrements of many kinds. In short, masked festivals employ many different kinds of objects, all of which are capable of transforming or revealing identity.

Celebrations from six communities are depicted in the pages that follow: San Lorenzo, Michoacán; Papalotla, Tlaxcala; the Río Fuerte region of Sinaloa; Zitlala, Guerrero; Suchiapa, Chiapas; and Acatlán, Puebla. The use of masks in these communities not only marks specific Roman Catholic holidays but also reflects local social organization, beliefs and customs, and the impact on these of historical and current events. As they did in the past, masked festivals continue to this day to serve and fulfill the needs of the people.

Acatlán, Puebla

Zitlala, Guerrero

Suchiapa, Chiapas

Suchiapa, Chiapas

Río Fuerte region, Sinaloa

Papalotla, Tlaxcala

Corupo, Michoacán

Papalotla, Tlaxcala

Procession in Zitlala,
Guerrero, 1981.

ommunity Preparations

Masks are used in festivals that
involve and incorporate the whole
community. Preparations for these
celebrations are costly, both in terms
of wealth and labor. The successful
outcome of a festival depends upon
the aid of many people. Responsibility
for supervising and paying for the
many details of the festival is often
assumed by sponsors or hosts who
serve with the community's approval.
A host may have a post in the
community's ceremonial organization
and is usually motivated by promises
made to Jesus, the Virgin Mary, or a
saint.

No one person or couple is able to
assume sole responsibility for a
festival *cargo*, as it is known.
The host and his spouse must rely on
the help of family, friends, and those
with whom they have special
relationships. Large quantities of
special dishes must be prepared
requiring contributions of ingredients,
firewood, utensils, and expertise.

Kitchen space must be found and cooks provided with refreshment. Services of dance directors and mask makers must be sought. Musicians must be hired, dancers rehearsed, and costumes sewn. The church, chapel, images of saints, and even the streets must be adorned. Participants must be advised as to appropriate behavior. A festival that is carefully planned and successfully executed reflects well on its sponsors and increases their standing in the community.

Cooking and feasting are important elements of the festival. Men and boys gather and carry firewood, while women and girls prepare the festival meals. If the occasion is very important the host may be responsible for several meals. Festival meals are lavish; special and luxury foods are served such as chocolate, sweet white-flour breads in special shapes, complex sauces, fruits from other regions, and much more meat than at ordinary meals. Bottled sodas and beer and distilled liquors are plentiful.

For many months before the festival, masks and costumes are prepared for the dancers. Mask makers almost always have other occupations and rarely work at their craft full time. Masks are usually made for use in the mask maker's community or in neighboring communities. Today, many carvers also sell their masks to people from outside their communities who purchase them for decorative use.

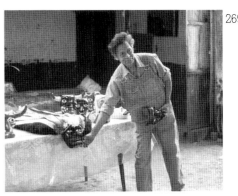

Right: Mask maker Victoriano Salgado. Uruapan, Michoacán. Below: Work bench of Victoriano Salgado with mask in progress. Uruapan, Michoacán. Left: Antonio Saldaña carving a mask. Nuevo San Juan Parangaricutiro, Michoacán.

Photos this page: Oliver Velásquez carving a mask at his home in Suchiapa, Chiapas, 1987. Overlay: Efrain Jiménez of Acatlán, Puebla, 1987. Right: workshop of mask maker Antonio Saldaña. Nuevo San Juan Parangaricutiro, 1987.

Woman stirring stew,
Capomos, Sinaloa.

Curundas (tamales)
cooking in copper pots,
Corupo, Michoacán,
1988.

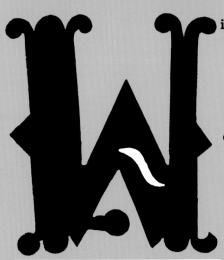

Winter Ceremonial Season

at San Lorenzo, Michoacán

San Lorenzo is a small, quiet village in the Tarascan highlands in the state of Michoacán. About 2,000 people live here, most of them housed in distinctive and traditional timber structures called *trojes*. Many of the townspeople speak no Spanish, but almost everyone is fluent in the indigenous language, *purepecha*. Known as "cold country" (*tierra fria*), the area surrounding San Lorenzo is characterized by pine- and oak-covered mountain slopes.

On January 1 in San Lorenzo, three different groups of dancers perform to honor the last year's ritual officers and to welcome the new officers who assume their obligations on New Year's Day. The dances are part of the winter ceremonial season in the Tarascan highlands that chronicle the birth and infancy of Jesus. Two of the dance groups, the *viejitos*, or "old ones," and the *negritos*, or "Blackmen," are elegantly dressed. In contrast, the third group, the *feos*, or "uglies," are dressed ridiculously and behave in ways that are aggressive and antisocial. These buffoons turn the normal social order upside-down. Each group teaches correct behavior: *viejitos* and *negritos* do so by expressing the seriousness and authority of the elders, while the *feos* demonstrate the dire (even if hilarious) consequences of flaunting society's rules. Additionally, the character of the *negrito* records the very real presence of black Africans in Colonial Mexico. In all cases, masks representing women are worn by male dancers.

Little Mary (*Maringuilla*)
San Lorenzo, Michoacán
Costume assembled and
  skirt, underskirt, and
  apron made by Maclovia
  Anguiano, Nuevo San
  Juan Parangaricutiro,
  Michoacán, 1987.
Mask made by Joaquín
  Amaro Bravo, Angahuan,
  Michoacán, 1987. Carved,
  painted wood.

Little Mary (*Maringuilla*), detail of back
San Lorenzo, Michoacán
Costume assembled and skirt, underskirt, and apron made by Maclovia Anguiano, Nuevo San Juan Parangaricutiro, Michoacán, 1987,

Little Mary (*Maringuilla*),
  detail
San Lorenzo, Michoacán
Costume assembled by
  Maclovia Anguiano, Nuevo
  San Juan Parangaricutiro,
  Michoacán, 1987.
Mask made by Joaquín
  Amaro Bravo, Angahuan,
  Michoacán, 1987. Carved,
  painted wood.

Little Mary (*Maringuilla*)
San Lorenzo, Michoacán
Costume assembled and
  skirt, underskirt, and
  apron made by Maclovia
  Anguiano, Nuevo San
  Juan Parangaricutiro,
  Michoacán, 1987.
Mask made by Joaquín
  Amaro Bravo, Angahuan
  Michoacán, 1987. Carved
  painted wood.

Old Man (*Viejo*), detail
San Lorenzo, Michoacán
Costume assembled by
  Maclovia Anguiano, Nuevo
  San Juan Parangaricutiro,
  Michoacán, 1987.

Old Man (*Viejo*)
San Lorenzo, Michoacán
Costume assembled by
  Maclovia Anguiano, Nuevo
  San Juan Parangaricutiro,
  Michoacán, 1987.
Mask made by Antonio
  Saldaña, Nuevo San Juan
  Parangaricutiro, Michoa-
  cán, 1987. Carved, painted
  wood.

Old Man (*Viejo*)
San Lorenzo, Michoacán
Costume assembled and
  headdress made by
  Maclovia Anguiano, Nuevo
  San Juan Parangaricutiro,
  Michoacán, 1987.
Mask made by Antonio
  Saldaña, Nuevo San Juan
  Parangaricutiro, Michoa-
  cán, 1987. Carved, painted
  wood.

Blackman (*Negrito*), detail of
  back
San Lorenzo, Michoacán
Costume made and
  assembled by Maclovia
  Anguiano, Nuevo San
  Juan Parangaricutiro,
  Michoacán, 1987.

Blackman (*Negrito*), detail of
  over-britches
San Lorenzo, Michoacán
Costume assembled and
  over britches made by
  Maclovia Anguiano, Nuevo
  San Juan Parangaricutiro,
  Michoacán, 1987.

Blackman (*Negrito*)
San Lorenzo, Michoacán
Costume assembled and
  over britches, headdress,
  and aprons made by
  Maclovia Anguiano, Nuevo
  San Juan Parangaricutiro,
  Michoacán, 1987.
Mask maker unknown.
  Undated. Carved, painted
  wood. Loan from collection
  of Dr. Ruth Lechuga,
  Mexico City.

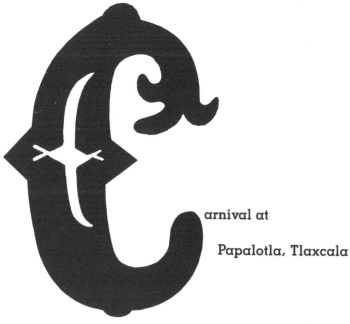

Carnival at

Papalotla, Tlaxcala

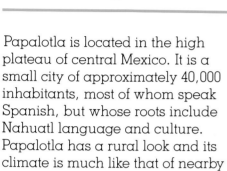

Papalotla is located in the high plateau of central Mexico. It is a small city of approximately 40,000 inhabitants, most of whom speak Spanish, but whose roots include Nahuatl language and culture. Papalotla has a rural look and its climate is much like that of nearby Puebla City.

Carnival in Papalotla is celebrated with an elaborate masked festival that begins on the Sunday before Ash Wednesday and continues for a week. At Papalotla the festival is not associated with the riotous behavior of Carnival celebrations elsewhere. Participation is a serious undertaking, reflecting deep concern for the success of the approaching planting season.

Papalotla is divided into six sectors, or *barrios*. Five of the *barrios* have their own dance groups that perform at Carnival. As many as forty dancers may appear in a single group. Most of the dancers are dressed as elegant hacienda owners. Their splendid costumes include sequined and embroidered capes and ostrich-plume headdresses. Each headdress contains forty-eight feathers and represents a considerable economic outlay for the dancer. Continuity of this tradition is insured by training small boys, dressed in miniature costumes, to perform.

Performances by women are a recent innovation. Until a few years ago, men impersonated the female role. It was the women themselves who initiated the change by expressing their desire to participate directly in the dance, rather than remaining in the audience.

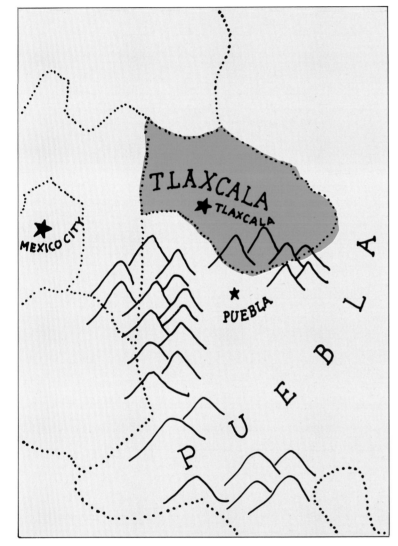

The map shows Mexico City, Tlaxcala, and Puebla.

Charro, detail
Papalotla, Tlaxcala
Collected by Dr. Ruth
  Lechuga, 1987.
Mask made by the Méndez
  Family, Puebla, Puebla.

Carved, gessoed, and
painted wood; glass eyes,
artificial eyelashes, metallic
fringe.

Charro
Papalotla, Tlaxcala
Collected by Dr. Ruth
  Lechuga, 1987.
Cape embroidered with
  national seal of Mexico.
Mask made by the Méndez
  Family, Puebla, Puebla.
Carved, gessoed, and
  painted wood; glass eyes,
  artificial eyelashes, metallic
  fringe.

Charro, detail of back
Papalotla, Tlaxcala
Collected by Dr. Ruth
  Lechuga, 1987. Central
  design of cape is national
  seal of Mexico.

Charro, detail of back
Papalotla, Tlaxcala
Collected by Dr. Ruth
Lechuga, 1987.
Cape embroidered with
national seal of Mexico.

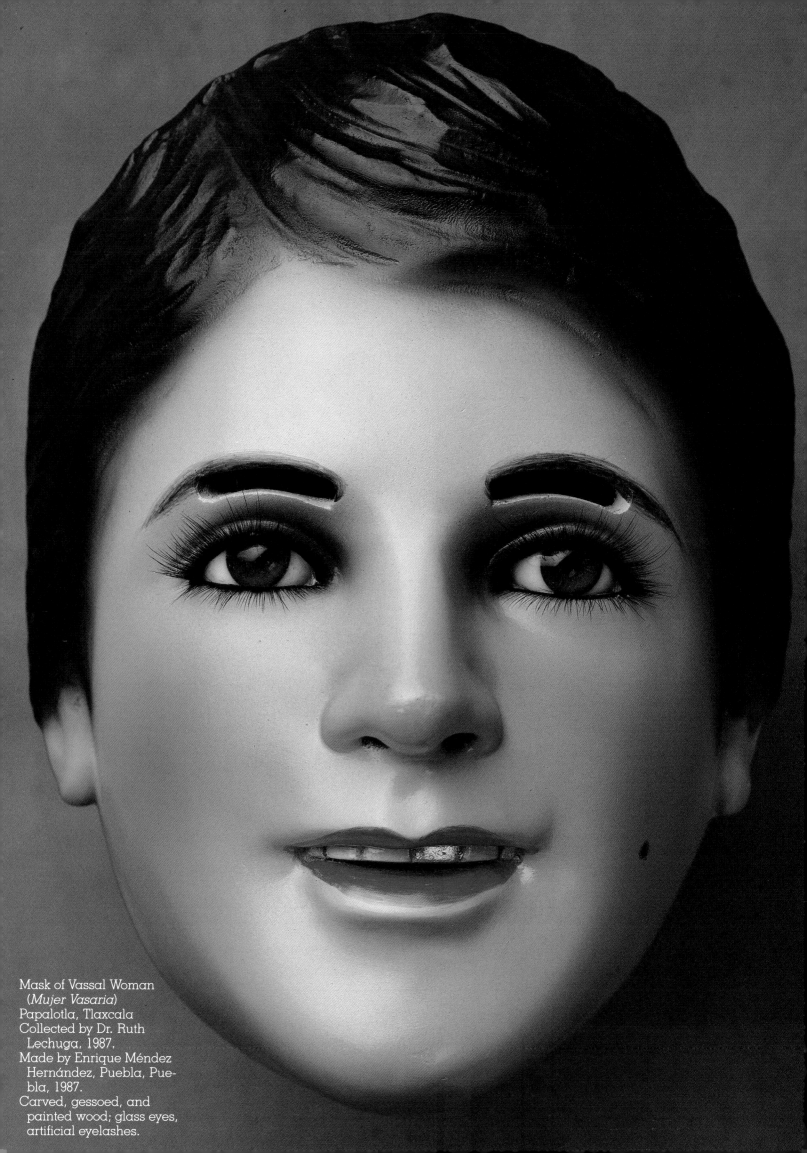

Mask of Vassal Woman
  (*Mujer Vasaria*)
Papalotla, Tlaxcala
Collected by Dr. Ruth
  Lechuga, 1987.
Made by Enrique Méndez
  Hernández, Puebla, Pue-
  bla, 1987.
Carved, gessoed, and
  painted wood; glass eyes,
  artificial eyelashes.

Charro
Papalotla, Tlaxcala
Collected by Dr. Ruth
  Lechuga, 1987.
Cape embroidered with
  national seal of Mexico.
Mask made by the Méndez
  family, Puebla, Puebla.
Carved, gessoed, and
  painted wood; glass eyes,
  artificial eyelashes, metallic
  fringe.

L ent in the

Río Fuerte Region, Sinaloa

Numerous small communities of Mayo Indians live along the Río Fuerte in northern Sinaloa. The river provides water for irrigation in this arid region. The city of Mochicahue has substantial populations of mestizos as well as Mayos. During Lent, the principal ceremonial season, Mayos from sixteen communities congregate at Mochicahue. Some of these communities are located within the city limits.

Lent, or *cuaresma*, begins on Ash Wednesday and continues for forty days until Easter Sunday. Jesuit missionaries introduced the Holy Week drama into northwest Mexico in the seventeenth and eighteenth centuries to various indigenous groups who adapted it to their own mythic world view.

Among the Mayo Indians of the Río Fuerte region, Sinaloa, masked personages called *judíos* (See Editor's note, page 63) are in charge of the Lenten and Holy Week activities. In other Mayo areas the terms *fariseos* or *chapokobam* are used to designate these sacred clowns. Early in the Lenten season, groups of *judíos* in full costume leave their communities to travel through the surrounding countryside. They collect alms, or *limosnas*, to support the Holy Week festivals. They visit other towns where they mutely request contributions of strangers. They dance for the contributors.

Judíos are charged with the most serious responsibilities for maintaining order in the society, encouraging traditional attitudes of respect, and mediating between life and death. *Judíos* participate in community processions, or *konti*, each Friday afternoon of Lent. Holy images are carried from the church to each of the Stations of the Cross in the churchyard and then returned. As the *judíos* accompany the procession they deliberately violate accepted social behavior by clowning and mocking the seriousness of the activities.

Mayo men in Mochicahui who serve as *judíos* agree to do so for three years as a result of having made a vow, or *manda*. Masks and costumes are usually made by individual participants at the beginning of their terms of obligation. On Holy Saturday masks and weapons generally are burned as part of the ceremony that cleanses participants of evil and enables them to resume ordinary life.

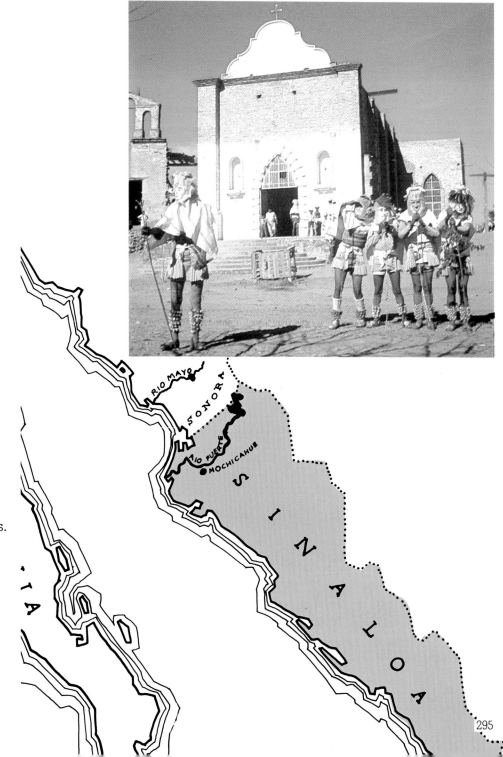

Judío Masks (*Máscaras de Judíos*)
Río Fuerte region, Sinaloa
Collected by Roberto Ruiz
1982.
Left: made by Juan Torres,
Rancho Igual, Sinaloa,
1980. Carved, painted
coral bean wood; sheep-
skin.
Right: made by Rafael
Alvarez, La Libertad,
Sinaloa, 1981. Carved,
painted coral wood.

Musical Instruments
Río Fuerte region, Sinaloa
Drum collected in San
  Xavier Choix, Sinaloa, by
  Dr. Barney T. Burns, 1986.
Belt made by Filiberto
  Valdón; undated. Collected
  by Dr. Barney T. Burns,
  1986.
Leg rattles (giant silk moth
  cocoon rattles) made by
  Serapio Gámez, San Pedro
  de Masiaca, Sonora.
  Collected by Dr. Barney T.
  Burns, 1984.

Judío Masks (*Máscaras de Judíos*)
Río Fuerte region, Sinaloa
Collected by Roberto Ruiz
1982.
Left: made by Eraglio
Zacarías, La Florida,
Sinaloa, 1974. Javelina
hide with paint.
Center: made by Rosario
López, La Florida, Sinaloa,
1981. Goat skin, leather,
paint.
Right: maker unknown, La
Florida, Sinaloa, 1981.
Painted goat skin.

Festival of the Holy Cross

at Zitlala, Guerrero

The village of Zitlala is situated on a mountain top in the Montaña de Guerrero near the large city of Chilapa. The approximately 14,000 inhabitants speak both Nahuatl and Spanish. Many women still wear the *huipil* and wrap-around skirts typical of Nahuatl culture since before the Conquest.

The Feast of the Holy Cross (Santa Cruz) is celebrated on May 3, only two days after May 1, the secular national holiday dedicated to labor. Many communities in Guerrero share with Zitlala the celebration of this critical time in the agricultural cycle when the earth is prepared for the arrival of the first rains of the wet season.

The celebration begins on May 1 when three crosses, each belonging to one of the town's *barrios*, are removed from the mountain top and carried to the riverside. On May 2, mass is performed at the riverside. Garlands of breads and flowers are brought to decorate the crosses, which are then carried through town and back to the mountain top. Masked dancers, including *tlacololeros* (farmers), accompany these processions. Men and women, dressed in their finest traditional clothing, help to carry the crosses.

Formerly, a battle between two dancers masked as jaguars took place on the main plaza at Zitlala during the festival of the Holy Cross while the crosses were carried in procession. Because of the fierceness of these contests, which involve pairs of dancers from rival *barrios*, the event was postponed to May 5. It now takes place on the plaza near the church. Other dance groups also perform on this plaza, but withdraw at the approach of the "jaguars." These adversaries dedicate themselves to San Nicolas, their patron saint, whom they identify with the Lord of the Jungle.

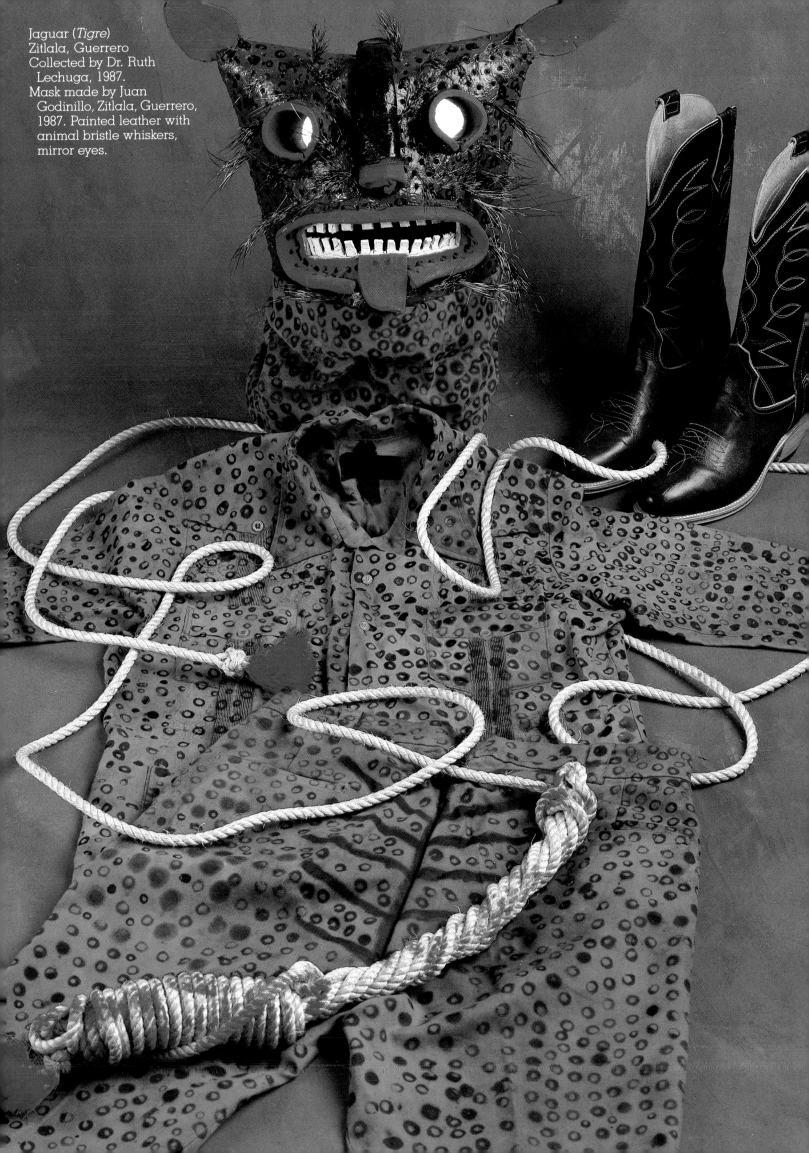

Jaguar (*Tigre*)
Zitlala, Guerrero
Collected by Dr. Ruth
    Lechuga, 1987.
Mask made by Juan
    Godinillo, Zitlala, Guerrero,
    1987. Painted leather with
    animal bristle whiskers,
    mirror eyes.

Farmer (*Tlacololero*)
Zitlala, Guerrero
Collected by Dr. Ruth
  Lechuga, 1987.
Costume assembled by José
  Colasillo, 1987.
Mask made by José
  Colasillo. Carved and
  painted wood.

Traditional Woman's Cos-
  tume
Zitlala, Guerrero
Collected by Dr. Ruth
  Lechuga, 1987

Suchiapa is a small town of 8,000 inhabitants lying at about 600 meters in altitude, and is near the state capital of Tuxtla Gutiérrez. Suchiapa's main street is full of color imparted by its houses and its lush, tropical foliage. Most of the town's inhabitants speak both Spanish and Zoque.

Corpus Christi, the Feast of the Sacrament, is a moveable feast that falls in May or June and coincides with the beginning of the rainy season in most of Mexico. Corpus Christi is celebrated here with a masked dance that tells two stories at the same time.

In most of Mexico, Corpus Christi festivals are associated with hunting; Suchiapa is no exception. The masked festival performed for this holiday includes a chase- and- hunt sequence between masked actors representing wild animals and those representing humans. Masked actors representing jaguars, *los tigres*, a deer, *kalalá* or *venado*, and the plumed serpent, or *gigantón*, confront white-faced clowns called *chamulas*, who carry live or stuffed wild animals. Actually, Chamula is a town of indigenous people located some eighty kilometers from and 2,000 meters higher than Suchiapa. A dance based on the story of David, the *gigantillo*, and Goliath is presented at the same time by a small boy and the masked dancer representing the plumed serpent.

Mexican masked dramas are always changing. New and different elements continue to be added every time a masked dance is performed. While the plumed serpent back-mask of Suchiapa may recall the pre-Hispanic image of Quetzalcoatl, it is not clear how this was introduced into the community. A plumed serpent was carved in stone at the ancient Mexican city of Teotihuacan, and it is this image that is replicated today in many popular forms, including the Mexican five peso coin in circulation a few years ago. Conceivably this ubiquitous, portable, and supremely accessible object could have provided a means of entry for this ancient deity.

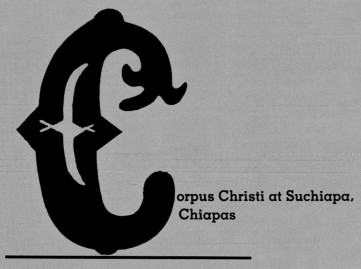

Corpus Christi at Suchiapa, Chiapas

Codex Dehesa, close-up

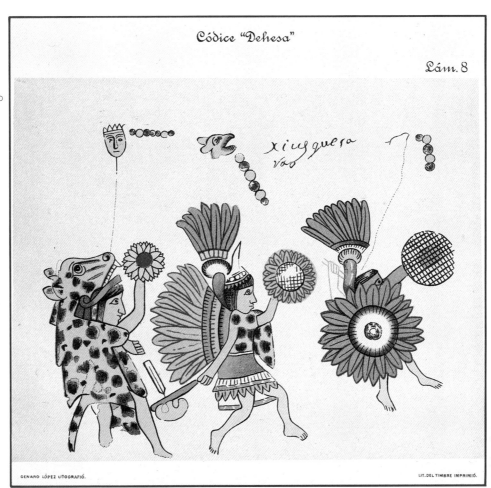

Jaguar (*Tigre*), detail
Suchiapa, Chiapas
Made by Oliver Velázquez
Serrano, Suchiapa, Chiapas, 1987.

Jaguar (*Tigre*)
Suchiapa, Chiapas
Made by Oliver Velázquez
 Serrano, Suchiapa Chia-
pas, 1987. Mask is carved,
 painted wood with cotton
 neck attached.

Serpent-Giant (*Gigantón*)
Suchiapa, Chiapas
Made by Oliver Velázquez
    Serrano, Suchiapa, Chia-
    pas, 1987. The "back
    mask" is carved, painted
    wood; feathers, metallic
    paper.

Coins (*Monedas*)
Mexican five-peso coins,
    showing a head of the
    Plumed Serpent from the
    Temple of Quetzalcoatl,
    Teotihuacán, Mexico.

Little David (*Gigantillo*)
Suchiapa, Chiapas
Assembled by Oliver
    Velázquez Serrano, Su-
    chiapa, Chiapas, 1987.

Deer (*Kalalá*)
Suchiapa, Chiapas
Made by Oliver Velázquez
Serrano, Suchiapa, Chia-
pas, 1987. The "body
mask" is a wooden frame
covered with deer hides,
log- and rolled-blanket
counterweights; sisal rope
reins; paper flowers.

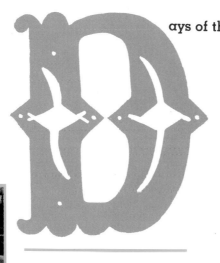

Days of the Dead at

Acatlán, Puebla

Acatlán is famous for its pottery. Wares are displayed in front of many houses and even, in some instances, on the roofs. This is a Spanish-speaking town of some 7,000 inhabitants located near Mixtec- and Popolocan-speaking groups.

All Saints Day is celebrated on November 1, and All Souls Day on November 2. This marks the occasion when the living remember deceased relatives and friends. In Acatlán, the public part of the festival takes place in the cemetery. On November 1 families clean, repaint, and refurbish the grave sites. The graves are adorned with masses of marigolds and cockscomb. Candles and incense burners are placed on the graves. Families gather at the graves throughout the night of November 1 to await the arrival of departed souls. The cemetery is illuminated by hundreds of candles.

On November 2 relatives continue to visit the cemetery. They place bouquets on the graves and pass the day visiting with family, friends, and neighbors.

All Souls Day in Acatlán includes a masked dance. On the afternoon of November 2, a dance of jaguars, or *tecuanes*, takes place at the entrance to the cemetery. Here performers dedicate their dance to the deceased. If a relative of a member of the group has died recently, the dance is performed at the grave site. In addition, masked dancers representing death and the Devil tease and pull children from the crowd, while *viejos rancheros*, or "old ranchers," perform a vigorous line dance. This same dance is performed on October 24 for the fiesta of San Rafael, patron saint of Acatlán.

Old Rancher (*Viejo Ran-
    chero*)
"*Viejo Moranchi*," detail
Acatlán, Puebla.
Mask collected by Pascual
    Domínguez Martínez and
    Dr. Ruth Lechuga, 1987.

Old Rancher (*Viejo Ran-
    chero*)
"*Viejo Moranchi*," detail
Acatlán, Puebla.
Collected by Pascual
    Domínguez Martínez and
    Dr. Ruth Lechuga, 1987.
The central design
represents the Virgin of
Guadalupe.

Old Rancher (*Viejo Ran-
    chero*)
"*Viejo Lucas*," detail
Acatlán, Puebla
Collected by Pascual
    Domínguez Martínez and
    Dr. Ruth Lechuga, 1987.

Old Ranchers (*Viejos Rancheros*)
Acatlán, Puebla
Collected by Pascual Domínguez Martínez and Dr. Ruth Lechuga, 1986, 1987.

"Viejo Lucas" (left): Mask made by Efraín Jiménez Ariza, Acatlán, Peubla, 1986. Carved, painted wood; horse teeth.

"Viejo Moranchi" (right): Mask made by Efraín Jiménez Ariza, Acatlán, Puebla, 1986. Carved, painted wood; horse hair.

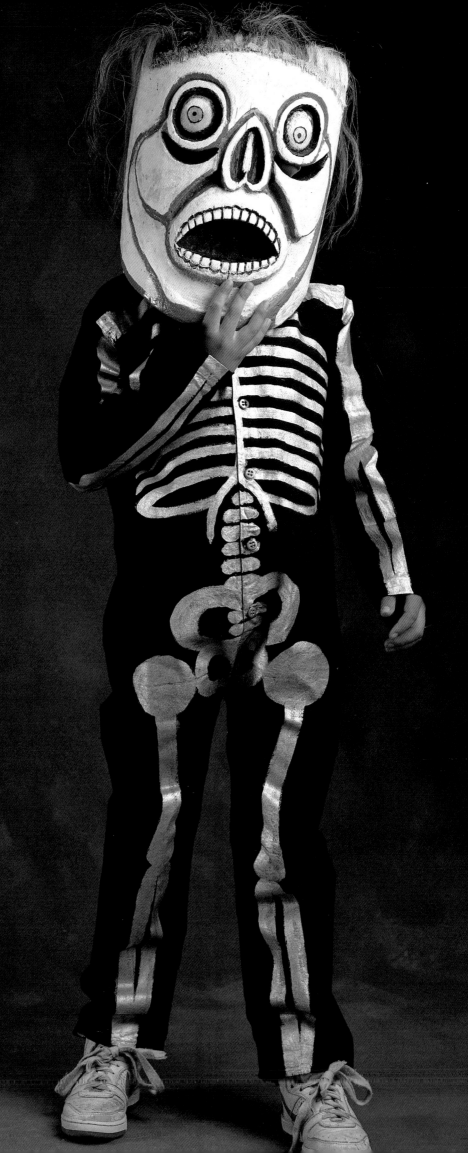

Death (*La Muerte*)
Acatlán, Puebla
Costume collected by
  Pascual Domínguez Martí-
  nez and Dr. Ruth Lechuga,
  1987.
Mask made by Efraín
  Jiménez Ariza, Acatlán,
  Puebla, 1986. Carved,
  painted wood; horse hair.

Dog (*Perro*) and Devil (*El Diablo*)
Acatlán, Puebla
Dog (left): Costume collected by Pascual Domínguez Martínez and Dr. Ruth Lechuga, 1987.
Mask maker unknown.
Collected ca. 1970 by Kathleen Kaupp and Robert Kaupp. From the Kathleen Kaupp and Robert Kaupp collection of the Museum of International Folk Art.
Devil (right): Costume collected by Pascual Domínguez Martínez and Dr. Ruth Lechuga, 1987.
Mask made by Norberto Simón, Ahuehuetitla, Puebla, 1987. Carved, incised, painted wood; leather.

Jaguar (*Tigre*), detail
Acatlán, Puebla
Costume collected by
  Pascual Domínguez Martí-
  nez and Dr. Ruth Lechuga,
  1987.

Jaguar (*Tigre*)
Acatlán, Puebla
Costume collected by
  Pascual Domínguez Martí-
  nez and Dr. Ruth Lechuga,
  1987.
Mask made by Efraín
  Jiménez Ariza, Acatlán,
  Puebla, 1986. Carved,
  painted wood; boar's tusks
  and teeth.

Devil (*El Diablo*), detail
Acatlán, Puebla
Costume collected by
  Pascual Domínguez Martí-
  nez and Dr. Ruth Lechuga,
  1987.
Mask made by Norberto
  Simón, Ahuehuetitla,
  Puebla, 1987. Carved,
  incised, painted wood;
  leather.

G L O S S A R Y

The following terms appear in the essays. They are used by many different ethnic groups and represent a complex pattern of retention and borrowing. Some of the words derive from indigenous languages, some are Spanish, and many are the result of adaptation and acculturation. Because of long years of usage, it is often difficult to ascertain the ultimate genesis of a word. The most probable source is given wherever feasible.

In general, pronunciation conforms to Spanish. While stress in Nahuatl always falls on the penultimate syllable, some Nahuatl words have become hispanicized. Wherever possible recognition has been given to current practice.
The symbol ['] stands for the glottal stop which is a sudden stopping of the breath.
The symbol [ą, ų] are nasalized forms of [a, u].
The symbol [ø] is like [o] but higher and more open.

abaso. Mayo. Forest. A cottonwood forest.

abuso. Spanish. Abuse, excess.

acatlaxqui. Nahuatl. Reed throwers.

afro-mestizo. Spanish. A person whose ancestry includes black Africans.

aje, axin. Nahuatl. A wax made from *coccids*. A material used in making indigenous lacquer.

alawasim. Mayo. Lowest ranking ritual hosts. *Paskome* who guard Jesus' tomb during Holy Week ritual.

alkandi. Tarascan. The highest rank in the San Lorenzo *cargo* system.

amapeapilli. Nahuatl. A band or decorative element used on clothing.

amate. Nahuatl. Bark paper.

antsayoh. Hñähñų. Flaying of dogs. A pre-Columbian festival.

archareos. Spanish. A dance performed in the state of Mexico.

Astucia. Spanish. Cunning. One of the devil characters in Shepherds' plays.

Atlaua. Nahuatl. A god of the *chinampa* district of Lake Xochimilco.

atole. Nahuatl. Flavored maize gruel. A festival beverage.

auto sacramental. Spanish. Religious play.

ayacahuite. Nahuatl. Pine tree. A wood used for dance masks in San Pablo Apetatitlán, Tlaxcala.

bahi mariam. Mayo. Women and children who participate in Holy Week performances.

bahi reyesim. Mayo. Little boy angels. Civil-church governors. Men of the pueblo. Three kings.

bailada. Spanish. Danced. A mask that has been used in a dance.

bailes. Spanish. Dances.

Barrabás. Spanish. A scoundrel. The prisoner released in preference to Jesus.

barrio. Spanish. Neighborhood, district.

Bartolo. Spanish. Name of shepherd in Christmas play. A clown figure who keeps order in dances and processions.

Bato. Spanish. A contraction for Bartolo.

bato achaim. Mayo. Godfathers.

bato ayem. Mayo. Godmothers.

botín. Spanish. Ankle boot.

caballo. Spanish. Horse.

cabilde, cabildes. From Spanish *cabildo*. Town council. An elder. Group of elders in village civic-ceremonial organization.

cabo. Spanish. Corporal or third in command. Lowest ranking officer in Mayo Lenten ceremonies.

cacique From Arawak. Term the Spaniards applied to indigenous rulers.

Caifás. Mayo. Name of the priest said to have condemned Jesus. The Devil in Mayo myths.

caimán. From Carib. Alligator.

calalá, kalalá.   Unknown. Possibly Zoque. Character representing deer in Corpus Christi dance in Suchiapa, Chiapas.

calpixque.   Nahuatl. In Colonial Mexico the overseer in charge of gangs of indigenous laborers.

calpulli.   Nahuatl. A neighborhood. Aztec social and political unit.

calzón.   Spanish. Trousers.

camada.   Spanish. A brood of young animals. A band of thieves or rogues. A group of playful people.

camisa.   Spanish. Shirt.

cantora.   Spanish. Female church cantor in Mayo Lenten ceremonies.

capitán.   Spanish. Captain; ritual officer in many ceremonies.

careta.   Spanish. Face mask.

cargo.   Spanish. Office, responsibility, obligation. Post in community ceremonial organization.

carguero.   Spanish. Officer in the *cargo* system.

Carnaval.   Spanish. Tuesday before Ash Wednesday. Period of revelry before Lent. Refers also to other occasions when celebrants wear masks and disguises.

carrizo.   Spanish. Cane

cascarón.   Spanish. Confetti-filled eggs.

casquetes.   Spanish. Helmet or skullcap masks.

catrín.   Spanish. City dandy. Elegant city-style clothing.

cha-chaac.   Mayan. Ceremony of summoning the *chaacs* or rain gods.

chachalmeca.   Nahuatl. Elite sacrificial priests among the pre-Conquest Aztecs.

Chalmecacihuatl.   Nahuatl. Aztec goddess associated with death and with the district of Chalma.

champurrada.   Spanish. Chocolate-flavored maize beverage.

chapakoba, chapayeca.   Mayo. Masked member of the Mayo *parisero* soldality. Lowest ranking member of *pariserom*.

charanda.   Tarascan. Distilled sugar cane spirits made in Michoacán.

chareo.   Spanish. Line dancer in performances of Moors and Christians in Juxtlahuaca, Oaxaca.

charro.   Spanish. Elegantly dressed Mexican horsemen. Dancers in Tlaxcala who are dressed to resemble them.

chichimeca.   Nahuatl. Various groups of warlike hunting people from the north who conquered and intermixed with settled agriculturalists in central Mexico from 900 A.D. onward.

Chicomecoatl.   Nahuatl. Seven Serpent. Aztec goddess of maize.

chicotero.   Spanish. Men who preserve discipline in Mayo Lenten ceremonies.

chiflando.   Spanish. Blowing, whistling.

chilolos.   Mixtec. Name given to line dancers in Juxtlahuaca, Oaxaca.

chilolo del ardilla.   Spanish. *Chilolo* of the squirrel. Masked dancer in Juxtlahuaca, Oaxaca.

chinampa.   Nahuatl. Artificially constructed gardens used by Aztecs for truck gardening. Floating gardens.

chinampaneca.   Nahuatl. A chinampa district.

chinelos.   Spanish. Dancers in Cuernavaca, Morelos, who wear large fringed headdresses and long black gowns of the medieval scholar.

chivarando.   Spanish. Dancer in Tlaxcala who uses trousers of cowhide.

chivo.   Spanish. Goat. Goat dance performed at Atzacoaloyan, Guerrero.

cigarro.   Spanish. Cigarette.

Cihuacoatl.   Nahuatl. Serpent woman. Aztec earth goddess.

cihuacoatl.   Nahuatl. Chief priest among pre-Conquest Aztecs. Assumed identity of goddess of the same name. Title of powerful advisor to Aztec rulers. De facto co-ruler. Leader of *chachalmecas*.

cimarrones.   Spanish. Insurgent, fugitive slaves.

códices. Spanish. Books made by indigenous artists in Colonial Mexico.

cofradía. Spanish. Religious brotherhood serving the Virgin or patron saint.

colorín. Spanish. A softwood from the coral tree used to make masks. Latin name: *Erythrina coralloides*.

comadre, compadre. Spanish. Ritual co-mother or co-father. Terms of deep respect used to designate relationships between parents and godparents.

conchero. Spanish. Urban dancers organized in para-military fashion. Name derives from use of armadillo shells. Also known as Aztec dancers because their costumes reflect romantic notions concerning Aztec appearance.

conquista. Spanish. The Spanish Conquest of Mexico led by Hernán Cortés, 1519–21.

conquista, danzas de. Spanish. Conquest dances. Variations on dances of Moors and Christians, performed in many parts of Mexico.

copal. From Nahuatl. Resin used as incense.

corona de quetzal. Spanish, Nahuatl. Quetzal bird crown. A headdress worn by the *quetzal* dancers in the Sierra Norte de Puebla.

Cortés, el. Spanish. Character in Conquest dances representing Hernán Cortés, conqueror of Mexico. Also known as *el marqués* (Cortés's title).

costumbre. Spanish. Custom.

costumbre ya'uchim. Spanish, Mayo. Ritual officers who enforce customs.

credo. Spanish. Articles of faith. Christian doctrine.

cuacuacuitlin. Nahuatl. Elite grade of Aztec priest.

cuadrillas. Spanish. Quadrilles. Courtly square dances brought from Europe.

cuauhehuetque. Nahuatl. The most elite grade of Aztec priest.

cuerudo. Spanish. Tlaxcalan dancer who wears cowhide.

cuexcochtechimalli. Nahuatl. Paper rosette and cone headdress element worn in Aztec rituals.

culebra. Spanish. Serpent. Part of *paragüero* dance in Tlaxcala.

cura. Spanish. Priest.

Curicaueri, Tirepenie Curicaueri. Tarascan. God of Tarascan ruling lineage in pre-Conquest period.

dama. Spanish. Lady.

danza. Spanish. Dance.

diablo. Spanish. Devil.

Doña Marina. Spanish. The name the Spaniards used for Malintzin, the Indian woman who was Hernán Cortés's mistress and interpretor. Her character appears frequently in Conquest dances where she is referred to as *La Malinche*.

ejido. Spanish. A parcel of land established by Mexican law after the Revolution. This land is owned and worked communally.

encabezado. Spanish. Headman. Leader of a dance group.

encargados. Spanish. Those responsible for the functioning of the group, including dance instruction and rehearsal.

enmascarado. Spanish. Masked one.

ermitaño, hermitaño. Spanish. Clown character who represents a Colonial friar in Shepherds' plays.

escribano. Spanish. Actuary, notary, scriviner. A post in the *cargo* system.

etzalcualiztli. Nahuatl. A month dedicated to Tlaloc. Seventh of the twenty-day periods into which the Aztec year was divided.

faja. Spanish. A belt or sash usually woven on the traditional back-strap loom.

fariseos. Spanish. Pharisees. Characters in Lenten ceremonial dances and dramas.

feos. Spanish. Uglies. A generic term in the Tarascan region for buffoon characters who participate in masked ceremonials.

feria primaveral. Spanish. Spring festival.

fiscal   Spanish. Attorney general, clerk, treasurer. A post in the *cargo* system.

flautero.   Spanish. Flutist.

gachupín.   Spanish. A contemptuous name for Spanish settlers in Mexico.

gallina.   Spanish. Hen.

gente de razón.   Spanish. People of reason. Indigenous people commonly use this term to refer to Spanish-speaking mestizos.

Gloria.   Spanish. Part of the observance of Holy Week, occuring on Saturday before Easter Sunday.

guarda de espaldas.   Spanish. Bodyguard. One of the officers in the Mayo ceremonial organization.

guare.   Tarascan. Woman. A woman dressed in traditional Tarascan finery.

hacienda.   Spanish. Landed estate, plantation.

herrero.   Spanish. Ironworker, blacksmith.

h'men.   Mayan. Indigenous priest.

Hñähñü.   Hñähñü. The term the Otomíes use to refer to themselves.

hortelanos.   Spanish. Truck gardeners. Buffoon characters in Uruapan festivals for patron saints.

hospital.   Spanish. Hospital. In Colonial times a place where the sick were cared for and the indigenous people were instructed in catechicism and crafts. The hospital was introduced into the New World by the Spaniards. Today, among the Tarascans, it is the place where those responsible for one of the most prestigious *cargos* live and hold feasts in honor of the Virgin whose chapel adjoins.

huacal.   Nahuatl. A wooden frame placed on the back and carried by means of a tump line. Traditionally, traders secured their wares to the *huacal. Huacales* have been in use in Mexico since long before the arrival of Europeans. A variation, in the form of a chair, is carried by the Blackman of Nuevo San Juan Parangaricutiro, Michoacán.

huacalero.   Nahuatl. Long-distance peddler with *huacal.*

huapango.   Spanish. Modern country dance native to the Sierra Norte de Puebla, the southern Huasteca in the state of Veracruz, and the adjacent Gulf Coast region.

huarache.   Tarascan. Sandal.

huehues.   Nahuatl. Old men, old ones. Another name for *catrín* dancers in Tlaxcala.

huehuetl.   Nahuatl. Wooden drum of pre-Conquest type. Drum used in Carnival dance at Mérida, Yucatán.

huetzquistle.   From Nahuatl. A character who accompanies the Mecos dance in Mochitlán. Guerrero.

huipil.   Nahuatl. Woman's woven garment. A traditional item of feminine apparel in pre-Conquest period, the *huipil* has survived into the present day.

humdø.   Hñähñü. Dancers representing old people.

indígenas.   Spanish. Indians, indigenous people.

Inmaculada, la.   Spanish. The Virgin of the Immaculate Conception. Her day, December 8, marks the beginning of the winter ceremonial season in Tarascan communities.

inspikuriri.   Tarascan. A long-distance trader or merchant who usually carries his wares on his back. Same as *huacalero.*

Itom Achai.   Mayo. Any form of Our Father, God, Jesus, Christ, the crucified Christ, other crosses, or manifestations of male divinity.

Itom Achai O'ola.   Mayo. God the Father, Our Father Old Man God.

Itom Achai Usi.   Mayo. Jesus, Our Father Son, the Holy Infant.

Itom Aye.   Mayo. Our Mother, the Virgin Mary.

ixtle.   Nahuatl. Agave fiber used for weaving cloth since pre-Hispanic times.

jarabe.   Spanish. Name given to various popular dances throughout Mexico.

jardinero.   Spanish. Gardener. Name for participants in a dance in Zapotecan towns of Oaxaca.

joyero mayor. Spanish. Leader of the *judíos* in Mayo Lenten ceremonies.

judíos. Spanish. Jews. Characters in Mayo Lenten ceremonies.

Kalbario. From Spanish *Calvario*. Calvary. Way of the Cross. The last station in the Mayo Way of the Cross.

Kao O'ola. Mayo. Old hill. Serves as Calvary in Lenten ceremonies.

kengyi. Tarascan. Steward. In pre-Conquest times, the keeper of the ruler's granary. Today, the *mayordomo* of the hospital.

konti. Mayo. The service of the Way of the Cross each Friday of Lent except Good Friday, and other services involving processions surrounding the church.

ladinos. Spanish. Hispanicized, Christianized blacks brought to Mexico usually from Seville and Lisbon.

lansam. Mayo, from Spanish. Swords.

latu nucaca. Mixtec. Old man. A clown figure.

letra, la. Spanish. A dance leader representing a blackman in Cherán, Michoacán.

liana. Spanish, from French *liane*. Vine. The ropes used by performers in the Flying Pole dance of the Sierra Norte de Puebla and Papantla, Veracruz.

limosna. Spanish. A contribution either to the church or to ceremonial organizations. Any small donation.

listones. Spanish. Ribbons. Ribbon dance. Resembles European maypole dance. Popular in Tlaxcala and Puebla.

locos. Spanish. Crazies. Name of dance group in Tepeyanco, Tlaxcala.

Loria Ultima. Mayo, from Spanish. The last *Gloria*. One of three sacred ways in Mayo Lenten rituals.

Luzbel. Spanish. The character of Lucifer in Shepherds' and Miracle plays.

machitos. Spanish. Little mule drivers. Dance performed in Zitlala, Guerrero.

macho. Spanish. Male, masculine. Name of a character in dance from Juxtlahuaca, Oaxaca.

madrina. Spanish. Godmother.

maestro. Spanish. Teacher and organizer of a dance. Lay minister in Mayo Lenten ceremonies.

mahoma. Spanish. Mohammed. Name of a black-faced clown character in Juxtlahuaca, Oaxaca.

mahoma de ardilla. Spanish. Mohammed of the squirrel. A masked clown who performs at Carnival in Juxtlahuaca, Oaxaca.

maizos. Spanish. Maize cultivators. Similar to dance of tlacololeros performed in Mochitlán, Guerrero.

Malinalxochitl. Nahuatl. Rebellious sister of Aztec patron Uitzilopochtli.

Malinche. From Nahuatl. Hernán Cortés's Indian mistress and interpreter. Also known as Doña Marina and Malintzin. This character is portrayed in Conquest dances by a man or boy dressed in woman's clothing.

manda. Spanish. A religious vow. Usually the motivation for participation in masked dances.

mandón. Spanish. Commander. High ranking officer in *cargo* system.

mantón de Manila. Spanish. A large overcoat-like cape.

manueles. Spanish. Emanuels. A dance performed in Tixtla, Guerrero.

maringuilla. Spanish. Mariquita, little Mary. A man or boy masked or otherwise disguised as a woman in ceremonial dances.

marqués, el. Spanish. Marquis. Character representing Hernán Cortés in Conquest dances.

maromero. Spanish. Acrobat. Tight-rope walker. Somersaulter.

mascada. Spanish. Scarf worn by dancers. Often worn across the chest.

máscara. Spanish. Mask.

mascaritas gritonas. Spanish. The little screaming masks. Characters who spread gossip in dance from Juxtlhuaca, Oaxaca.

maso. . Mayo. Deer dancer.

matachines. Spanish. A performance by elegantly dressed dancers whose costumes incorporate many ribbons. Widely performed, especially in northern Mexico.

matachini. From Spanish. Dancers. A church dance society among the Mayos.

mayordomo. Spanish. Steward. *Carguero* in the civil-ceremonial organization.

maxtlatl. Nahuatl. Apron-like loin cloth worn by Aztec men in the pre-Conquest and Colonial periods. Part of dance costume in Sierra Norte de Puebla.

mecos, los. From Nahuatl. Contraction of *chichimecos,* pre-Hispanic hunting groups known for their war-like nature. A dance performed in Mochitlán, Guerrero.

media careta. Spanish. Half-face masks. A small mask covering part, but not all, of the face.

mercaderes. Spanish. Merchants, dealers, tradesmen. Dance performed in Chapa, Guerrero.

merino. Spanish. Magistrate, supervisor of sheep. A post in the *cargo* system.

mescal. From Nahuatl. Liquor made from distilled agave juice.

meseta tarasca. Spanish. The high plateau in Michoacán where many Tarascan villages are located.

mestizaje. Spanish. Racial mixing.

mestizo. Spanish. A person of mixed racial ancestry.

mexica. Nahuatl. The historical name for the people we call Aztecs.

Mictlantecuhtli. Nahuatl. Lord of the land of the dead.

Micticacihuatl. Nahuatl. Death deity.

michuaque. Nahuatl. People from the place of fish. Aztecs' name for Tarascans.

mole. Nahuatl. Sauce made from chiles and other ingredients. Meat or fowl prepared with this sauce.

moro. Spanish. Moor.

moro cabezón. Spanish. Big-headed Moor.

moro chino. Spanish. Curly-haired Moor. An Islamicized black.

mo'oro. From Spanish. An advisor in Mayo Lenten ceremonies.

moros y cristianos. Spanish. Moors and Christians. Combat dances introduced by the Spaniards to Mexico, where they were reinterpreted as conflict between *indígenas* and conquerors.

muertos, días de los. Spanish. Days of the Dead. All Saints Day, November 1; and All Souls Day, November 2.

municipio. Spanish. A political division similar to a county in the United States.

nacimiento. Spanish. Nativity scene.

nahual. Nahuatl. A dialect related to Nahuatl.

nahuas. Nahuatl. Name of the indigenous group that speaks Nahuatl.

Nahuatl. A member of the Ute-Aztecan language family. The language spoken by pre-Conquest Aztecs and still spoken by thousands of contemporary Mexicans.

nakatamales. Tarascan. Maize dumplings filled with *mole.*

negrito comilludo. Spanish. Black masks with tusks danced by Zapotecs in Oaxaca.

negritos. Spanish. Dancers wearing masks representing black Africans who were brought to Mexico in large numbers during the Colonial period. Variations of these masks are used all over Mexico. When referring to participants in a dance, the use of the term *negrito* implies affection and familiarity.

negro de la pastorela. Spanish. Character representing a black pageboy in the Shepherds' dance of Uruapan, Michoacán.

negros. Spanish. Blacks. Dancers in Blackman performances.

negros sordos. Spanish. Deaf blacks. Name of a dance in the state of Mexico.

Nochebuena. Spanish. Christmas Eve.

nochebuenas.   Spanish. Poinsettias.

nortes.   Spanish. Winds from the United States and Canada that bring rain and cold weather to the eastern portions of Mexico.

obraje.   Spanish. Woolen mill. During the Colonial period Indians were forced to work in such mills as a form of tribute payment or punishment. In Mexico, blacks frequently served as overseers in these mills.

ocote.   Nahuatl. Resinous pine tree.

octava.   Spanish. Octave. The eighth day of a festival. A repetition of celebrations held a week after the initial date of the festivity.

ochpaniztli.   Nahuatl. A harvest festival in pre-Conquest times. Twelfth of the eighteen twenty-day periods into which the Aztec year was divided.

o'ola.   Mayo. Old. Old man. An image that is captured in Lenten rituals. An actor who impersonates the old man character who is said to represent Christ.

palito.   Spanish. Little stick or rod.

palenques.   Spanish. Palisades. Settlements of insurgent blacks in Colonial Mexico.

palo volador.   Spanish. Flying Pole used by the *voladores* in the Flying Pole dance.

pan dulce.   Spanish. Sweet pastries and rolls.

panquetzaliztli.   Nahuatl. Sixteenth period of twenty days in the Aztec calender.

paragüeros.   Spanish. Dancers from Tlaxcala whose headdresses resemble umbrellas.

parisero.   Mayo. Pharisee. Character in Mayo Lenten rituals, a member of a sodality.

pariserom.   Mayo. Performers in Lenten rituals. Name of Lenten sodality.

parota.   Tarascan. A tropical soft wood used in mask making.

pascola.   Spanish. Ritual host of every Mayo and Yaqui fiesta.

pascoleros.   Spanish. Term for Lenten performers among the Tarahumaras.

paskome.   Mayo, from Spanish. Ritual hosts.

pastorela.   Spanish. A play of shepherds. A traditional play or dance with religious content, usually performed at Christmas time.

pastores.   Spanish. Shepherds.

patria, la.   Spanish. The fatherland. Mexico.

Pecado.   Spanish. Sin. A devil figure in the Shepherds' and Miracle plays.

penitente.   Spanish. Penitent.

Perra.   Spanish. Bitch. A mask that represents a female dog in the *tecuanes* dance in Guerrero.

pescado.   Spanish. Fish. Dance of the Fish. Dances honoring fisherman are performed in several places in Mexico.

Pilato.   Spanish. Pontius Pilate.

pilatom.   Mayo, from Spanish. The highest *parisero* office and the head of the *pariserom.*

pluma.   Spanish. Feather. Name given to dance performed by Zapotec communities in the state of Oaxaca.

pozole.   Nahuatl. Festival stew of pork and hominy.

principales.   Spanish. Principal persons. Members of a *cabildo.*

purépecha.   Tarascan. Tarascan language and culture. Commoners in pre-Conquest days.

quecholli.   Nahuatl. Fifteenth of the twenty day periods in the pre-Conquest Aztec calendar.

quetzalcoatl totec tlamacazqui.   Nahuatl. The leader of one half of the Aztec priesthood.

quetzales.   Nahuatl. Tropical birds with blue-green plumage. Dancers in Cuetzalan, Puebla, who dress to resemble the birds.

Ra Zitu.   Hñąhñų. Deity. Eater of the dead.

ramada.   Spanish. Bower.

ranchería.   Spanish. Hamlet.

rancho.   Spanish. Small farm, ranch. A small, isolated community.

ranchero.   Spanish. A person who lives on a *rancho. Ranchero* characters are often burlesqued in masked dances.

reconquista. Spanish. The Reconquest. Refers to centuries of war waged by Spanish Christians to free Spain from Moslem rule.

reina de los huipiles. Spanish. The queen of the *huipiles.* A woman dressed in traditional indigerous clothing in the Sierra Norte de Puebla.

relato. Spanish. Account. The story of Jesus' birth.

remate, el. Spanish. The end and culmination of festivities.

reto. Spanish. Challenge. Challenges of the Saints.

rubios. Spanish. Blonds. Dancers dressed like cowboys in Juxtlahuaca, Oaxaca.

Sabario. Spanish. Sabarius. Men who wear heavy aluminum masks in the dance of the *Archareos,* state of Mexico. Companion of Pilate in dances from Sierra Norte de Puebla.

sabio. Spanish. Man of knowledge.

San Juan. Spanish. Saint John.

San Marcos. Saint Mark.

San Martín Caballero. Spanish. Saint Martin the horseman.

Santa Cruz. Spanish. Holy Cross.

Santa Kurus paskome. From Spanish. Ritual hosts in Mayo Lenten ceremonies devoted to the Holy Cross.

santero. Spanish. Carver of religious images. Sometimes a carver of masks.

Santiago. Spanish. Saint James the Elder, Patron saint of Spain. Character in Mexican combat masquerades.

Santiago Caballero. Spanish. Saint James riding his white horse as he appeared in visions to Spanish Christian soldiers during the *reconquista.* Dance character of Saint James with a hobby horse around his waist.

Santo Niño. Spanish. The Holy Child. An image representing the infant Jesus.

santo sewam. Spanish, Mayo. The Holy Flowers.

Santísima Tiniran paskome. From Spanish. Ritual hosts in Mayo Lenten ceremonies devoted to the Holy Trinity.

segadores. Spanish. Harvesters. Name of dance in state of Mexico.

segundo. Spanish. A dance leader in Cherán, Michoacán.

semaneros. Spanish. In Michoacán, an association comprised of married couples who take turns caring for the chapel of the Virgin adjacent to the hospital.

sewateri. Mayo. One of three sacred ways in Mayo Lenten rituals.

siete vicios. Spanish. The seven vices. Represented by masks in plays with religious content performed especially at Christmas and Easter.

soldados. Spanish. Soldiers.

soldados razos. Spanish. Rank-and-file soldiers. Characters in Mayo Lenten ceremonies.

sonaja. Spanish. Rattle.

suela. Spanish. Sole. Leather.

sunni. Mayo. Cane.

tamboleros, tampoleros. From Spanish. Drummers in Mayo Lenten ceremonies.

taras, thare. Unkown. Said by colonial missionaries to refer to deities worshipped by Tarascans.

tastoanes. From Nahuatl. Masked characters in combat dramas performed in state of Jalisco.

tatanake. Mayo. To throw down.

tebatpo kurusim. Mayo, Spanish. House crosses.

tecolote. Nahuatl. Owl.

tecomate. Nahuatl. Wooden platform affixed to the pole used in the Flying Pole dance.

tecuacuiltin. Nahuatl. Category of priests among the Aztecs.

tecuani. Nahuatl. Jaguar. Wild beast, man-eater. Dances of *tecuanes* are performed in Guerrero.

tecuilhuitontli. Nahuatl. Eighth of the twenty-day periods into which the Aztec year was divided.

tejorones.   Unkown. Characters in dances performed in coastal Mixteca region, state of Oaxaca, who employ small masks.

templo.   Spanish. Church.

tenebarim, tenabares, tenovaris.   Mayo. Strings of dried moth cocoons filled with small pebbles and wrapped around the legs of dancers.

teocalli.   Nahuatl. Aztec temple or pyramid.

Teocalli de la Guerra Sagrada.   Nahuatl, Spanish. Pyramid of the Sacred War. A miniature stone pyramid found in the foundations of Moctezuma II's palace.

teponaxtle.   Nahuatl. Indigenous wooden slit drum.

tequila.   Unknown. A liquor distilled from fermented maguey juice.

tequilma.   Nahuatl. Tribute laborers. Officers in ceremonial organization in Tlaxcala.

tequio.   Nahuatl. Labor paid as tribute to the community.

terroncillo.   Spanish. Dance of cowboys in Chapa, Guerrero.

tigre.   Spanish. Jaguar. Many masks representing this character are danced in Mexico, especially in the southern part of the nation.

tilma.   Nahuatl. A large cloak worn knotted over one shoulder by Aztec men in pre-Conquest and early Colonial times.

tititl.   Nahuatl. Seventeenth of the twenty-day period into which the Aztec year was divided.

tlacuache.   Nahuatl. Opossum.

Tlaloc.   Nahuatl. Aztec god of rain and water.

tlaloc totec tlamacazqui.   Nahuatl. Leader of one half of Aztec priesthood.

tlaloque.   Nahuatl. Assistants of the rain god, Tlaloc. Aztec priests dedicated to his service.

tlamacazque.   Nahuatl. Priest. The priests of Tlaloc.

tlenamacaque.   Nahuatl. Fire priests. Rank below cuacuacuitlin in priestly hierarchy.

tlimetl.   Nahuatl. A cleft reed staff.

Toci/Tlazolteotl.   Nahuatl. Aztec earth goddeses. Our Grandmother (Toci); Eater of Filth (Tlazolteotl).

Tonatiuh.   Nahuatl. Aztec sun god.

topiles.   Nahuatl. Policemen. Officers in *cargo* system.

topiltzin.   Nahuatl. Title of high priest among Aztecs.

torero.   Spanish. Bullfighter.

torito.   Spanish. Little bull. A framework with a bull's head in front that is carried over the dancer's head. Often it has firecrackers attached. European in origin.

toro.   Spanish. Bull. Bull dancer in Mérida, Yucatán.

traje indio.   Spanish. Traditional homespun cotton suit of the Mexican peasant consisting of *camisa* and *calzón*—cotton tunic shirt and trousers.

trecena.   Spanish. Period of thirteen days. Twenty such periods constituted the 260-day ritual calendar of the Aztecs.

trojes.   Spanish. Granaries. Tarascan timber houses.

tuisi litila.   Mayo. Very tired.

tumba.   Spanish. Tomb. A mound of earth that symbolizes the tomb of Jesus in Mayo Lenten ceremonies.

tuno, el.   Spanish. The fruit of the prickly pear cactus. A masked character who represents the father of "Beauty" in Juxtlahuaca, Oaxaca.

turí uarari, or turísha uarani.   Tarascan. Black dancers. Term for those who participate in Blackman dances. Foreigners.

turía, turíacha.   Tarascan. Blacks, black lords, blackmen. Beings who control the air.

tzoalli.   Nahuatl. A paste of amaranth seeds shaped into images of gods in pre-Columbian times. Thought to represent their flesh.

tzompantle.   Nahuatl. Coral tree. Soft wood used in mask making.

Tzontemoc.   Nahuatl. Aztec death god.

uacusecha.   Tarascan. Eagles. Eagle lineage.

ueitecuihuitl.   Nahuatl. Aztec period of twenty days.

uixachtlan.   Nahuatl. Name of hill where Aztec priests drilled new fire.

Uixtocihuatl.   Nahuatl. Aztec salt goddess. Older sister of the Tlaloques.

uixtoti.   Nahuatl. Aztec sacrificial priests who wore the eagle claw headdress.

urna.   Spanish. Glass case containing image of Jesus.

vaquero.   Spanish. Cowboy.

vara.   Spanish. Ceremonial staff symbolic of governance. Cared for by a *carguero*. Originally given by Spaniards to leaders of indigenous communities.

varitas.   Spanish. The little rods. A warrior dance from Huasteca, San Luis Potosí, in which dancers fence with small decorated canes.

vasario.   From Spanish *vasallo*. Vassal. Costumed couples in Tlaxcala dances.

venado.   Spanish. Deer. Deer dance. Clown performers who mimic the serious Deer dancers in Mayo Lenten ceremonies.

viejo, viejito.   Spanish. Old man, little old man. Popular dance character all over Mexico. The meaning of this character may vary from region to region and from dance to dance.

voladores.   Spanish. Performers in the Flying Pole dance.

wakavaki.   Mayo. Special fiesta stew.

warehma, warezma.   Mayo, from Spanish *cuaresma*. Lent.

wikosa.   Mayo. Waist band and rope used by Mayo *o'ola* in Holy Week ceremonies.

xicolli.   Nahuatl. A short jacket worn by men and boys in pre-Conquest Aztec society.

Xilonen.   Nahuatl. Aztec maize goddess.

Xipe Totec.   Nahuatl. Deity of springtime, seeding, and planting.

Xochimilco, Lake.   Nahuatl. A lake with chinampas, or floating gardens near Mexico City.

xochipayo.   Nahuatl. Festive sash worn by the *Sabario* character in the Sierra Norte de Puebla.

xtoles.   Maya. Dancers in Mérida, Yucatán, who perform during Carnival season costumed in romanticized version of indigenous dress.

ya'uchim.   Mayo. Officers in the *parisero* sodality.

yonxitzá.   Hñähñü. Dry leaves.

zapateado.   Spanish. A tap dance in which the dancers wear *botines*, rather than *huaraches*.

BIBLIOGRAPHY

Cecelia F. Klein
Tlaloc Masks as Insignia of Office in the Mexica-Aztec Hierarchy

Acosta Saignes, Miguel

1946 "Los Teopixque." *Revista Mexicana Estudios Antropológicos* 8: 147–205.

Broda, Johanna

1978 "Relaciones políticas ritualizadas: El ritual como expresión de una ideología." In *Economía política e ideología en el México prehispanico*, Pedro Carrasco and Johanna Broda, eds. Mexico City: Centro de Investigaciones Superiores del Instituto Nacional de Antropología e Historia, Editorial Nueva Imagen, pp. 251–55.

Brown, Betty Ann

1979 "All around the Xocotl Pole: Reexamination of an Aztec Sacrificial Ceremony." Paper presented at Forty-third International Congress of Americanists, Vancouver, B.C., August.

1984 "Ochpaniztli in Historical Perspective." In *Ritual Human Sacrifice in Mesoamerica*, Elizabeth H. Boone, ed. Washington, D.C.. Dumbarton Oaks, pp. 195–210.

Caso, Alfonso

1927 "El teocalli de la guerra sagrada: Descripción y estudio del monolito encontrado en los cimientos del Palacio Nacional." *Monografías del Museo Nacional de Arqueología, Historia y Etnografía*, no. 3. Mexico City: Publicaciones de la Secretaria de Educación Pública.

1929 "El Uso de los máscaras entre los antiguos mexicanos." *Mexican Folkways* 5: 111–13.

1958 *The Aztecs: People of the Sun.* Norman: University of Oklahoma Press.

1967 *Los calendarios prehispánicos.* Mexico City: Instituto de Investigaciones Históricas, Universidad Nacional Autónoma de México.

Codex Borbonicus

1974 *Codex Borbonicus*, K. A. Novotny, ed. Graz, Austria: Akademische Druck-u. und Verlagsanstalt.

Codex Magliabecchiano

1970 *Codex Magliabecchiano: CL XIII. 3 (B.R.) 232*, Ferdinand Anders, ed. Graz, Austria: Akademische Druck-u. und Verlagsanstalt.

Codex Ramírez

1975 "Códice Ramírez." In *Crónica mexicana/Códice Ramírez*, 2d ed., D. Manuel Orozco y Berra, ed. Mexico City: Editorial Porrúa, S.A., pp. 77–149.

Codex Rios

1964 "Códice Vaticano Latino 3738 o Códice Vaticanus Rios." In *Antigüedades de México basadas en la recopilación de Lord Kingsborough*, José Córona Núñez, ed. Mexico City: Secretaria de Hacienda y Crédito Público, vol. 3, pp. 7–313.

Durán, Fray Diego

1967 *Historia de las indias de Nueva España e islas de la tierra firme*, Angel Ma. Garibay K., ed. Mexico City: Editorial Porrúa, S.A., 2 vols.

1971 *Book of the Gods and Rites and the Ancient Calendar*, Fernando Horcasitas and Doris Heyden, trans. and eds. Norman: University of Oklahoma Press.

Hvidtfeldt, Arild

1978   *Teotl and Ixiptlatli: Some Central Conceptions in Ancient Mexican Religion.* Reprint of 1958 ed. Ann Arbor, Mich.: University Microfilms International.

Jiménez Moreno, Wigberto, ed.

1974   *'Primeros memoriales' de Fray Bernardino de Sahagún,* Colección Científica 16. Mexico City: Instituto Nacional de Antropología e Historia, Consejo de Historia.

Klein, Cecelia F.

1976   "The Identity of the Central Deity on the Axtec Calendar Stone." *Art Bulletin* 58(1): 1–12.

1980   "Who Was Tlaloc?" *Journal of Latin American Lore* 6(2): 155–204.

1984   "¿Dioses de la lluvia o sacerdotes ofrendadores del Fuego? Un estudio socio-político de algunas representaciones mexicas del dios Tláloc." *Estudios de Cultura Náhuatl* 17: 33–50.

1986   "Masking Empire: The Material Effects of Masks in Aztec Mexico." *Art History* 9(22): 136–66.

n.d.   "Rethinking Cihuacoatl: Political Imagery of the Conquered Woman." In *Smoke and Mist: Meso-american Studies in Memory of Thelma D. Sullivan,* J. Kathryn Josserand and Karen Dakin, eds. BAR International Series. Oxford: BAR. In press.

Padden, R. C.

1970   *The Hummingbird and the Hawk: Conquest and Sovereignty in the Valley of Mexico, 1503–1541.* New York: Harper & Row.

Palacios, Enrique Juan

1929   "La Piedra del Escudo Nacional de México." *Publicaciones de la Secretaría de Educación Pública* 22, no. 9. Mexico City: Dirección de Arqueología.

Parsons, Jeffrey R.

1976   "The Role of Chinampa Agriculture in the Food Supply of Aztec Tenochtitlan." In *Cultural Change and Continuity: Essays in Honor of James Bennett Griffin,* Charles E. Cleland, ed. New York: Academic Press, pp. 233–57.

Pomar, Juan Bautista

1975   *Relación de Tezcoco.* Reprint ed. of 1891 work, Joaquín García Icazbalceta, ed. Biblioteca Enciclopédica del Estado de México.

Rounds, J.

1977   "The Role of the Cihuacoatl in Succession to the Aztec Throne." Term paper, Department of Anthropology, University of California, Los Angeles.

Sahagún, Fray Bernardino de

1950–1969   *Florentine Codex: General History of the Things of New Spain,* Arthur J. O. Anderson and Charles E. Dibble, trans. Monographs of the School of American Research and the Museum of New Mexico, no. 14, pt. 2. 13 vols. Santa Fe, N.M.: School of American Research and University of Utah.

1977   *Historia general de las cosas de Nueva España,* 3d ed. Mexico City: Editorial Porrúa, S.A., Mexico City: 4 vols.

Seler, Eduard

1939   *Gesammelte Abhandlungen zur Amerikanische Sprach und Altertumskunde,* J. Eric S. Thompson and Francis B. Richardson, eds. Mimeographed English translation of selected articles from the 1902–3 work. Cambridge, England: Carnegie Institution of Washington, 5 vols.

1960–1961   *Gesammelte Abhandlungen zur Amerikanischen Sprach und Altertumskunde.* Graz, Austria: Akademische Druck-u. und Verlagsanstalt.

Sullivan, Thelma D.

1976 "The Mask of Itztlacoliuhqui." *Actas del XLI Congreso Internacional de Americanistas, México 2 al 7 de Septiembre de 1974*, 2: 252–62.

Tibón, Gutierre
1975 *Historia del nombre y de la Fundación de México.* Mexico City: Fondo de Cultura Económica.

Townsend, Richard Fraser
1979 *State and Cosmos in the Art of Tenochtitlán.* Studies in Pre-Columbian Art and Archaeology, no. 20. Washington, D.C.: Dumbarton Oaks.

Zantwijk, Rudolf van
1963 "Principios organizadores de los mexicas, una introducción al estudio del sistema interno del régimen azteca." *Estudios de Cultura Náhuatl* 4: 187–222.
1966 "Los seis barrios sirvientes de Huitzilopochtli." *Estudios de Cultura Náhuatl* 6: 177–85.

María Teresa Pomar
Mexican Masks and Ceremonial Dances

Brown, Betty Ann
1978 *Máscaras: Dance Masks of Mexico and Guatemala.* University Museum, Illinois State University.

Carrillo A., Rafael
1971 *Introducción lo efímero y eterno del arte popular mexicano.* Mexico: Fondo Editorial de la Plástica Mexicana.

Cook de Leonard, Carmen
1953 *Máscaras.* Vol. 1 + 1. Mexico: Editorial Yañez.

Cordry, Donald
1980 *Mexican Masks.* Austin: University of Texas Press.

Covarrubias, Miguel
1945 *Máscaras mexicanas.* Mexico: Sociedad de Arte Moderno.

Durán, Fray Diego

1967 *Historia de los indios de Nueva España.* Mexico: Porrúa.

Griffith, James S., and Felipe S. Molina
1980 *Old Men of the Fiesta: An Introduction to the Pascola Arts.* Phoenix: Heard Museum.

Landa, Fray Diego de
1959 *Relación de las cosas de Yucatán.* Mexico: Porrúa.

Lechuga, Ruth D.
1981 Unedited conference paper on a psychosomatic interpretation of mask use. Mexico.

Luna Parra de García Sanz, Georgina, and Graciela Romandia de Cantú
1979 *El Paisaje de México en el mundo de la máscara.* Mexico: Fomento Cultural Banamex.

Mompradé, Electra L., and Tonatiúh Gutiérrez
1976 *Danzas y bailes populares.* Mexico: Hermes.

Montenegro, Roberto
1926 *Máscaras mexicanas.* Mexico: Secretaria Educación Pública.

Moya Rubio, Victor José
1978 *Máscaras: La otra cara de México.* Mexico: Universidad Nacional Autónoma de México.

Sahagún, Fray Bernardino de
1956 *Historia de las cosas de la Nueva España.* Mexico: Porrúa.

Sodi, Demetrio M.
1975 *Máscaras: Arte popular mexicano.* Mexico: Herrero.

Toor, Frances
1939 *Mexican Popular Arts.* Mexico.

Villaurrutia, Xavier
1926 *Máscaras mexicanas.* Mexico: Secretaria Educacional Pública.

Vogt, Evan Z.
1979 *Ofrendas para los dioses.* Mexico: Fondo de Cultura Económica.

Marsha C. Bol
Mexican Masked Festivals at the Turn of the Century, as Witnessed by Frederick Starr

Calderón de la Barca, Frances
1966   *Life in Mexico. The Letters of Fanny Calderón de la Barca, with New Material from the Author's Private Journals.* Howard T. Fisher and Marion Hall Fisher, eds. New York: Doubleday. Originally published 1843.
Cole, Garold
1978   *American Travelers to Mexico, 1821–1972; A Descriptive Bibliography.* Troy, N.Y.: Whitson Publishing Company.
Gardiner, Clinton Harvey
1952   "Foreign Travelers' Accounts of Mexico, 1810–1910." *Americas* 8: 321–51.
Lameiras, Brigitte B. de
1973   *Indios de México y viajeros extranjeros, siglo XIX.* Mexico: Secretaria de Educación Pública.
Lumholtz, Carl
1902   *Unknown Mexico.* 2 vols. New York: Charles Scribner's Sons.
Starr, Frederick
1892   "Anthropological Work in America." *Popular Science Monthly,* 41 (July 1892): 289–307.
1894–   Field Notes and Papers.
1928   Special Collections. Joseph Regenstein Library, University of Chicago.
1896a   "Popular Celebrations in Mexico." *Journal of American Folk-lore* 9: 161–69.
1896b   "How We Saw the Tastoanes." *Outlook,* January 18.
1898   *Catalogue of a Collection of Objects Illustrating the Folklore of Mexico.* Wiesbaden: Publications of the Folklore Society; Nendelm: Kraus, 1967 edition.
1899   *Indians of Southern Mexico: An Ethnographic Album.* Chicago: [the author].
1900–   *Notes upon the Ethnography of Southern Mexico.* Davenport, Iowa: Putnam Memorial Publication Fund. Reprinted from vols. 8 (Part 1) and 9 (Part 2), *Proceedings of Davenport Academy of Natural Sciences.* 1900, Part 1; 1902, Part 2.
1902a   "The Tastoanes." *Journal of American Folk-lore* 15(57): 73–82.
1902b   *The Physical Characteristics of the Indians of Southern Mexico.* Chicago: Decennial Publications, University of Chicago.
1908   *In Indian Mexico: A Narrative of Travel and Labor.* Chicago: Forbes and Co.; reprint ed. 1978, New York: AMS Press.

James S. Griffith
Holy Week in Los Patos, Sinaloa

Crumrine, N. Ross
1977   *The Mayo Indians of Sonora: A People Who Refuse to Die.* Tucson: University of Arizona Press.
Griffith, James S., and Felipe Molina
1980   *Old Men of the Fiesta: An Introduction to the Pascola Arts.* Phoenix: Heard Museum.
Painter, Muriel Thayer
1986   *With Good Heart: Yaqui Beliefs and Ceremonies in a Pascua Village.* Tucson: University of Arizona Press.
Spicer, Edward H.
1980   *The Yaquis: A Cultural History.* Tucson: University of Arizona Press.

N. Ross Crumrine
Ritual Mediation of the Life-Death Opposition: The Meaning of Mayo *Parisero* Lenten Masks

Beals, Ralph L.
1943   "The Aboriginal Culture of the Cahita Indians." *Ibero-Americana* 19.

1945 "The Contemporary Culture of the Cahita Indians." *Bureau of American Ethnology, Bulletin* 142. Washington.

Crumrine, N. Ross

1964 "The House Cross of the Mayo Indians of Sonora, Mexico: A Symbol of Ethnic Identity." *Anthropological Papers of the University of Arizona*, no. 8. Tucson: University of Arizona Press.

1969a "Función del ritual y del simbolismo sagrado en la aculturación y el pluralismo. Con especial referencia al ceremonial Mayo." *Anuario Indigenista* 39: 331–46.

1969b "Capakoba, the Mayo Easter Ceremonial Impersonator: Explanations of Ritual Clowning." *Journal for the Scientific Study of Religion* 8: 1–22.

1973 "La tierra te devorará: un análisis estructural de los mitos de los indígenas mayo." *America Indígena* 33(4): 1119–50. English version published in Katunob 10(3): 26–62, September 1977, issued 1979.

1974a "Anomalous Figures and Liminal Roles: A Reconsideration of the Mayo Indian Capakoba, Northwest Mexico." *Anthropos* 69: 858–73.

1974b El Ceremonial de Pascua y la Identidad de los Mayos de Sonora (Mexico). *Seplini* 31. Mexico: Instituto Nacional Indigenista.

1974c "God's Daughter-in-law, The Old Man, and the Olla: An Archaeological Challenge." *Kiva* 39 (3–4): 277–81.

1975 "A New Mayo Indian Religious Movement in Northwest Mexico." *Journal of Latin American Lore* 1 (2): 127–45.

1976 "Mediating Roles in Ritual and Symbolism: Northwest Mexico and the Pacific Northwest." *Anthropologica* 18(2): 131–52.

1977a *The Mayo Indians of Sonora, Mexico: A People Who Refuse to Die.* Tucson: The University of Arizona Press. Prospect Heights, Illinois: Waveland Press (reprint in progress: 1988).

1977b "El Ceremonial Pascual Mayo de Banari, Un Drama Ritual Sagrado." *Folklore Americano* 24: 111–39.

1979 "Folk Drama in Latin America: A ritual type characterized by Social Unification and Cultural Fusion." Paper presented at the 78th Annual Meeting of the American Anthropological Association, under revision for publication.

1981a "The Mayo of Southern Sonora: Socio-economic Assimilation and Ritual-symbolic Syncretism—Split Acculturation." In *Themes of Indigenous Acculturation in Northwest Mexico*, Thomas B. Hinton and Phil C. Weigand, eds., Anthropological Papers of the University of Arizona, no. 38, pp. 22–35. Tucson: The University of Arizona Press.

1981b "The Ritual of the Cultural Enclave Process: The Dramatization of Oppositions Among the Mayo Indians of Northwest Mexico." In *Persistent Peoples*, George P. Castile and Gilbert Kushner, eds., pp. 109–31. Tucson: University of Arizona Press.

1981c "Folk Drama in Latin America: A Ritual Type Characterized by Social Group Unification and Cultural Fusion." North South: *Canadian Journal of Latin American Studies* 6(12): 103–25.

1982 "Transformational Processes and Models: with Special Reference to Mayo Indian Myth and Ritual. In *The Logic of Culture*, Ino Rossi, ed., pp. 68–87. J.F. Bergin Publishers, Inc.

1983a "Mayo." In *Handbook of North American Indians*, William C. Sturtevant, ed. Alfonso Ortiz, vol. ed., vol. 10, Southwest pp, 264–75. Washington: Smithsonian Institution.

1983b "Mask Use and Meaning in Easter Ceremonialism: The Mayo Parisero." In *The Power of Symbols*, N. Ross Crumrine and Marjorie Halpin, eds., pp. 93–101. Vancouver: University of British Columbia Press.

1986 "Drama Folklorico en Latino America: Estructura y significado del ritual y simbolismo de Cuaresma y de la Semana Santa." *Folklore Americano* 41/42:5–31.

1987a "Reflections, Contrasts, and Directions, by Ralph L. Beals and N. Ross Crumrine. In *Ejidos and Regions of Refuge in Northwest Mexico*, N. Ross Crumrine and Phil C. Weigand, eds. Anthropological Papers of the University of Arizona, no. 46, pp. 1–10. Tucson: University of Arizona Press.

1987b "Mechanisms of Enclavement: Maintenance and Sociocultural Blocking of Modernization Among the Mayo of Southern Sonora." In *Ejidos and Regions of Refuge in Northwest Mexico*, N. Ross Crumrine and Phil C. Weigand, eds. Anthropological Papers of the University of Arizona, Number 46, pp. 21–30. Tucson: University of Arizona Press.

Erasmus Charles J.
1961 *Man Takes Control: Cultural Development and American Aid*. Minneapolis: University of Minnesota Press.

1967 Culture Change in Northwest Mexico. In *Contemporary Change in Traditional Societies*. Julian Steward, ed. vol.III. Mexican and Peruvian Communities. Urbana: University of Illinois Press.

Leach, Edmund R.
1961 *Two Essays Concerning the Symbolic Representation of Time. Rethinking Anthropology.* London: The Athlone Press. Reprinted in *Reader in Comparative Religion: An Anthropological Approach*, William Lessa and Evon Vogt, eds., New York: Harper and Row.

Levi-Strauss, Claude
1963 "The Structural Study of Myth." In *Structural Anthropology*, pp. 206–31. New York: Basic Books.

Spicer, Edward H.
1940 *Pascua, A Yaqui Village in Arizona.* Chicago: University of Chicago Press.

1954 "Potam, A Yaqui Village in Sonora." *American Anthropological Association. Memoir* No. 77.

1964 Apuntes Sobre el Tipo de Religión de los Uto-aztecas Centrales. *Actas y Memorias del XXXV Congreso International de Americanistas*, México. pp. 27–38.

Spicer, Rosamond B.
1939 The Easter Fiesta of the Yaqui Indians of Pascua, Arizona. Unpublished M.A. Thesis, Department of Anthropology, University of Chicago.

Janet Brody Esser
Those Who Are Not From Here: Blackman Dances of Michoacán

Aguirre Beltrán, Gonzalo
1946 *La población negra de México, 1519–1810.* Mexico: Fonda de Cultura Económica.

1952   "La etnohistoria y el estudio del negro en México." In *Acculturation in the Americas*, Sol Tax, ed. Chicago: University of Chicago Press, pp. 161–68.

Beals, Ralph

1946   *Cherán: A Sierra Tarascan Village*. Institute of Social Anthropology, Publication 2. Washington, D.C.: Smithsonian Institution.

Borah, Woodrow, and Sherburne F. Cook

1963   *The Aboriginal Population of Central Mexico on the Eve of the Spanish Conquest*. Ibero-Americana 45. Berkeley: University of California Press.

Bowser, Frederick P.

1975   "The Free Person of Color in Mexico City and Lima: Manumission and Opportunity, 1580–1650." In *Race and Slavery in the Western Hemisphere. Quantitative Studies*, Stanley L. Engerman and Eugene D. Genovese, eds. Princeton: Princeton University Press, pp. 331–68.

Carrera Stampa, Manuel

1954   *Los gremios mexicanos: La organización gremial en la Nueva España. 1521–1861*. Mexico.

Chevalier, François

1963   *Land and Society in Colonial Mexico*. Alvin Eustis, trans. and L. B. Simpson, ed. Berkeley: University of California Press.

Esser, Janet Brody

1981   *Faces of Fiesta: Mexican Masks in Context*. San Diego: San Diego State University Syllabus Service.

1983   "Señores del aire y principales: Máscaras de los 'negros' de Michoacán, México. (Conservaciones y transformaciones: El arte popular como historia popular.)" Ruth Lechuga, trans. In *Foro Inter-Americano "la cultura popular y la educación superior."* Colima:

Universidad de Colima, pp. 94–101.

1984   *Máscaras ceremoniales de los tarascos de la sierra de Michoacán*. Mexico: Instituto Nacional Indigenista.

Foster, George

1960   *Culture and Conquest*. Viking Fund Publications in Anthropology 27. Chicago.

Gage, Thomas

1958   *Travels in the New World*. J. Eric S. Thompson, ed. Norman: University of Oklahoma Press.

Gorenstein, Shirley, and Helen Perlstein Pollard

1983   *The Tarascan Civilization: A Late Prehispanic Cultural System*. Vanderbilt University Publications in Anthropology 28. Nashville: Vanderbilt University Press.

Guillot, Carlos Federico

1961   *Negros rebeldes y negros cimarrones: Perfil afro-americano en la historia del Nuevo Mundo durante el siglo XVI*. Buenos Aires: Editores Fariña.

Jenkins, Katherine D.

1967   "Lacquer." In *Handbook of Middle American Indians*, Manning Nash ed., vol. 6, pp. 125–37. Austin: University of Texas Press.

Herskovitz, Melville J.

1970   *The Myth of the Negro Past*. Boston. Originally published 1941.

INEGI (Instituto Nacional de Estadística, Geografía, e Informática)

1983   *X Censo General de Población y Vivienda, 1980*. Estado de Michoacán. Volumen II, Tomo 16. Mexico.

Instituto Nacional Indigenista

1982   *Grupos étnicos de México*. 2 vols. Mexico: Instituto Nacional Indigenista.

López Lara, Ramón, ed.

1973   *El Obispado de Michoacán en el siglo XVII: Informe inédito de beneficios, pueblos y lenguas*. Morelia: Fimex. Originally published 1631.

Martínez de Lejarza, Juan José

1974   *Analisis estadístico de la provincia de Michoacán en 1822*, Xavier Tavera Alfaro, ed. Morelia: Fimax.

Miranda, Francisco, ed.

1980   *Fray Jerónimo de Alcalá, La relación de Michoacán*. Morelia: Fimax.

Mörner, Magnus

1967   *Race Mixture in the History of Latin America*. Boston: Little, Brown and Company.

Ms. C. IV. 5 de El Escorial

1541   *Relación de las ceremonias y ritos y población y gobernación de los indios de la provencia de Mechoacán, hecha al ilustrisimo señor don Antonio de Mendoza, vírrey y governador desta Nueva España por su magestad, etc*. El Escorial.

Ricard, Robert

1966   *The Spiritual Conquest of Mexico*. L. B. Simpson, trans. Berkeley: University of California Press. Originally published 1933.

Rosenblat, Angel

1954   *La población indigena y el mestizaje en America*. 2 vols. Buenos Aires.

Rout, Leslie B., Jr.

1976   *The African Experience in Spanish America*. Cambridge: Cambridge University Press.

Seler, Eduard

1908   "Die alten Bewohner der Landschaft Michuacan." In *Gesammelte Abhandlungen zur Amerikanischen Sprach und Altertumskunde* 3: 33–156. Berlin.

Toor, Frances

1947   *A Treasury of Mexican Folkways*. New York: Crown Publishers.

West, Robert C.

1948   "Cultural Geography of the Modern Tarascan Area." Smithsonian Institution, Institute of Social Anthropology, Publication 7. Washington, D.C.

Ruth D. Lechuga
Carnival in Tlaxcala

Benítez, Fernando

1970   *Los indios de México*. 5 vols. Mexico: ERA.

Brown, Betty Ann

1978   *Máscaras, Dance Masks of México and Guatemala*. Bloomington: University Museums, Illinois State University.

Clavijero, Francisco Javier

1974   *Historia antigua de México*. Mexico City: Editorial del Valle de México.

Durán, Fray Diego

1967   *Historia de las Indias de Nueva España y Islas de Tierra Firme*. 3 vols. Mexico: Editorial Nacional.

Esser, Janet Brody

1984   *Máscaras ceremoniales de los tarascos de la sierra de Michoacán*. Mexico: Instituto Nacional Indigenista.

Kingsborough, Lord [Edward King]

1964   *Codex Mendoza*. In *Antigüedades de México*, vol. 1. Mexico: Secretaria de Hacienda y Crédito Público.

Lumholtz, Carl

1904   *El México desconocido*. 2 vols. New York: Charles Scribners' Sons.

Mendoza, T. Vicente

1976   "La música y la danza." In *El esplendor del México antiguo*. 2 vols. Mexico: Editorial Valle de México. 2nd edition.

PRI-IEPES

1977–1982   *Estado de Tlaxcala*. Mexico: PRI-IEPES.

Sahagún, Fray Bernardino de

1955 *Historia general de las cosas de la Nueva España* 3 vols. Mexico: ALFA.

Scheffler, Lilian

1986 *Grupos indígenas de México.* Mexico: Panorama.

Sodi Morales, Demetrio

1976 *The Maya World.* Mexico: Minutiae.

Timón Tiemblo, María Pía

1979 "Datos folklóricos de Lagunilla." In *Narria: Estudios de artes y costumbres populares,* nos. 15 and 16. Madrid: Universidad Autónoma de Madrid.

Warman, Irene, and Arturo Warman

1971 "Danzas." In *Lo efímero y eterno del arte popular mexicano,* vol. 2. Mexico: Fondo Editorial de la Plástica Mexicana.

James Dow
Sierra Otomí Carnival Dances

Boilés, Charles

1969 "Cognitive Processes in Otomí Cult Music." Ph.D. Dissertation, Tulane University.

1971 "Síntesis y sincretismo en el carnival Otomí." *América Indígena* 31(3): 555–63.

Dow, James

1974 *Santos y supervivencias: Funciones de la religión en una comunidad Otomí.* Mexico City: Instituto Nacional Indigenista y Secretaria de Educación Pública.

Foster, George M.

1966 *Culture and Conquest: America's Spanish Heritage.* Viking Fund Publications in Anthropology, 27. Chicago: Quadrangle Books.

Gluckman, Max

1956 *Custom and Conflict in Africa.* Oxford: Blackwell.

Inchón, Alain

1973 *La religión de los Totonacas de la Sierra.* Mexico City: Instituto Nacional Indigenista y Secretaria de Educación Pública.

Norbeck, Edward

1961 *Religion in Primitive Society.* New York: Harper and Row.

1963 "African Rituals of Conflict." *American Anthropologist* 65(6): 1254–79.

Provost, Paul Jean

1974 "Culture and Anti-Culture among the Nahua of the Huaxteca Region of Northern Veracruz, Mexico." Paper presented at the Central States Anthropological Association Meetings, Chicago, March 28.

1981 *Carnaval en La Huasteca: Un análisis de su significancia funcional en las comunidades indias tradicionales.* Cuadernos Antropológicos 3.

Wallace, Anthony F. C.

1966 *Religion: An Anthropological View.* New York: Random House.

Williams García, Roberto

1963 *Los Tepehuas.* Jalapa, Veracruz: Universidad Veracruzana.

Ted J. J. Leyenaar
Dances of the Nahuas and Otomíes of Sierra Norte de Puebla

Arizpe Schlosser, Lourdes and Vera B. Kandt

1972 La Sierra de Puebla. *Artes de México.* Año XIX, no. 155.

Clavijero, Francisco Javier

1958 *Historia antigua de México,* 2a ed. Tomo II, Mexico: Porrúa.

Códice Fernández Leal

1895 Mexico: Antonio Peñafiel.

Esser, Janet Brody

1984 *Máscaras ceremoniales de los Tarascos de la Sierra de Michoacán.* Mexico: Instituto Nacional Indigenista.

Leyenaar, Ted J.J.

1981 *De Indianen Van Mexico, "Azteken in 't Verleden Nahua's van Heden'.* Leiden: Rijksmuseum voor Volkenkunde.

Mompradé, Electra and Tonatiúh Gutiérrez

1976 *Danzas y bailes populares.* Mexico: Hermes.

1977 Mensajeros del cielo: mito y magía de los hombres voladores. *Revista de geografía universal,* vol. I, no. 1, pp. 78–97.
Papousek, D.A.
1980 *Mexico.* The Hague: Staatsuitgeveri.
Reuter, Jas
1980 *La música popular de México.* Mexico: Panorama.
Toor, Frances
1947 *A Treasury of Mexican Folkways.* New York: Crown Publishers.
Torquemada, Juan de
1976 *Monarquía indiana* 3a ed. vol. III. Mexico: Universidad Nacional Autónima de México.

Ruth D. Lechuga
Mask Making in Guerrero

Cordry, Donald
1980 *Mexican Masks.* Austin: University of Texas Press.
Gutiérrez Casillas, Manuel
1981 *Las artesanías populares de madera en México.* Mexico: Subsecretaria Forestal y de la Fauna.
Sepulveda Herrera, María Teresa
1982 *Catálogo de máscaras del Estado de Guerrero de la colecciones del Museo Nacional de Antropología.* Mexico: Instituto Nacional de Antropología e Historia.

Betty Ann Brown
Mixtec Masking Traditions: Juxtlahuaca, Oaxaca

Bernal, Ignacio
1965 "Archeological Synthesis of Oaxaca." In *Handbook of Middle American Indians.* Gordon Wiley, ed. vol. 3. Austin: University of Texas Press.
Blaffer, Sarah C.
1972 *The Black-man of Zinacantan.* Austin: University of Texas Press.
Bode, Barbara

1961 "The Dance of the Conquest in Guatemala." In *The Native Theater in Middle America.* Middle American Research Institute, Publication 27. New Orleans: Tulane University.
Bricker, Victoria
1973 *Ritual Humor in Highland Chiapas.* Austin: University of Texas Press.
Brown, Betty Ann
1983 "Mixtec Masking Traditions in Oaxaca." In *Arte Vivo: Living Traditions in Mexican Folk Art,* James R. Ramsey, ed. Memphis: Memphis State University.
Cancian, Frank
1965 *Economics and Prestige in a Maya Community. The Religious Cargo System in Zinacantan.* Stanford: Stanford University Press.
Caro Baroja, Julio
1966 *El Carnaval—Analisis Histórico-Cultural.* Madrid. Taurus.
Caso, Alfonso
1965 "Mixtec Writing and Calendar." In *Handbook of Middle American Indians,* Gordon R. Willey, ed. vol. 3. Austin: University of Texas Press.
1969 *El tesoro de Monte Albán.* Instituto Nacional de Antropología e Historia. Mexico: Memorias del Instituto Nacional de Antropología e Historia, 3.
Clark, James Cooper
1912 *The Story of "Eight Deer" in Codex Colombino.* London.
Cordry, Donald
1973 *Mexican Masks* (exhibit catalog). Fort Worth, Tex.: Amon Carter Museum.
1980 *Mexican Masks.* Austin: University of Texas Press.
Dahlgren de Jordan, Barbro
1954 *La mixteca: su cultura e historia prehispánica.* Mexico.
The Ephemeral and the Eternal of Mexican Folk Art
1971 *The Ephemeral and the Eternal of Mexican Folk Art.* Mexico: Fondo Editorial de la

Plástica Mexicana. 2 vols.

Esser, Janet Brody

1983   "Tarascan Masks of Women as Agents of Social Control." In *The Power of Symbols: Masks and Masquerades in the Americas,* N. Ross Crumrine and Marjorie Halpin, eds. Vancouver: University of British Columbia Press, pp. 116–27.

Foster, Elizabeth Andros

1950   *Motolinía's History of the Indians of New Spain.* Documents and Narratives Concerning the Discovery and Conquest of Latin America, n.s. 4. Berkeley: Cortés Society.

Foster, George

1960   *Culture and Conquest: America's Spanish Heritage.* New York: Wenner-Gren Foundation for Anthropological Research.

Fraser, Douglas, and Herbert M. Cole, eds.

1960   *African Art and Leadership.* Madison: University of Wisconsin Press.

Furst, Jill Leslie

1977   *Codex Vindobonensis Mexicanus I: A Commentary.* Institute for Mesoamerican Studies, State University of New York at Albany, Publication 4. Albany: State University of New York.

1978   "The Year 1 Reed, Day 1 Alligator: A Mixtec Metaphor." *Journal of Latin American Lore* 4(1).

Griffith, James

1972   "Cahitan Pascola Masks." *Kiva* 37(4).

Kurath, Gertrude Prokosch

1949   "Mexican Moriscas: A Problem in Dance Acculturation." *Journal of American Folklore* 62(244).

1956   "Dance Relatives of Mid-Europe and Middle America." *Journal of American Folklore* 69.

Miller, Virginia, Dudley M. Varner, and Betty Ann Brown

1975   "The Tusked Negrito Mask of Oaxaca." *Masterkey* (49)(2).

Moya Rubio, Victor José

1974   *Máscaras mexicanas. Exposición del museo nacional de antropología.* Mexico: Imprenta Madero.

1978   *Máscaras, la otra cara de México.* Mexico: Universidad Nacional Autónoma de México.

Nuttall, Zelia

1902   *Codex Nuttall.* Facsimile of an ancient Mexican codex belonging to Lord Zouche of Harynworth, England. Cambridge: Peabody Museum of American Archaeology and Ethnology. Pamphlet with introduction by Zelia Nuttall.

Ravicz, Marilyn Ekdahl

1970   *Early Colonial Religious Drama in Mexico from Tzompantli to Golgotha.* Washington: Catholic University of America Press.

Ravicz, Robert, and Kimball Romney

1967   "The Mixtec." In *Handbook of Middle American Indians,* Evan Z. Vogt, ed. vol. 7. Austin: University of Texas Press.

Ricard, Robert

1933   *La Conquête spirituelle du Méxique.* Université de Paris, Travaux et Memoires de l'Institut d'Ethnologie, 20. Paris.

Romney, Kimball, and Romaine Romney

1966   *The Mixtecans of Juxtlahuaca, Mexico.* Huntington, N.Y.: Robert E. Krieger Publishing Company.

Sahagún, Fray Bernardino de

1951   *Florentine Codex, General History of the Things of New Spain,* Book 2, *The Ceremonies.* Arthur J. O. Anderson and Charles E. Dibble, trans. Santa Fe, N.M. School of American Research and University of Utah.

Santiago, Frederico

1978 *Fiestas in Mexico.* Mexico: Ediciones Lara, S.A.

Siroto, Leon
1972 "Gon: A Mask Used in Competition for Leadership among the Bakwele." In Fraser and Cole 1972.

Smith, Mary Elizabeth
1973 *Picture Writing from Ancient Southern Mexico, Mixtec Place Signs and Maps.* Norman: University of Oklahoma Press.

Smith, Waldemar R.
1977 *"The Fiesta System and Economic Change.* New York: Columbia University Press.

Spores, Ronald
1967 *The Mixtec Kings and Their People.* Norman: University of Oklahoma Press.

Thompson, Robert F.
1972 "The Sign of the Divine Kings: Yoruba Bead-Embroidered Crowns with Veil and Bird Decorations." In Fraser and Cole, 1972.

Toor, Frances
1947 *A Treasury of Mexican Folkways.* New York: Crown Publishers.

Troike, Nancy
1979 "The Arrow Sacrifice Ceremony in the Mixtec Historical Codices." Paper delivered at the Forty-third International Congress of Americanists, Vancouver, B.C., August.

Very, Francis George
1962 *The Spanish Corpus Christi Procession, a Literary and Folklore Study.* Valencia, Spain: Tipografía Moderna.

A

A Treasury of Mexican Folkways, 247
Abrajám, Adelfo, 229; Ernesto, 229; Nolberto, 225, 229–233; Ruperto, 225–29
Acapetlahuaya, 32, 162 (Pl.99)
Acatlán, 264, 313–321
Accoutrements, 83–84
Acuitlapilco, 158
Advisors. *See* Mo'oro
African dance rhythms, 109
Africans, (black), 31, 108, 195
Age groups, 91
Aggressive behavior, 65–71. *See also* Mock battles
Aging of masks, 233
Alawasim, 97–98. *See also* Ritual hosts.
Alkandi, 110, 128 (Pl.77)
All Saints Day, 313
Alligators, 219, 224 (Pl.151), 242 (Pl.151)
Alms, 64, 65
Altar, 68
Altar women, 91
Amaxac de Guerrero, 157, 161, 163; *catrines* of, 161
Amuzgo Indians, 215
Angels (characters), 45, 86, 91, 216 (Pl.133)
Animal masks. *See* Perra; Perro.
Anota, Aurelio, 233; Cecilio, 233
Anthropology, beginnings of American, 39; departments of, 39; physical, 41
Aranza, 122
Archangel Michael, 193
Army of Pilate (characters), 83, 91; in Mayo myth, 81, 82; role of, 91–93. *See also* Pharisees (characters)
Aro, Julián, 157
Arrow ceremonies, 250
Asians, 31
Assimilation, 80, 145, 215
Astucia, 47
Atlaua, 14, 15, 18, 24 (Pl.14)
Aztec deities, 7–9, 14–15
Aztec Indians, 6–27, 247; deities of, 7–9; masks of, 7, 8; ritual objects among, 7; society described, 7, 8; spoils system, 9; territorially expansion, 8
Aztec influences, 41
Aztec language, 41
Aztec map, 6
Aztec masks, 7–27; socio-political significance of, 9
Aztec priests, 8–10, 18; 20 (Pl.10); economic advantages of, 22; group served a class of deity, 9; hierarchy of, 18–22; in New Fire ceremony, 16, 17 (Pl.7); involved in human sacrifice, 15, 21 (Pl.11).
Aztecs of today. *See* Nahua Indians

B

Backward performance, 93
Baez, Marcelino, 117
Bahena family, 229
Bahi Reyesim. *See* Three Kings
Baile del Calalá, 55
Banari, 81–101
Banks, 80
Baptism, 81
Bartolo, 45
Beards; of Blackmen, 107
Bells, 54
Bisexual behavior, 79
Black Africans, 195; as slaves, 123–24; contributions to New World, 123–31; from Tarascan perspective, 131–40; in Colonial Mexico, 122–40. *See also* Blackmen
Black (color), 18, 123, 131
Blackmen, 107, 118 (Pl.72), 119 (Pl.73), 275–285; analysis of, 123–40; as foreigners, 131, 140; as policemen, 116; beardless, 117; before the Revolution, 117; costumes of, 107, 116, 117, 123, 140; dance of, 116; dance discontinued, 122; expense of, 122; headdresses of, 116; impersonators, 131; masks of, 108, 109, 110; motivation for dance, 122–23; noises of, 116; of Aranza, 122; of Caltzontzin, 122; of Charapan, 122; of Cherán, 108–109, 118 (Pl.72), 119 (Pl.73), 122; of Nahuatzen,

122; of Nuevo San Juan Parangaricutiro, 110–14, 129 (Pl.78); 135 (Pl.82), 138–39 (Pl.85); of Paricutín, 122; of San Lorenzo, 109; of the *meseta*, 117; of Uruapan, 114–115; 141 (Pl.86); of Zacán, 115; with Huacal, 110, 129 (Pl.78), 135 (Pl.82)
Blacks. *See* Africans (black), Blackmen, *Negritos*
Blanco, Jesús, 233
Blanco, Rodolfo, 233
Board of directors, 146 (Pl.88)
Body paint, 32, 55
Bowers, 86, 97
Bravo Joaquín Amaro, 276
Bricker, Victoria, 247
Broda, Johanna, 8, 22
Brown, Betty Ann, 8, 22
Bull dancer, 254
Bullfighters (characters), 218
Bull's head, 218, 238 (Pl.147)
Burning of masks, 64. *See also* Masks, ritual burning of

C

Cabildo, 130–31 (Pl.79)
Cabo, 91, 93; responsibilities, 93
Caifás, 79
Calalá. *See* Jaguar dance
Calendrical systems, 246
Calvary. *See* Kalbario
Camada, 153, 165
Campo Morado, 221
Candles, 86, (Pl.54)
Canes, 86, 98
Cantora, 91, 92 (Pl.60)
Cantors. *See* Cantora
Capes, 158–59 (Pl.97), 160 (Pl.98), 169, 289, 290, 291. *See also* Cloaks, *tilma*
Capitán, 193
Capitanes, 40, 65, 83, 91, 93; responsibilities, 93
Captains, 117. *See also* Capitanes
Cargo of the Holy Child, 108–109
Cargos, 65, 107, 108, 265; expense of, 108; of the Holy Child, 108–109
Carguero, 108, 109, 110, 116, 117, 126–27 (Pl.76); of the Holy Child, 116
Carnival, 54, 55, 56–57 (Pl.33), 58–59 (Pl.34), 142–71; 253; 286–293; among indigenous peoples of Mexico, 143; Catholic practices incorporated into, 163; church disapproval of, 163; expense of, 169; function today among Westerners, 143; importations in Tlaxcala, 169; pre-Hispanic roots, 163, 165; rain-petitioning function, 163. *See also* Tlaxcala Carnival
Carnival dances, 253; seriousness of, 165; *See* fertility, rain-petitioning ceremonies
Carnival Monday, 153
Carnival Sunday, 145, 153, 161–62
Carnival Tuesday, 145, 153
Caso, Alfonso, 7, 9, 10, 246
Casques, 225
Catholic calendar, 250
Catholicism, 79
Catrines (characters), 151 (Pl.92), 155 (Pl.95), 161–63; costumes of, 161–63; female partners of, 151 (Pl.92); of Amaxac de Guerrero, 161
Chichimecas (tribes), 123
Center for Indian Affairs (Tarascan region), 108
Ceremonial centers, 80, 81, 83
Ceremonial labor, 96
Ceremonies, 245; analysis of, 79; functions of, 79
Chachalmeca, 14, 15, 18, 17 (Pl.18) (Pl.19); 24 (Pl.15); recruitment into, 22; represented wealthy lineages, 22; Tlaloc facial features, 18, 22
Challenges, 215
Chalman, 15
Chalmecacihuatl, 15
Champurrada, 253
Chapa, 221, 225
Chapakobam (characters), 80, 83, 91, 97, 98; and found items, 86; behavior of, 93; carry out orders, 93; length of service, 91; links to the dead, 93;

masks of, 82, 83; myths concerning, 94–96
Chapala, 45, 48 (Pl.28–30)
Chapel of the Virgin, iii
Charapan, 115–22
Chareos, 250
Charging the church, 68
Charros, 35, 158, 161, 163; costumes of, 163; masks of, 288, 289, 291
Che Guevara mask, 148 (Pl.90)
Cherán, 54, 117, 118 (Pl.118), 120–21 (Pl.74), 122; Blackmen of, 117
Chiapas, 55
Chichimecas, 116; as dancers, 117, 123
Chicomecoatl, 10
Chicoteros, 65
Chihuahua, 35
Children, 141 (Pl.86); dance participants, 54, 108, 109, 116, 117
Children, and masks, ix
Chilolos, 250
Chilolos de la ardilla (of the squirrel), 254; as characters, 251
Chinampa, 14, 22
Chinampaneca, 22, 24 (Pl.15)
Chivarandos, 164 (Pl.100), 165
Cholula, 153
Christ, birth of, 45–47; crucifixion of, 64; resurrection of, 95 (Pl.63)
Christmas Day, 108–109
Christmas Day dances, 116
Christmas Eve, 108–109
Christmas season, 109, 135 (Pl.82)
Church, in Amaxac de Guerrero, 152 (Pl.93)
Church, Mayo Indian, 83, 88 (Pl.54), 94
Cihuacoatl, 8, 10, 13 (Pl.4), 14 (Pl.5), 18, 22, 26 (Pl.17;) costume as reflection of priest, 8; priest impersonator of, 8, 14 (Pl.5)
Cimarrones, 122
City-states, 247
Clavijero, Francisco Xavier, 163
Cloaks, 163
Clowning behavior, 45, 65, 67, 93–94, 161. *See also* Mockery
Clowns, 45–47, 64, 195, 245, 250, 251; maintenance of order by, 109
Codex Borbonicus, 10, 12, 14 (Pl.5), 16 (Pl.7), 17 (Pl.8), 18, 19 (Pl.9), 20 (Pl.10), 25 (Pl.16)
Codex Durán, 195
Codex Magliabecchiano, 10, 13 (Pl.4)
Codex Nuttall, 246
Codex Ríos, 15
Codex Vienna, 250
Codices, 246
Cofradías, 247, 253
Colima, 107
Colonial dress in dances, 116
Colonial bureaucracy, 247
Columbian quincentenary, 39
Combat drama, 45
Comic masks, 49, 51. *See also* Clowns
Commander, 110
Confession, 96
Conquest, 247
Conquest, dance of, 215–216. *See* Danza de la conquista
Conquest of Mexico, 215
Cordry, Donald, 219–241; manipulated by dealers, 241
Corpus Christi, 307–311
Cortés, Hernán, 203
Corupo, 116, 264; blackmen of, 117
Costumbre ya'uchim. *See* Pharisees, protectors of custom
Costumes, 35; contest, 218; expense of, 145; like ancient Mayan, 54. *See also* trousers (slit); location of magic, 7; male and female distinctions in Tlaxcala, 166–67 (Pl.101); nineteenth century, 163; of Blackmen, 117; of *Quetzales*, 205; reflection of wearer, 8; Tlaxcala carnival, 161; transformative power of, 7. *See also* transvestism
Court dance. *See* cuadrilla

Cowboys (characters), costumes, 254
Crazy ones. *See* locos
Cremation, 19 (Pl.9)
Crosses, church, 95 (Pl.63), finding of, 65; house, 65, 86, 96, 97; planting of, 65; shooting of, 65, 67; uprooting, 65, 86, 91 (Pl.59), 94
Crowns, 54
Crucifixes, 85, 93
Crucifixion. *See* Jesus, crucifixion of
Cuacuacuiltin. *See* Human sacrifice, priests involved
Cuadrilla, 32, 165; costumes of, 165
Cuauhuehuetque, 15. *See* Human sacrifice, priests involved in
Cuerudos, 164 (Pl.100), 165
Cuexcochtechimalli, 10, 14, 18, 21 (Pl.11)
Curing, in Mayo myth, 81
Custom. *See* Pharisees, protectors of custom.

D

Dance, around uprooted cross, 65; as intermediary device, 29–30; as theater, 29; cowboy (spurious), 225; devil, 221; farmer's, 226 (Pl.138); fisherman's, 224 (Pl.137); harvest celebration, 219–20; magical elements, 29; Moors and Christians, 34; of Blackmen, 107, 108–109, 122; of little mule drivers, 230 (Pl.142); of *los manueles*, 233, 237 (Pl.146); of Malinche, 203; of *mecos*, 227 (Pl.140); of Old Ones, 222 (Pl.135); of *paragüeros*, 165; of *tecuanes*, 33; of the *chichimecas*, 116, 117; of the children, 116, 117, 141 (Pl.86); of the Conquest; 203–205; of the devils, 218; of the fish, 35; of the Fisherman, 221, 233; of the gardeners, 32; of the harvesters, 32; of the mutes, 233; of the *Negritos*, 195; of the Old Ones, 117; of the *pascolas*, 67, 68; of the *Quetzales*, 203–205; of the Santiagos, 203–205; of the Seven Vices, 233; of the *tejorones*, 33; of the *viejos*, 47–54; of the voladores, 193–95; of the *xtoles*, 55; rain-petitioning, 163, 219; reenactment of Conquest, 215–16; ribbon, 154 (Pl.94), 163; serpent, 165, 166–67 (Pl.103); social, 68; teacher of, 217; *tecuani*, 233; the mutes, 233; tightrope walkers, 228 (Pl.141); traditional, 29; use of masks in, ix; Voladores, 33; with food, 217; with references to daily life, 217
Dance drama, 250; leaders, 108–109
Dance of the Flying Men. *See* Dance, of the voladores
Dancers, motivation of, 31; strolling bands of, 55
Dances, change with time, 31; Colonial, 215; farmers, 217; humorous, 217. *See also* clowning behavior; joking behavior, mockery; Nahuatl, 215–18; no complete inventory, 31; of animals, 217; of Moors and Christians, 32, 250; *See also* rehearsals
Danza de la conquista, 47
Danza de listones. *See* ribbon dance
Days of the Dead, 313–321
Deaf blacks (characters), 32
Dealers, 241
Death, 93, 99; as transition, 79; opposition to life, 96, 98–99; deities, 9–10, 12, 15; as character, 34
Deer dance, 55, 82, 91, 94
Deer head, 83
Deer-Jaguar Claw, 246
Delgado, Santiago Martínez, 221, 225
Devil (character), 29, 32, 34, 47, 240 (Pl.149), 250, 251
Diablos de pastorela, 32
Dioscuri, 79
Disguises, 143. *See also* Masks, Costumes
Disguises, allow mocking behavior with impunity, 143
Dolls, 35, 162 (Pl.99), 165, 168 (Pl.102)
Dramas, performances of, 47; passed from town to town, 47
Drum, 4, 217, decorated, 83, 86
Drummers, 67, 91
Drunken behavior, 45

E

Eagle claw headdress, 10, 18, 20 (Pl.10)
Easter celebrations, 247
Easter ceremonial, 91. *See also* Lenten ceremonial
Easter ceremonialism, 80, 81
Easter fiesta, Yaqui and Mayo Indian, 64, 68, 69, 81, 86
Easter Sunday, 64, 67, 68–69, 83, 86, 101
Easter Week ceremonial, 94, 143
Egalitarian societies, 8
El remate, 145, 153, 161–63, 165, 169

El tuno, 255
Elders, 134 (Pl.81)
Encabezados, 145, 153
Encargados, 153
Enculturation, 93. *See also* Assimilation
Enmascarados, 161
Epiphany, dances, 116–17
Ermitaño, 45
Escobar, Jesús, 117
Etzalcualiztli, 22
Expense of dances, 145. *See also* Fundraising
Eyebands, 8

F

Face coverings, 83
Face paint, 55
Falsetto voices, 55
Fans, 54
Fariseos. *See* Pharisees
Farmers (characters), 32
Feasting, 64, 96, 110, 134 (Pl.81), 145
Feathers, 33, 35, 54, 163, 169
Female characters, 79, 161, 165; increasingly performed by females, 161, 165; unmasked, 153
Female impersonators, 147 (Pl.89), 153, 161, 165, 166–67 (Pl.101), 203, 221
Female participants, 10, 91, 109, 143, 153, 161, 165. *See also* angels
Feos. *See* Uglies
Feria primaveral, 195
Fertility, 165
Festival of the Holy Cross, 303–305
Fiesta of San Marcos, 50–51 (Pl.31)
Fiesta stew, 68, 272
Fiesta system, economic structure, 250; function in indigenous groups, 153
Fife, 54
Fire priests, 22
Fireworks, 69, 145. *See El remate*
Fiscales, 152 (Pl.93), 156 (Pl.96), 161
Fisherman (character), 221
Flauteros. *See* Flutists
Flowers, 110
Flutists, 91
Folk arts collections, 41
Folk drama, 79
Food, 110, 265–274; collection of, 65; dancers eating, 236 (Pl.145); dancing with, 217, 234–35 (Pl.144); holiday, 253, 254. *See also* Feasting
Foreigners, 99, 122, 123. *See also* Others
Friars, 247
Fringes, 32
Fuente, Jr., Fidel de la, 218
Fundraising, 93
Funerary customs, 79, 80, 98, 99
Furst, Jill, 250
Fusion, 79, 122, 169. *See also* Assimilation

G

Gabriel, José Antonio, 241 (Pl.150)
Gamecock fighting, 169
Gente de razón. *See* Mestizos
Gifts, to dancers, 109
Glasses, 32, 83
Gloria, 67, 68
Goat (character), 225 (Pl.137)
God, 79, 80; conflict with Devil, 94
Godmothers, 97
God-the-Sun, 96
Good Friday, 64–67, 69, 82, 84
Gorilla, 111
Gourd, 33
Grande, Máximo Juárez, 241
Guarda de Espaldas, 65
Guares, 110
Guatemala, 250
Guerrero, 107
Guerrero, 33, 215, 246; dances, held on civic celebrations, 218; dances, inventive, 217; dances, pre-Hispanic in origin, 217; dances, Spanish in origin, 215–16; masks, metal, 241; (state), 214–243
Gutiérrez Casillas, Manuel, 233–241

H

Hair, 83
Harp, 68
Harper, blind, 45
Hats, 83

Headdresses, 34
Headdresses, 45, 54, 107, 116; Aztec, 10; of Blackmen, 107; of charros, 165
Headdresses, of Moors, 215
Headdresses, of Sabarios, 205
Helmet masks, 233–41
Hernández, Eladio, 155 (Pl.95), 157, 163
Herod, 163
Hidalgo, 35, 173
Hieroglyphic notations, 246
Hill-of-the-Mask, 247
Historia general, 15
Hobby horses, 35, 47, 164 (Pl.100), 165, 205
Holy Child (image), 108, 116, 117, 123
Holy Cross, Feast of the, 303
Holy Saturday, 64, 67–68, 69
Holy Thursday, 64, 68
Holy Week, 32, 33, 39, 221; drama of, 64
Horned serpent, 229
Horns, 32, 45, 47
Hospital, 129
Hosts of Mayo and Yaqui fiestas, 67–68
House crosses. *See* crosses, house
Huacalero, 111
Huehues, 153, 161
Huehuetl. *See* Drum
Huejotzingo, 157, 158–59 (Pl.97)
Huetzquistles, 228 (Pl.141)
Huitzuco, 22, 27
Human sacrifice, 10, 14, 169; intimidation and propaganda function of, 22; priests involved, 15–16, 24 (Pl.15), 25 (Pl.16)
Hunter (character), 223 (Pl.136)
Hvidtfeldt, Arild, 7

I

Icons. *See* religious images
Iguala, 221, 233, 241
Imitation, 7
Incense bags, 9
Independence Day, 221, 225; ceremonies, 218
Indian Mexico, 41
Indian revolt, 79
Initiation, 79
Inspikuriri. *See* Huacalero
Inverted behavior, 65, 79
Ironwork industry, 116
Islam, 250
Isolation, 173
Itom Achai O'ola. *See* Our Father
Itom Aye, 82

J

Jaguar dance, 55
Jalisco, 45
Jarabe folk dance, 251
Jesuits, 64, 79
Jesus, 79, 91; as curer, 98; birth of, 81, 82; coffin of, 86, 96; crucifixion of, 81, 82, 85, 91–93, 94, 97; funeral of, 97; image, 93–94. *See also* crucifixes; image of, 86, 94 (Pl.62), 97, 99 (Pl.66); Mayo myths concerning, 81, 82; meets Mary, 86, 94; pursuit of, 81–82; related to life/death opposition, 79; removed from cross and carried to coffin, 94 (Pl.62); resting of, 93, 100 (Pl.66); resurrection of, 82, 94, 99; tomb of, 86, 97; why killed, 82; *See also* O'ola
Jewelry, 246
Jewish characters, 163
Jews (characters), *See* Judíos
Joking behavior, 51. *See also* Clowning behavior, Mocking behavior
Joseph, in Mayo myth, 81–82
Joyero mayor, 65
Judas (character), 65–75
Judíos, 65–67; organization of, 65
Jupare, 81–101; masks of, 83
Juquila, 47
Juxtilahuaca, 250

K

Kalbario, 85 (Pl.49 and 50); 86 (Pl.51), 94
Kao O'ola, 65–67, 69
Kengyi, 110–111
Knives, decorated, 83
Konti, 81
Ku Klux Klan, 255

L

La culebra. *See* Serpent
La Magdalena's Day, 116, 117
La patria, 218
La raza, 218
Ladies (characters), 221
Ladinos, 123
Lake Patzcuáro, 49–54
Lake Xochimilco, 14
Land ownership, 80
Land reform, 80
Lansam, 83
Latu Nucaca, 253
Lay ministers. *See* Maestros
Leaders of dance groups, 51, 55
Lent, 64, 143, 253, 295–301; Carnival dances during, 145; three sacred areas of, 86
Lenten ceremonial, 91; Mayo explanation, 94; method of analysis, 94; planning for, 93; replications within, 94. *See also* Easter ceremonial
Lenten ceremonialism, 79, 80, 295–301
Lévi-Strauss, Claude, 79
Life/death opposition, 79, 80
Locos, 165, 166, 167 (Pl.101)
Lord of Miracles, 116
Lord of the Mountains, 193
Loria Ultima, 86
Los pastores, 45–47, 54
Los Patos, 64–75
Los semaneros, 111
Lost-wax-cast gold, 246
Lumholtz, Carl, 41
Luzbel, 47

M

Machetes, 68, 69
Macho troupe, 254
Madrinas. *See* Godmothers
Maestro, 217, 228 (Pl.141)
Maestros, 69, 91, 92 (Pl.60), 101, 109, 122
Magic, 163; and masks, 7, 8; in dance, 29; location within masks and costumes, 7; type related to social structure, 8
Mahoma. *See* Mohammed
Maize goddess. *See* Xilonen
Male roles, 79. *See also names of specific characters*
Malinalxochitl, 22
Malinche. *See also Maringuillas*
Malintzín. *See* Malinche
Mandas. *See* Religious vows
Mandón. *See* Commander; Sponsors of fiestas
Maranguillas, 144, 116, 120–21 (Pl.74), 126–27 (Pl.76), 153, 276–279
Mary, 245, 253; as symbolic figure, 82; brotherhood of, 122; in Mayo myth, 81; meets Jesus, 86, 94; (character), 81; *See also* Our Mother
Máscara. *See Chapakoba* (character), mask of
Mascaritas gritonas, 254; 255
Mask, angel, 229; black, 254; *caretas* shapes, 32; cowboy (spurious), 225; devil, 221; devil (spurious), 225; female, 229; half-face masks, 32; helmet shapes, 32; Moor, 229; of *Pilato*, 205; of *Tastoanes*, 60 (Pl.35–38); of the Santiagos, 205; represents eagle head, 33
Mask makers, xi, 35, 153–161, 218, 221–233, 241 (Pl.150), 242 (Pl.152), 269; as guardian of tradition, 35–36; how taught, 218
Masked festival, increasing vitality in Mexico, 55
Masks, and children, ix; and female characters, 153; and political power, 8–9; artificial aging of, 221–25; as art, 34; as art form, ix; as disguises, 143, 163; as identification, 29; Aztec, 7–8; back, 33; bearded, 31, 155 (Pl.95), 161, 205, 219, 241; burning of, 83, 94, 101 (Pl.67); change with fashion, 157; clay, 34; combination, 33; comic, 33, 49; creator of, ix; dance/decorative distinction, 225, 233; death, 233; decorative, 37; definition of, ix; devil, 218, 221, 225, 251; dual, 233; extracted from context, ix; false aging of, 233; feminine. *See also* female characters, female impersonators; fine craftsmanship, 219; fringes as, 32; from molds, 149 (Pl.91); function separate from art, 69; harvest celebration masks (spurious), 229; helmet, 33; hair of, 83; humorous, 108; in drama, 41–45; integral part of dance, 31; interaction with environment, ix; jaguar, 35; leather, 218; materials in, 45; materials used in, ix; Mayo, 82; metal, 34, 241, 243 (Pl.153); of Acatlán, 313–321; of Blackmen, 108, 110, 116, 117; of Blacks, 34; of Cantinflas, 157; of Chapakoba, 82, 83; of chareos, 251; of charros, 163; of Che Guevara, 148 (Pl.90), 157; of cloth, 31; of clowns, 45; of deer head, 83; of famous actors, 169; of goat hide, 65; of goat or lamb skin, 32; of hide, 83; of jaguar, 33; of Jorge Negrete, 157; of *judíos*, 69; of Jupare, 83; of lambskin, 33; of leather, 31, 33, 149 (Pl.91), 157–161, 158–159 (Pl.97); of leather painted, 60 (Pl.35–38); of metal, 33; of Moors, 251; of negros, 54; of old men, 149 (Pl.91); of papier-mâché, 155 (Pl.95); of Papalotla, 287–293; of *perro*, 45; of Pharisees, 82; of Pilate, 82; of Río Fuerte region, 295–301; of San Lorenzo, 275–85; of shell, 31; of Suchiapa, 307–311; of terra cotta, 45; of the Devils, 32; of the hermit, 45; of the Matachines, 32; of the Queen, 45; of the Sierra Otomíes, 173; of the Tastoanes, 45; of Three Kings, 45; of Tlaloc, 9–22; of *viejos*, 47; of wax, 32, 157; of *xtoles*, 54; ownership of, 83, 109, 117; painted, 153–57; papier-mâché, 33, 218; past and present compared, 35; pre-Hispanic, Mixtec, 251; racial types in, 45, 54; ritual burning of, 33, 64, 69; ritual removal of, 88; ritually thrown into water; role in present-day Mexico, 29; serious, 108; shopping for, 35, 219; skullcap, 32, 33; small, 33; social functions of, 83; spurious, 34, 37, 229; standards for, 157; stone, 247; symbolism, 219; techniques used in making, 65; tin, 33; Tlaxcala Carnival, 169; transformative, 7, 34; unpainted, 51; uses of, ix, 79, 218; wooden, 31, 33, 34, 35, 47, 49, 51, 54, 68, 153, 157, 158–59 (Pl.97), 161, 218; works of art, 219; wrinkled, 35, 149 (Pl.91)
Maso dancers. See Deer dance
Maso. See Deer dance
Matachines (characters), 32
Matachini, 91
Maya Indians, 250
Mayan dress, 54; language, 55
Mayo ceremonialism, 79–101; cycle curtailed, 80
Mayo Indians; 32; 64, 79–101; and Spanish contact, 79; assimilation of, 80; Easter ceremonial calendar, 81; *ejidos* of, 80; everyday way of life, 80; history of, 79–80; myths about Jesus, 81; sodalities of; belief in efficacy of ritual and prayer, 99; view of their own ceremonies, 79
Mayordomo, 110, 111, 129; 217, 253
Maypole, 163; dance, 195
Mazotecochco, 158
Mecos. *See* Savages
Mediation, 99; devices, 79
Men wearing cowhide. *See Cuerudos*
Men who use trousers of cowhide. *See Chivarandos*
Méndez family, 153, 158–59 (Pl.97)
Mendoza, Baldomero, 218, 221; Vicente, 169
Mercaderes. *See* Merchants (characters)
Merchants, 218; (characters), 239
Mérida, Yucatán, 54, 56–57 (Pl.33)
Mermaid, 221
Mescal, 254
Mesquitán, 38 (Pl.23), 40 (Pl.24), 41, 44 (Pl.26), 46 (Pl.27)
Mestizos, 79, 80, 205, 215, 246, 253
Mexica court, 18
Mexican Revolution, 79–80, 218; sierra, 107
Mexico, central. See Tlaxcala. Frederick Starr in, 39–54; independence from Spain, 123; Indian cultures in, 39–41. *See also* Tarascans. northern, 41; northwest, 64; southern, 41
Mexico, mestizo culture, 205
Mexico City, 157
Michoacán, 34, 47, 54, 107–141
Micticacihuatl, 10
Mictlantecuhtli, 10, 12 (Pl.3)
Midnight Mass, 109
Mixtec arts, 246
Mixtec Indians, 215, 245
Mixtec Indians, ancient, 246
Mixteca zone, 33
Mochitlan, 217, 229
Mock battles, 203, 218, 250
Mockery, 143, 169. *See also* clowning behavior
Moctezuma, ii, 9
Mohammed (character), 250, 251
Mole, 253
Monte Albán, Tomb 7, 246
Moors, 203, 247; sub-groups in Guerrero, 215; Moors and Christians, 215, 250; (characters), 38 (Pl.23), 41–45
Moros. *See* Moors
Motolinía, Fray Toribio de, 247
Mo'oro, 91
Museo Nacional de Antropología e Historia, 18, 22
Museo Nacional de Artes e Industrias Populares, xi, 32, 34, 157, 219, 233
Musical instruments, 55
Musicians, 145, 161. *See also* Flutists, Harpers
Myths, 79, 80; about Pharisees, 99; Mayo Indian, 81–82, 94–96

N

Nacimientos. *See* Nativity scenes
Nahua dances, 191–213; Indians, 191
Nahuatl culture, 215; Indians, 215; language, 165
Nahuatzen, 122
Nativity scenes, 198; in headdresses, 107
Nature worship, 7
Nayarít, 33
Negritos, 107; (characters), 32, 110, 195–203; dance, music for, 203
Negros, 107
New Fire ceremony, 9, 10, 16 (Pl.7), 18; priests, 18
New Testament, 163
New Year's Day, 109, 120–21 (Pl.74), 132–33 (Pl.80), 135 (Pl.82), 267; dances, 116
Noche buenas. *See* Flowers
Noises, of Blackmen, 116
Nortes, 191
Nuevo San Juan Parangaricutíro, 110–114; 117, 129 (Pl.78)

O

Oaxaca, 34, 35, 215, 245
Oaxaca City, 247
Obrajes, 123
Obscenity, 47
Octava, 145, 153
Old Man-God, 96
Old men. *See viejos*
Old Ones, 53 (Pl.32), 109, 110, 122. *See also Viejos*
Old Ones (characters), 34
Olvera, Isaías, 241
Opposition, life/death, 98
Order, maintenance of, 109
Ortega, Javier Juarez, 241
Otomí Voladores, 193
Otomíes, 32, 34, 173–213
Our Father, Mayo Indian religious image, 86
Our Grandfathers, 131
Our Mother, Mayo Indian image, 82, 86
O'ola, 81; and his *madrinas*, 88 (Pl.54), capture of, 94; costume of, 97; falling, 97; represents Jesus, 81; running of, 89 (Pl.55), 94

P

Pacific Ocean, 107
Padden, R.C., 22
Padre Tomas, 54
Pages (characters), 45
Paint, body and face, 55
Paintings, 246
Palacios, Enrique Juan, 9
Palitos, 55
Palm Sunday, 97
Pan dulce, 254
Panotla, 150–51 (Pl.92), 161
Panotla Carnival dances, 163; dates of, 145; organization, 145
Panquetzaliztli, 24
Papa mayor, 18
Papalotla, 158, 264, 286–293; Carnival dances, 65, 171; masks of, 287–293
Parade, Carnival in Tlaxcala, 145
Paragüeros, 158, 161, 162 (Pl.99), 163; costumes of, 163; dance of, 165
Paricutín, 110, 122
Pariserom ya'uchim. *See* Pharisee officers
Pariseros. See Pharisees
Pascolas, 67, 68; costumes of, 68; masks of 68
Paskola, 82; dance group, 91
Paskome, 81, 85, 91, 93
Passion Plays, 64
Pastores, 48 (Pl.28–30)
Patron saints, 247, 250, 253
Pecado, 45
Penitentes, 255
Pérez, Francisco, 157, 163
Perra (character), 32
Perro (character), 41–45
Phallic representations, 86
Pharisee officers, 83; ritual, and Way of the Cross, 84, 85 (Pls.49 and 50), 86 (Pl.51). 89 (Pl.56); bap-

tism of, 81; burning of masks, 81, 83; capture Jesus, 81; charging the church, 88 (Pl.54); cry in the wilderness, 81; meaning of, 94–99; sodality, 81, 91–93; hierarchy of, 91–92; responsibilities of, 91; subgroups in, 91
Pharisees, 64, 65, 82, 98; and individual power, 82, 96; face coverings, 82, 83; feeding of, 94; fund-raisers, 93; head coverings, 82–83; in church, 83; in Mayo myth, 81–82; in processions, 84, 94; myths about, 94–96; organization of. See Pharisee sodality; protectors of custom, 91, 93; reflection of social structure, 98; ritual of, 91–94; ritual processions, 81, 83; role of, 91–93; scarves of, 83; symbolism of, 98–99; visiting households, 93
Pharisees (characters), 79, 80, 81–105, 87 (Pl.52), 88 (Pl.53); costumes, 82; flutists, 89 (Pl.55); masks of, 82, 83; on Easter Sunday, 83; struggle for power, 91–92; uprooting crosses, 86 (Pl.51); See also Judíos
Physical labor, 93
Pilate, 203. See also Pontius Pilate
Pilato (character), 205. See also Pontius Pilate
Pilatom, 83; face coverings of, 83; ribbons of, 83
Pilatotom O'owim. See Army of Pilate
Pito. See Fife
Plaster casts, 41
Polka, 108
Pontius Pilate, 83; in Mayo myth, 81, 82; power of, 91–93
Pontius Pilate (character), 82; mask of, 82
Pot, 80, 99
Praying, 67–68, 82, 84
Priests, Aztec, 8; trumpet-blowing, 20 (Pl.10). See also Aztec priests
Primero memoriales, 14, 18
Primeros
Primitive, 7, 8
Processions, 64, 65, 67, 68–69, 81, 84 (Pl.48), 94, 98, 110, 217, 232 (Pl.143)
Progreso, 55, 58–59 (Pl.34)
Puebla, 35, 145, 153, 229, 246
Purepecha, 107
Purification, function of Carnival, 143
Pyramid of the Sacred War, 9, 14, 18

Q

Quecholli, 193
Quechultenango, 233
Queen (character), 41
Queretaro, 107
Quetzalcoatl, 8
Quetzalcoatl (historic), 18
Quetzalcoatl Totec Tlamacazqui, 18, 22
Quetzales (characters), costumes

R

Rain god, 9, 10. See also Tlaloc
Rain-petitioning ceremonies, 143, 157, 161–63, 165
Rattles, 54, 82; cocoon, 82
Rebellion, ritual of, 79
Reconquista. See Moors and Christians; dances of
Rehearsals, 108
Relación de Michoacán, 123
Religious dramas, 247
Religious images, 7, 81, 86, 97, 109, 110, 111, 116, 117, 126–27 (Pl.76), 128 (Pl.77), 217, 253.
Religious vows, 91, 96, 108, 109, 110
Resurrection Pot, 80, 99
Retos. See Challenges
Reyes, Carlos, 150–51; family, 150–51 (Pl.92)
Ribbon dance, 154 (Pl.94), 163, 169
Ribbons, 83, 116, 117
Río Fuerte region, 295–301
Rites of passage, 79
Ritual hosts, 69–71, 81
Ritual Humor in Highland Chiapas, 250
Ritual officer. See Carguero
Rodríguez masks, 233–237
Rooster killing, 169
Rosaries, 82
Rosary, in costume, 45
Rosette and cone headdress. See Cuex-cochtechimalli
Rosettes, 22. See also Cuexcochtechimalli
Rubios, 254

S

Sabario, 203

Sacred history, 79
Sacrifice, 169. See also Human sacrifice
Sacristans, 91
Sahagún, Fray Bernardino de, 9, 10–14, 15, 169
Saignes, Acosta, 18–22
Saint Francis of Assisi, 193
Saint James, 29, 33, 203, 215, 217 (Pl.133), 218, 245, 250
Saint James Day, 38 (Pl.23), 41 (Pl.24), 42–43 (Pl.25), 44 (Pl.26), 47 (Pl.27)
Saints, 69; masks resembling face of, 108; taking them home, 68–69. See also names of specific saints; Patron saints
Saints' days, 80–81, 116
Saldaño, Antonio, 271
Salgado, Victoriano, 117, 269
Salt goddess. See Uixtocihuatl
San Bernardino Contla, 146 (Pl.88)
San Cosme Mazotecochco, 160 (Pl.98), 165, 169 (Pl.102); Carnival dances, organization, 145–53
San Felipe de Herreros, 116
San Francisco Ozomatlán, 233
San Juan. See St. John
San Juan Quemada's Day, 116, 117
San Juan Totolac, 161–63; Carnival dances, 161
San Lorenzo, 120–21 (Pl.74), 124–25 (Pl.75), 126–26 (Pl.76), 128 (Pl.77), 129 (Pl.78), 130–31 (Pl.79); masks of, 275–285
San Lorenzo (village), 109–110, 275
San Lucas Cuauhtelulpan, 143; Carnival dances, organization of, 145
San Marcos, Juquila, Oaxaca, 50–51 (Pl.31)
San Marcos (fiesta of), 47
San Martín de Porres, 108
San Miguel's Day, 116, 117
San Pablo Apetatitlán, 148 (Pl.90), 153
San Pedro Zacán, 117
San Sebastian Atlahuapa, 169
Santa Cruz, 65–67, 68, 69
Santa Cruz Techachalco, 154 (Pl.94); Carnival dances, 163
Santa Fe de Laguna, 49, 53 (Pl.32)
Santiago de Compostela, 250
Santiagos (characters), 33, 41, 215, 250; costume of, 205; fiesta, 250; image, 253
Santo Cristo. See Our Father
Savages, 217
Serpent, 165
Sevilla, 255
Sevina, 122
Sewateri. See Loria Ultima
Sextons. See sacristans
Sexual behavior, 93; by masked characters, 64
Shepherds (characters), 45–47
Shepherds' Play, 117
Shields, 45, 205
Sierra Norte de Puebla, 191–213; climate, 191
Sierra Otomíes, 173–189; isolation of, 173
Sinaloa, 64
Sixteenth of September, 218
Skulls, 9
Slavery, 122–23
Snake, 203
Social control, 258. See also Custom
Social unification, 79, 80, 98
Soldados. See Army of Pilate
Soldados razos, 65
Sombreros, 195
Songs, to the baby Jesus, 47
Specialists, 69
Sponsors of fiestas, 67
Squirrel, 254
Staff, Aztec, 15–16
Staff of office, 110, 130–31 (Pl.79)
Standard, of xtoles, 54
Standards, of dancing parties, 54, 55
Starr, Frederick, field trips to Mexico, 39–54; measurement of skulls by, 41; pictorial records by, 41; research plan, 41
Stepdance, 68
Step-in figures, 229
Steward of the hospital, 110–111
Stewards, of the Holy Child, 117
Sticks, 45, 67. See also Wands, Palitos
Stratification, 8
Structural analysis, 79, 98; variants, 79
St. James Day (July 25), 41–45
St. John, 86; image of, 97
St. Joseph, 110
Suchiapa, 55, 264; masks of, 313–321
Swords, 83

Symbols, 98
Syncretism. See Fusion

T

Tamboleros, 65, 67
Tarahumara Pascoleros, 32
Tarascan Indians, 41, 107; Black Africans' relationship with, 122–23; cosmology of, 123, 131; empire of, 107; of the meseta, 107. See also Blackmen, Old Ones, Uglies
Tariacuri, 123
Tastoanes (characters), 32, 42–43 (Pl.25), 45
Tecomate. See Voladore platorm
Tecuacuiltin. See Human sacrifice, priests involved
Tecuilhuitontli, 10, 14, 21 (Pl.11)
Teloloapan, 218
Temple, of Tlaloc, 18
Tenebarim. See Rattles, cocoon
Tension, reduction of, 79
Teocalli, 10, 14–15, 18; headdress of, 10
Teocalli de la Guerra Sagrada. See Pyramid of the Sacred War
Tepexicotlan, 233
Tepeyanco, 157, 167 (Pl.101), 169
Teponaxtle. See drum
Tequila, 254
Three Kings, 41–45, 81–82, 86, 91
Throne, 44 (Pl.26), 47 (Pl.27)
Thrones, 45
Tigre (character), 32, 224 (Pl.136), 254; importance of, 35; Tabasco, 35
Tilma, 163, 169
Tinieblas, 81, 88 (Pl.54)
Tiripemencha, 123
Tiripenie Curicaueri, 123
Tixtla, 225–29
Tlacaelel, 22
Tlaloc, 9, 11 (Pl.2), 14, 18, 22; diagnostic features, 9, 18; headdress of, 10; images as reflections of priests, 9; masks of, 9–22; temple of, 18
Tlaloc priesthood. See Aztec priests, Tlaloc branch
Tlaloc Totec Tlamacazque, 9, 18
Tlaloque, 10, 22
Tlamacazque, 22
Tlapanec Indians, 215
Tlaxcala, 35, 142–171
Tlaxcala Carnival, 169
Tlaxcala Carnival costumes, 161; dances, 142; dates of, 145; general sequence of events, 145; many importations in, 169; music in, 169; northern, 161; organization of, 145–153; southern, 161; See also Amaxac de Guerrero, Guerrero, Panotla, San Bernardino Contla, San Lucas Cuauhtelulpan, Tlaxcala City, Tlaxcala masks
Tlaxcala Carnival music, 169
Tlaxcala City, 145; Carnival dances, dates, 145
Tlaxcala masks, 153–161; Caucasian features, 153; eyes of, 157; precious, 153
Tlenamacaque, 22
Tlimetl, 14
Tonatiuh, 8
Toor, Frances, 247
Topiltzin, 18
Torito, 164 (Pl.100), 165
Totonac dances, 193
Townsend, Richard, 7, 9
Trader, long-distance. See huacalero
Tradition. See Pharisees, protectors of custom
Transvestism, 55, 109. See Female impersonators
Troike, Nancy, 250
Trojes, 110, 111
Trousers (slit), 51
Trumpet, 20 (Pl.10)
Tumba, 86
Turí uarari. See Blackmen, of Charapan
Turía. See Blackmen
Twelve Peers of France, 215
Tzontemoc, 15

U

Ueitecuilhuitl, 10, 14, 25 (Pl.16)
Uglies, 109, 110, 111, 138–39 (Pl.85)
Uitzilopochtli, 22
Uixtocihuatl, 10, 18
Uixtoti, 10, 17 (Pl.8), 18
Umbrellas, 161, 163
United States, 225
University of Chicago, anthropology department, 39, 41
Unknown Mexico, 41

Uprooting of house crosses, 65
Uruapan, 33, 107, 114–115, 110, 116–117; barrios
    of, 116, 117; Blackmen of, 116–117

V

Vara, 128 (Pl.77), 130–31 (Pl.79)
Vasarios. *See* Vassals
Vassals, 165, 169 (Pl.102)
Veils, 32, 45
Velasquez, Oliver, 270
Venados, 65, 67
Viejito, 110, 253
Viejos, 47–54. *See also* Old Ones (characters)
Violin, 68
Virgin, 110, 111
Voices. *See* Falsetto voices
Voladores, 33; bird disguise, 195; changed number
    of fliers, 195; cosmic events, 195; costumes, 193–
    95; dance in front of church, 193; description of
    descent, 193; eagle disguises, 195; linkage of
    heaven and earth, 195; ladder, 193; music, 193;
    Nahua, 195; of Cuetzalan, 193; Otomí, 195; plat-
    form, 193; pre-Hispanic elements; Totonac, 195
Volcano. *See* Paricutin
Vra. *See* Staff of office

W

Waltz, 108
Wands, 45
War goddess, 10
Warehma. *See* Lenten ceremonialism
Way of the Cross, 67, 83, 86 (Pl.51), 93, 94, 97;
    procession, 81, 84 (Pl.48). *See also* Crosses
Weapons, of ritual characters, 82
Weeklies, 138–39 (Pl.85)
Whipping, of earth, 99
Whips, 83, 99, 165, 169
Wigs, 51; of Blackmen, 107, 108, 110, 117. *See also*
    Headdresses; of horsehair, 124–25 (Pl.75); of Old
    Ones, 124–25 (Pl.75)
Winds of the Four Quarters, 193
Winter ceremonies, 275–285
Witchcraft, 93
Women, in festive dress, 120–21 (Pl.74;) of San
    Lorenzo, 126–27 (Pl.76)
World's Columbian Exposition (1898), 39

X

Xametla, 164 (Pl.100)
Xicolli tunics, 9
Xilonen, 10, 14, 18
Xtoles, 54, 56–57 (Pl.33)

Y

Yaqui Indians, 32, 64
Year bundle, 19 (Pl.9)
Yopico, 169
Yucatán, 54, 55

Z

Zacán, 115, 117
Zacatlanzillo, 221
Zantwijk, Rudolph de, 22
Zapotec Indians, 246
Zinacantán, 250
Zitatla, 264

CONTRIBUTORS

Marsha C. Bol

Marsha Bol is curator of Latin American folk art at the Museum of International Folk Art, Santa Fe, New Mexico, and project director of "Behind the Mask in Mexico." As project director, she is curator of the exhibition, coordinator of the catalogue portion of this volume, and director of the two supporting grants from the National Endowment for the Humanities. She received her M.A. in Spanish Colonial art history from the University of New Mexico, where she is currently a Ph.D. candidate in Native American art history. She has researched and published on Lakota, New Mexican Colonial, and Mexican folk arts.

Betty Ann Brown

Betty Brown has been an avid researcher in the field of Oaxacan masks for many years. Her many publications include studies of pre-Conquest and early Colonial art of Mexico, with an emphasis on the art of the Aztecs. She has lived in Spain and Mexico and has served both as director of the Visual Arts Program, University of Southern California, and as resident director of that university's Madrid Center. She has done intensive field research and film work in Oaxaca since the early 1970s. Her M.A. degree in art history is from the University of Texas at Austin, and her Ph.D. from the University of New Mexico. She makes her home in the Los Angeles area and is assistant professor in the department of art, general studies, California State University, Northridge.

N. Ross Crumrine

Ross Crumrine is professor of anthropology at the University of Victoria, B.C., and has been researching and publishing on the culture of the Mayo Indians of Sonora, Mexico, since the 1960s. His Ph.D. in anthropology was earned at the University of Arizona. His interest in the symbolic content of ritual has led him to Peru, as well as many times to the north of Mexico. He was co-editor of *The Power of Symbols: Masks and Masquerades in the Americas* (1983), University of British Columbia Press, and has authored numerous monographs and journal articles on ritual and ceremony.

James Dow

James Dow received his B.S. in mathematics from the Massachusetts Institute of Technology and his Ph.D. in anthropology from Brandeis University. He is associate professor of anthropology at Oakland University, Rochester, Michigan. Since 1967 he has conducted research among the Otomí Indians of the Sierra Norte de Puebla, Mexico. He has been the recipient of numerous grants, has published many articles and books, and has been a tireless and valuable contributor to professional societies. His most recent book is *The Shaman's Touch: Otomí Indian Symbolic Healing* (1986), University of Utah Press.

Janet Brody Esser

Janet Esser has been researching mask use in the Tarascan sierra of Michoacán since 1970. She received a B.F.A. degree in studio art from the University of Iowa. Her Ph.D. in art history is from the University of California, Los Angeles, and her dissertation on Tarascan masquerades was translated into Spanish and published by the Instituto Nacional Indigenista of Mexico. Many of her published articles have investigated the relationship between past and present in Mexican folk art. She has also been especially interested in the contribution to this art made by the many Africans introduced into Mexico during the Colonial period. Although she grew up in New York City she has made her home in California for many years and is professor of art at San Diego State University.

James S. Griffith

Jim Griffith was born in southern California but has called the Tucson area home since the mid-fifties. He received his undergraduate and graduate degrees from the University of Arizona. He earned his Ph.D. in cultural anthropology and art history. In the 1960s he worked documenting traditional arts and folklife in the Mexican states of Sonora and Sinaloa. Since 1979 he has been director of the University of Arizona's Southwest Folklore Center. He has authored numerous books and articles on the traditional arts of southern Arizona and northwest Mexico.

Cecelia F. Klein

Cecelia Klein is associate professor of art history at the University of California, Los Angeles. She has a broad background in studio arts and art history. Her Ph.D. degree in pre-Columbian art history was received from Columbia University. As a productive and meticulous scholar she has long been recognized as an expert on pre-Conquest Aztec art. In this area she has focused her interest on the relationship of complex imagery to ideology and politics. Her investigations have brought a new dimension to our understanding of these important people.

Ruth D. Lechuga

Ruth Lechuga has been profoundly attracted to Mexican folk culture from the time of her arrival to that country from her native Austria as a teenager. Learning Spanish rapidly and fluently, she soon enrolled in a course of study leading to a medical degree. A pathologist by training, she supervised her own laboratory for many years. But Mexico provided her with more than refuge and a medical career. It gave her the opportunity to study, collect, and photograph the folk life which stirred her deeply. For many years she has held a leading position at the Museo Nacional de Artes e Industrias Populares in Mexico City. Both as an avid scholar and superb photographer, she has served her beloved adopted nation with singular devotion.

Ted J. J. Leyenaar

Ted Leyenaar is deputy director of the Rijksmuseum voor Volkenkunde (National Museum of Ethnology) in Leiden, the Netherlands, as well as director of their Latin American collection, which of course includes the famous Maya treasure, the Leiden Plate. He has done extensive field work among the Nahuas and Otomíes of the Sierra Norte de Puebla and is well published in this area. His Ph.D. in anthropology is from the University of Leiden. He is also an expert on the pre-Columbian ball game, the subject of his published dissertation, and is currently preparing an exhibition on this theme to open in Amsterdam in 1988.

María Teresa Pomar

Teré Pomar has been the director of the numerous museums throughout the country under the direction of the Museo Nacional de Artes e Industrias Populares for many years. The scope of her responsibilities is equalled only by the unflagging devotion she brings to her many tasks. She grew up in Guanajuato where, as the daughter of a reknowned musician, she was surrounded by many of Mexico's most notable personalities in those days of intellectual and artistic ferment. Married to art historian Rafael Carillo, she has devoted her life to the study and preservation of the rich and varied folk art traditions of her people. Tirelessly, she has written, lectured, and organized collections and exhibitions. The success of her mission to educate the public at large while encouraging indigenous artisans to maintain the integrity of their traditions was recognized by the Mexican government, which bestowed upon her one of it highest honors—the Premio Gamio—in 1985.

Photo Credits/Permissions

Pages i, ii, x, front and back cover photos, 312—313 by **Miho**. Page vi photo by **Tom McCarthy**. Pages iv, xii, xiv, figs. 87—103, 133—53 photos by **Ruth D. Lechuga**. Pages 4—5, fig. 39 (from Faces of Fiesta by Janet Brody Esser, 1981. Courtesy San Diego State University), figs. 69—70, 72—82, 84—86, 273 photos by **Janet Brody Esser**. Pages 30, 36, 264, 268—69, 286—87, 302—303, 306—307 photos by **Marsha C. Bol**. Fig. 1 courtesy **Emily Umberger**. Fig. 3 from *The Aztecs: People of the Sun*, by Alfonso Caso. Courtesy University of Oklahoma Press. Figs. 2—10, 14, 16 courtesy Akademische Druck- und Verlagsanstalt, Graz, Austria. Figs. 11, 13, 15, 17, 18 courtesy Museo Nacional de Antroplogia e Historia, Mexico City. Fig. 19 from Historica del Nombre y de la Fundacion de México, by Gutiérre Tibon. Courtesy Fondo de Cultura Economica, Mexico City. Fig. 156 courtesy Dover Publications, New York. Figs. 23—34 photos by Frederick Starr. Figs. 23, 26, 27, 32, 34 courtesy University of Chicago Library. Figs. 25, 33 courtesy Colorado Springs Fine Arts Center. Figs. 35—38, and all studio photographs pages 275—321 by **Michel Monteaux**. Photos page 225 by Donald Cordry; from *Mexican Masks*, by Donald Cordry, © 1980 the University of Texas Press. Courtesy the Publisher. Figs. 40—46 photos by **James S. Griffith**. Figs. 47—68 photos by **N. Ross Crumrine**. Figs. 71, 83 photos by **Robert Radlow**. Figs. 104—113 photos by **James Dow**. Figs. 119, 120, 125, 129 courtesy Rijksmuseum voor Volkenkunde, Leiden, Netherlands. Figs. 114, 117, 128 photos by **Ted J.J. Leyenaar**. figs. 115, 116, 118, 121—24, 126, 127, 130, 131, 132 photos by **Ted and Paula Leyenaar**. Figs. 154—66 photos by **Betty Ann Brown. Pages 264-65 photos by Barney T. Burns, Marsha C. Bol, Marilee Schmidt, Miho**. Pages 266—76 photos by **Marsha C. Bol, Miho, James Griffith**. Pages 270—71 photos by **Ruth D. Lechuga, Marilee Schmidt, Juan Alvarez**. Pages 274—75, 294—95 photos by **Marsha C. Bol** and **Marilee Schmit**. Color photos of Guerrero, pages 303—305 by **Dr. Marion Oettinger, Jr.**